Careers in Technical Services
&
Equipment Repair

Careers in Technical Services

&

Equipment Repair

Editor
Michael Shally-Jensen, Ph.D.

SALEM PRESS
A Division of EBSCO Information Services, Inc.
Ipswich, Massachusetts

GREY HOUSE PUBLISHING

Publisher's Cataloging-In-Publication Data
(Prepared by The Donohue Group, Inc.)

Careers in technical services & equipment repair / editor, Michael
  Shally-Jensen, Ph.D. -- [First edition].

    pages : illustrations ; cm. -- (Careers in--)

  Edition statement supplied by publisher.
  Includes bibliographical references and index.
  Contents: Publisher's note -- Editor's introduction -- Aircraft Mechanic -- Automotive Technician -- Biomedical Equipment Technician -- Computer Service Technician -- Diesel Service Technician -- Electronics Engineering Technician -- Electronic Equipment Repairer -- Engineering Technician -- Farm Equipment Mechanic -- General Maintenance Mechanic -- Heating & Cooling Technician -- Heavy Equipment Service Technician -- Home Appliance Repairer -- Home Entertainment Equipment Technician -- Industrial Machinery Mechanic -- Laser Technician -- Locomotive Engineer -- Maintenance Supervisor -- Office Machine Repairer -- Renewable Energy Technician -- Robotics Technician -- Small Engine Mechanic -- Stationary Engineer -- Telecommunications Equipment Installer/Repairer -- Vending Machine Repairer -- Appendix A: Holland Code -- Appendix B: Bibliography --Index.
  ISBN: 978-1-61925-780-1 (hardcover)

  1. Industrial technicians--Vocational guidance--United States. 2. Mechanics (Persons)--Vocational guidance--United States. 3. Repairing trades--Vocational guidance--United States. I. Shally-Jensen, Michael. II. Title: Careers in technical services and equipment repair III. Series: Careers in--

TA158 .C375 2015
620.00023

First Printing

PRINTED IN THE UNITED STATES OF AMERICA

CONTENTS

PUBLISHER'S NOTE

Careers in Technical Services & Equipment Repair contains twenty-five alphabetically arranged chapters describing specific fields of interest in this broad industry segment. Merging scholarship with occupational development, this single comprehensive guidebook provides students pursuing careers in technical services and equipment repair insight and instruction on what they can expect in terms of training, advancement, earnings, job prospects, working conditions, relevant associations, and more. *Careers in Technical Services & Equipment Repair* is specifically designed for a high school and undergraduate audience and is edited to align with secondary or high school curriculum standards.

Scope of Coverage

Understanding the wide net of jobs in these segments is important for anyone preparing for a career within them. *Careers in Technical Services & Equipment Repair* comprises twenty-five lengthy chapters on a broad range of occupations including traditional and long-established jobs such as Automotive Technician and Heating & Cooling Technician, as well as more recent jobs like Home Entertainment Equipment Technician and Renewable Energy Technician. This excellent reference also presents possible career paths and high-growth and emerging occupations within the technical services and equipment repair fields.

Careers in Technical Services & Equipment Repair is enhanced with numerous charts and tables, including projections from the US Bureau of Labor Statistics, and median annual salaries or wages for those occupations profiled. Each chapter also notes those skills that can be applied across broad occupation categories. Interesting enhancements, like **Fun Facts, Famous Firsts**, and dozens of photos, add depth to the discussion. A highlight of each chapter is **Conversation With** – a two-page interview with a professional working in a related job. The respondents share their personal career paths, detail potential for career advancement, offer advice for students, and include a "try this" for those interested in embarking on a career in their profession.

Essay Length and Format

Each chapter ranges in length from 3,500 to 4,500 words and begins with a Snapshot of the occupation that includes career clusters, interests, earnings and employment outlook. This is followed by these major categories:

- **Overview** includes detailed discussions on: Sphere of Work; Work Environment; Occupation Interest; A Day in the Life. Also included here is a Profile that outlines working conditions, educational needs, and physical abilities. You will also find the occupation's Holland Interest Score, which matches up character and personality traits with specific jobs.

- **Occupational Specialties** lists specific jobs that are related in some way, like Aircraft Mechanic and Small Engine Mechanic, Computer Service Technician and Home Appliance Repairer, and Electronic Equipment Repairer and Biomedical Equipment Technician. Duties and Responsibilities are also included.
- **Work Environment** details the physical, human, and technological environment of the occupation profiled.
- **Education, Training, and Advancement** outlines how to prepare for this field while in high school, and what college courses to take, including licenses and certifications needed. A section is devoted to the Adult Job Seeker, and there is a list of skills and abilities needed to succeed in the job profiled.
- **Earnings and Advancements** offers specific salary ranges, and includes a chart of metropolitan areas that have the highest concentration of the profession.
- **Employment and Outlook** discusses employment trends, and projects growth to 2020. This section also lists related occupations.
- **Selected Schools** list those prominent learning institutions that offer specific courses in the profiled occupations.
- **More Information** includes associations that the reader can contact for more information.

Special Features

Several features continue to distinguish this reference series from other career-oriented reference works. The back matter includes:
- Appendix A: Guide to Holland Code. This discusses John Holland's theory that people and work environments can be classified into six different groups: Realistic; Investigative; Artistic; Social; Enterprising; and Conventional. See if the job you want is right for you!
- Appendix B: General Bibliography. This is a collection of suggested readings, organized into major categories.
- Subject Index: Includes people, concepts, technologies, terms, principles, and all specific occupations discussed in the occupational profile chapters.

Acknowledgments

Special mention is made of editor Michael Shally-Jensen, who played a principal role in shaping this work with current, comprehensive, and valuable material. Thanks are due to Allison Blake, who took the lead in developing "Conversations With," with help from Vanessa Parks, and to the professionals who communicated their work experience through interview questionnaires. Their frank and honest responses provide immeasurable value to *Careers in Technical Services & Equipment Repair*. The contributions of all are gratefully acknowledged.

EDITOR'S INTRODUCTION

An Occupational Overview

For those interested in how things work, a career in technical services, maintenance, and repair may be just the thing. Technical services and repair work provides millions of jobs across the United States, in virtually all regions and all local economies. Wages are often strong—generally higher than the average. In many of these occupations, moreover, the employment picture is reasonably good, with opportunities continuing to present themselves to job seekers. In addition, most maintenance and repair jobs do not require a 4-year college degree; they usually demand no more than a 2-year associate's degree or only a high school diploma.

Workers particularly in demand include heating and cooling technicians, industrial machinery mechanics, renewable energy technicians, and biomedical equipment technicians. But many other occupations, from automotive technician to telecommunications equipment installer/repairer, can be expected to see at least average growth in terms of employment opportunities.

In today's job market, of course, maintenance and repair workers need more than mechanical ability in their skill set. A facility with numbers (basic math or beyond) and communications skills are useful for workers in many of the fastest growing repair occupations. Even as technology makes work ever more error-proof and work results ever more reliable, workers must understand the essentials of the equipment they employ on the job. Increasingly, too, technicians of all kinds interact with staff members and customers, placing a higher premium on communications than was the case in the past.

Employment and Wages

Most every product, from airplanes to Zamboni machines (ice resurfacers), requires fixing at some point, thus creating job opportunities for repair and maintenance workers. All repair technicians help to restore equipment, machinery, or other devices to good working order. They usually perform routine maintenance, as well, in order to prevent major problems later on. Many technicians also install the products that they maintain.

In some cases a job is physically demanding and requires heavy lifting or working in awkward positions. Such is the case, for example, with some automotive repair occupations. Injury rates for these repair occupations are, on average, higher than those of other occupations. In other cases, however, a technician may work in an office environment or at a "bench" in a repair shop. In these situations, the environment is clean and there is no heavy lifting to do.

Employment Outlook

In 2013, more than 5 million workers were employed in installation, maintenance, and repair occupations, according to the U.S. Bureau of Labor Statistics. And the overall job outlook for maintenance and repair workers is fairly good, with nearly a half million job openings expected between 2015 and 2022. The projected rate of increase stands at 9.6 percent, close to the average (11 percent) for all occupations combined.

Openings are expected to come from ongoing growth in particular industries and occupations as well as from the need to replace workers who leave a job. Naturally, the more jobs there are in an industry the more opportunities there are for job seekers. Even occupations that are not especially fast growing can still have job openings because of the need to replace retiring workers or workers who leave for other reasons.

As with all occupations, many factors—including changing consumer tastes, demographic changes, and technological advances—can affect job prospects for those interested in technical services careers. Employment rates for these occupations are influenced by the prospect that someone will pay to have a product fixed. Many items are increasingly being replaced rather than repaired. Products also tend to be more reliable (within their specific lifespan) than before. Televisions, for example, used to be expensive to buy and often required costly maintenance. Today, televisions are relatively inexpensive and quite reliable; they are more often replaced when the time comes than repaired. As a result, television repairers are not in high demand, although there still is some demand. Moreover, someone with the background and skills to repair televisions most likely will be able to apply his or her talents to other electronic equipment, because the industry has moved in the direction of "convergent" technologies. At the same time, some equipment, such as medical equipment, is more specialized and very costly to replace. Because there is a continuing need for medical equipment, including well maintained older equipment, there is a continuing demand for medical equipment repair technicians.

Wages

Workers in repair and maintenance occupations earned an average annual wage of $44,420 in 2013, compared with a mean annual wage of $46,440 for employees (including managers) in all occupations. To put things in context, maintenance and repair occupations stood just behind construction and extraction occupations in terms of average annual wages, and ahead of such occupations as healthcare support, protective services, food services, building and grounds maintenance, sales, office administration, and agriculture/forestry. The overall wage picture, then, for maintenance and repair workers is solid.

Among the highest paying repair and maintenance occupations in 2013 were powerhouse, substation, and relay electrical and electronics repairers ($68,270), aircraft mechanics and service technicians ($57,610), telecommunications equipment installers and repairers ($54,030), precision instrument and equipment repairers

($51,600), and industrial machinery mechanics ($49,560). Working with electricity or heavy equipment is dangerous and requires special training—a factor that usually leads to increased pay. Similarly, working with precision instruments and advanced technology requires special training, patience, and skill. Maintenance and repair workers in all fields who go on to become supervisors or managers also typically earn higher wages.

Education and Training

As noted, most repair jobs do not require a 4-year college degree; they do, however, often carry some specific requirements. Background skills, formal training, and professional licenses and certificates are important for many repair careers.

Skills

Basic mechanical know-how and essential fix-it skills are expected in most technical services and repair personnel. Such knowledge and skills include mechanical aptitude and being adept at working with your hands and with a variety of tools and technologies. Interest in machinery, technology, and engineering comes with the territory. A willingness to diagnose a problem—also called troubleshooting—is important because technicians must be able to quickly and efficiently identify the source of an issue and address it. Analytical thinking, reasoning ability, manual dexterity, and flexibility of approach also help in working out what needs to be done and how best to do it. And, increasingly, mechanics and technicians need good communication skills to enable them to explain problems and likely solutions to customers and employers.

Training

Most repair and maintenance technicians can claim at least a high school education or its equivalent, such as a GED. Some go on to complete educational programs at community colleges or commercial vocational schools.

In *high school,* potential maintenance technicians learn basic math, reading, and vocational skills that they can later apply to their careers. They will need math to determine the amount of materials needed and the cost of repairs, or to calculate the lengths and positions of ductwork when installing a heating and air conditioning system. Reading is needed to understand repair manuals and to keep current on new technologies and techniques. Science and engineering are valuable for understanding electrical circuits or hydraulics in automobiles. Additional high school courses that are useful for future technicians are mechanical drawing, blueprint reading, electrical or electronics training, and automotive classes.

Postsecondary courses at a community college or vocational school may also prove beneficial. Increasingly, employers prefer to hire workers with some formal training. Such programs usually combine classroom learning with hands-on experience. The U.S. Armed Forces can also provide training opportunities for maintenance and repair workers, as can, where available, apprenticeship programs and other forms of on-the-job learning. Heating and cooling technicians, for example, often learn their jobs through an apprenticeship program. Such programs can last between 3 to 5 years and involve both technical instruction and paid on-the-job training. Workers start out as helpers to other, more experienced workers and slowly increase the complexity of their work assignments as they learn more advanced repair techniques. In all cases, workers must learn proper safety procedures to avoid injuries and must practice documenting their work in maintenance logs.

Licensing and Certification

Some repair technicians, including those who perform electrical work and plumbing services, require licensing, depending on their employer and the state or locality in which they work. Other technicians benefit from optional certification, which can demonstrate an added level of expertise based on skill testing and practical knowledge. Automotive service technicians, for example, often choose to become certified in one or more specialty areas, such as engines, brakes, or transmissions. Certification offered through the National Automotive Technicians Education Foundation involves passing an exam and having two or more years of experience.

Whatever approach you take, learning about and training for a career in technical services can reward you with valuable skills and knowledge that will put you in good stead for many years to come.

—Michael Shally-Jensen, Ph.D.

Sources

Bureau of Labor Statistics. *Occupational Outlook Handbook, 2014-2015.* Blue Ridge Summit, PA: Bernan Press, 2014.

Denning, Greg. "Maintenance and Repair Industry Trends for 2012." http://www.facilitiesnet.com/site/pressreleases/Maintenance-and-Repair-Industry-Trends-for-2012--24861#

Torpey, Elka Maria. "Fix-It Careers: Jobs in Repair," *Occupational Outlook Quarterly* 3 (Fall), 2010: 27-33.

Aircraft Mechanic

Snapshot

Career Cluster: Engineering; Maintenance & Repair; Technology

Interests: Aerodynamics, machinery, mechanics, aircraft, engine repair

Earnings (Yearly Average): $57,610

Employment & Outlook: Slower than Average Growth Expected

OVERVIEW

Sphere of Work

Aircraft mechanics work to ensure the safety and efficiency of private and commercial air travel. To this end, they perform scheduled maintenance, conduct Federal Aviation Administration (FAA)–mandated inspections, and make repairs on airplanes, helicopters, and other aircraft. Some aircraft mechanics specialize in one particular area, such as engine repair, while at smaller airports, mechanics are typically expected to work on all aspects of the planes housed there. This includes testing and repairing brakes, ventilation and air conditioning systems, radios, landing gear, and instruments. When operating issues arise, aircraft mechanics

determine the cause, select the proper tools and equipment, and repair or replace the malfunctioning systems while maintaining detailed logs of those repairs.

Work Environment

Aircraft mechanics work in airport hangars, repair areas, and flight lines. Airports, in general, are very busy environments, with planes and other vehicles, as well as people, constantly moving from place to place. Mechanics frequently work with heavy equipment and perform physically challenging work, often in potentially dangerous or uncomfortable locations, such as on an airplane's wing or on top of its fuselage (the main body). The work areas can be extremely noisy, and when working outside of a hangar, aircraft mechanics are exposed to all types of weather. Aircraft mechanics generally work forty-hour weeks, but due to the essential nature of the work, some late night and holiday shifts may be required. There is pressure for this work to be done quickly and correctly, which adds an element of stress to the job.

Profile

Working Conditions: Work both Indoors and Outdoors
Physical Strength: Medium Work
Education Needs: On-The-Job Training Technical/Community College
Licensure/Certification: Required
Physical Abilities Not Required: N/A
Opportunities For Experience: Apprenticeship, Military Service, Part-Time Work
Holland Interest Score*: REI, RIE

* See Appendix A

Occupation Interest

A career as an aircraft mechanic appeals to detail-oriented people who enjoy working with their hands and repairing a variety of complex machines. Aircraft mechanics frequently have to solve mechanical problems under strict time constraints, so workers must excel in fast-paced environments.

A Day in the Life—Duties and0 Responsibilities

Daily responsibilities for aircraft mechanics vary based on the type of aircraft in need of maintenance or the area of specialization in which they work. Airframe mechanics work on all parts of the aircraft aside from the instruments, engines, and propellers, while powerplant mechanics work with engines and some propeller systems. Avionics technicians specialize in navigation, radio, radar, and other flight control systems. Many mechanics who work at small regional airports or with private jets and smaller planes, are combined airframe and powerplant (A&P) mechanics, fulfilling dual roles.

In general, aircraft mechanics conduct routine inspections of systems and equipment, make repairs when necessary, and handle any emergency mechanical problems that may occur. They check gauges and instruments for operating difficulties and perform routine preflight maintenance as needed. When issues arise, aircraft mechanics make repairs in a hangar or along the flight line, sometimes climbing on top of the fuselage or wings in order to fix or replace malfunctioning equipment.

In addition to mechanical work, aircraft mechanics are responsible for logging the results of their FAA-mandated equipment inspections, as well as keeping records of maintenance performed. They may also participate in the ordering and tracking of inventory.

Duties and Responsibilities

- Repairing, replacing and assembling aircraft parts and frames
- Maintaining or replacing hydraulic units, oxygen systems, fuel and oil systems, fire extinguisher systems and electrical systems
- Repairing electronic systems, such as computerized controls
- Maintaining and replacing aircraft engines, propeller pumps and fuel, oil and water injection systems
- Certifying that an aircraft is ready for operation

OCCUPATION SPECIALTIES

Airframe and Powerplant (A&P) Mechanics

Airframe and Powerplant Mechanics are certified general mechanics who can independently perform maintenance and alteration tasks on aircraft. A&P mechanics repair and maintain most parts of an aircraft, including the engines, landing gear, brakes, and air conditioning systems. Some specialized activities require additional experience and certification.

Avionics Technicians

Avionics Technicians are specialists who repair and maintain a plane's electronic instruments, such as radio communications, radar systems, and navigation aids. As the use of digital technology increases, more time is spent maintaining computer systems. The ability to repair and maintain many avionics and flight instrument systems is granted through the Airframe rating, but other licenses or certifications may be needed.

Inspection Authorized (IA) Mechanics

Inspection Authorized Mechanics are mechanics who have both Airframe and Powerplant licenses and who may perform inspections on aircraft and return them to service. IA mechanics are able to do a wider variety of maintenance and alterations than any other type of maintenance personnel, such as comprehensive annual inspections or returning aircraft to service after a major repair.

WORK ENVIRONMENT

Physical Environment

Aircraft mechanics work primarily at airports and airfields, working in hangars as well as outdoor repair areas and flight lines. The work environment is busy and often very loud, and mechanics are frequently expected to work in all types of weather conditions. Mechanics may perform maintenance and repairs while on top of an aircraft's fuselage or wings or in tight spaces within the fuselage.

Relevant Skills and Abilities

Organization & Management Skills
- Paying attention to and handling details
- Performing duties that change frequently

Technical Skills
- Performing technical work
- Working with machines, tools or other objects

Unclassified Skills
- Being physically active

Human Environment

Aircraft mechanics frequently work in collaboration with their fellow mechanics, some of whom may specialize in particular areas. They may also interact with members of the airport staff, pilots and other flight crew members, and government officials.

Technological Environment

In addition to the handheld tools used to maintain and replace equipment, aircraft mechanics use metal cutters, mechanical lifts and test stands, electrical test equipment, X-ray machines, and magnetic inspection equipment. They must also use mobile computers to log completed maintenance, manage inventory, and analyze engine performance, among other tasks.

EDUCATION, TRAINING, AND ADVANCEMENT

High School/Secondary

High school students should study industrial arts, including welding and metalworking, engine repair, machine repair, and electronics. Math courses, such as trigonometry and geometry, are also highly useful. Classes in physics and chemistry provide aspiring aircraft mechanics with an understanding of the effects of environmental conditions on a plane's external skin and internal systems.

Suggested High School Subjects
- Algebra
- Applied Math
- Applied Physics
- Blueprint Reading
- Chemistry
- Electricity & Electronics
- English
- Machining Technology
- Trigonometry
- Welding

Famous First

The first commercial aircraft to be designed by computer was the Boeing 777, which entered service in 1995. The jetliner was designed using computer-aided design (CAD) software, allowing the manufacturer to avoid constructing a costly mock-up and to identify any assembly problems before the start of manufacturing. Compared to the older Boeing 747, the 777 has much lower maintenance costs.

College/Postsecondary

Aircraft mechanics must take and pass an FAA-approved aviation maintenance training course. Depending on the level of training sought or required, the program may last two to four years. Additionally, mechanics must receive practical training from a certified aircraft mechanic, who, in turn, must log the hours and systems on which the mechanic-in-training has worked.

Related College Majors
- Aircraft Mechanics Airframe
- Aircraft Mechanics Powerplant
- Aviation Systems & Avionics Maintenance Technology

Adult Job Seekers

Qualified aircraft mechanics may apply directly to positions listed online or in print. Professional trade associations such as the Professional Aviation Maintenance Association (PAMA), as well as regional and international unions, can provide information about available positions and present valuable networking opportunities.

Professional Certification and Licensure

The FAA requires that working aircraft mechanics either be certified or work under a certified mechanic. They must have at least eighteen months of general experience before choosing to specialize in an area such as airframe or powerplant mechanics, while A&P mechanics must have at least thirty months of experience working on both airframes and engines. In order to become certified, mechanics must take and pass written, oral, and practical exams administered by the FAA. Avionics mechanics must also be certified, unless they previously worked in the field while serving in the military, and in the case of avionics mechanics working on communications systems, they must obtain a restricted radiotelephone operator's license from the Federal Communications Commission (FCC).

Additional Requirements

Aircraft mechanics must be skilled in working with complex mechanical systems and equipment. Computer skills are also beneficial. Mechanics must be energetic, motivated, and able to quickly diagnose problems. Heavy lifting, climbing to high points on large aircraft, and working in tight spaces are often part of the job, so mechanics must be physically fit and possess a full range of motion. They must also be effective communicators, able to clearly explain maintenance issues to individuals from different professional backgrounds.

Fun Fact

So you want to be an aircraft mechanic? Plan for rigorous schooling, and be prepared for testing and regular "check ups" by the Federal Aviation Administration throughout your career.

Source: https://www.faa.gov/mechanics/become/basic/

EARNINGS AND ADVANCEMENT

Earnings depend on the employer, geographic location, union affiliation and mechanic's training, experience, seniority and responsibilities. Earnings of aircraft mechanics generally are higher than other types of mechanics.

Mean annual earnings of aircraft mechanics were about $57,610 in 2013. The lowest ten percent earned less than $34,580, and the highest ten percent earned more than $84,960.

Aircraft mechanics may receive paid vacations, holidays, and sick days; life and health insurance; and retirement benefits. These are usually paid by the employer. Aircraft mechanics may also receive free or reduced rates on flights and uniform cleaning allowances.

Metropolitan Areas with the Highest Employment Level in this Occupation

Metropolitan area	Employment [1]	Employment per thousand jobs	Hourly mean wage
Los Angeles-Long Beach-Glendale, CA	4,890	1.23	$31.92
Miami-Miami Beach-Kendall, FL	2,630	2.57	$26.16
Chicago-Joliet-Naperville, IL	2,300	0.62	$29.82
San Antonio-New Braunfels, TX	2,260	2.55	$22.70
Seattle-Bellevue-Everett, WA	2,250	1.55	$33.22
Phoenix-Mesa-Glendale, AZ	2,250	1.26	$27.43
Houston-Sugar Land-Baytown, TX	2,040	0.74	$32.13
Dallas-Plano-Irving, TX	2,010	0.93	$28.52
New York-White Plains-Wayne, NY-NJ	2,000	0.38	$29.13
Oklahoma City, OK	1,950	3.27	$24.69

[1]Does not include self-employ ed. Source: Bureau of Labor Statistics

EMPLOYMENT AND OUTLOOK

Aircraft mechanics held about 139,000 jobs in 2012. Most aircraft mechanics work at major airports near large cities. Employment of aircraft mechanics is expected to grow slower than the average for all occupations through the year 2022, which means employment is projected to increase 1 percent to 6 percent. Most job openings for aircraft mechanics will stem from replacement needs. Because the airlines offer relatively high wages and attractive travel benefits, competition for these jobs is high. Job opportunities will be best with smaller airlines and in general aviation.

Experienced aircraft mechanics who keep up on technological advances in electronics and other areas and who are trained to work on complicated aircraft systems will be in the greatest demand.

Employment Trend, Projected 2012–22

Total, All Occupations: 11%

Avionics Technicians: 3%

Aircraft Mechanics and Avionics Technicians: 2%

Aircraft Mechanics: 2%

Note: "All Occupations" includes all occupations in the U.S. Economy. Source: U.S. Bureau of Labor Statistics, Employment Projections Program

Related Occupations
- Automotive Technician
- Diesel Service Technician
- Electrician
- Heavy Equipment Service Technician

Related Military Occupations
- Air Crew Member
- Aircraft Mechanic
- Flight Engineer
- Transportation Maintenance Manager

Conversation With . . . DOUGLAS M. CLARKE

Retired, Corporate Aviation Mechanic, 42 years
Richmond, VA

1. What was your individual career path in terms of education/training, entry-level job, or other significant opportunity?

I've always been mechanical; as a teenager, I worked on cars, and even bicycles and lawnmowers. I went into the U.S. Air Force after high school and that got me into the aviation end of mechanics, which is what I wanted to do. After basic training, I went to technical school for aircraft engine school. I received additional training at a local Fixed Base Operator – known as an F.B.O., which is an airport's private sector service provider – and took my required Airframe and Powerplant license tests at the local FAA office.

After I got out of the Air Force, I went to work in Richmond, Va., for four years with Aero Industries, then spent 32 years in the same city with the Ethyl Corporation, and two more years with the Albemarle Corporation. Employers always send you to school for the aircraft type, as well as the engine; that's critical in aviation. Mechanics learn a particular aircraft's mechanics in ongoing training, just like pilots learn how to fly those same aircraft. That's how aviation works.

2. What are the most important skills and/or qualities for someone in your profession?

The most important skills come from getting all the training you can: hands-on books help, and seminars and schools – attend all you can – as well as on-the-job training. If you're mechanically-inclined, this will be an enjoyable challenge.

3. What do you wish you had known going into this profession?

The aircraft mechanic field requires extra training, always. Luckily I realized that in a short period of time. You will be going to school until you retire. Ongoing training by your employer is always required so you are up to date on the aircraft they operate and new repair techniques.

4. Are there many job opportunities in your profession? In what specific areas?

There are opportunities in my profession as aircraft technicians in different fields: airframe or powerplant, electrical, and hydraulics. The easiest way into the industry is to go to aircraft school.

5. How do you see your profession changing in the next five years, what role will technology play in those changes, and what skills will be required?

Technology is an ever-changing thing in aircraft. There will be a need for advanced skills in the computerized field of avionics.

6. What do you enjoy most about your job? What do you enjoy least about your job?

I was chief of maintenance for most of my career in corporate aviation and I enjoyed it. A bit hectic at times, but I would not trade it. It's what I wanted when I joined the Air Force way back when. I'm retired now, but I had a 42-year career in aviation and have no regrets.

7. Can you suggest a valuable "try this" for students considering a career in your profession?

I think you have to want this field. Get a mechanical background and that will help you decide your direction. If you would like a career as an aircraft mechanic the best way is to attend one of the aircraft tech schools to get your A&P license because all work done on aircraft has to be signed off by a licensed mechanic.

SELECTED SCHOOLS

A college degree is not necessary in most cases to work as an aircraft mechanic. For those interested in the field, however, a technical or community college is a good place to start. Many commercial trade schools are also available. For a position in avionics maintenance, courses in electronics and computers are usually required. Students are advised to consult with their school guidance counselor or research area post-secondary schools to find the right program.

MORE INFORMATION

Aircraft Maintenance Professionals (AMT Society)
801 Cliff Road East, Suite 201
Burnsville, MN 55337
800.827.8009
www.amtsociety.org

Association for Women in Aviation Maintenance
2330 Kenlee Drive
Cincinnati, OH 32132
386.416.0248
www.awam.org

ATEC (Aviation Technician Education Council)
2090 Wexford Court
Harrisburg, PA 17112
717.540.7121
www.atec-amt.org

Federal Aviation Administration
800 Independence Avenue, SW
Washington, DC 20591
866.835.5322
www.faa.gov

Professional Aviation Maintenance Association
717 Princess Street
Alexandria, VA 22314
703.778.4647
www.pama.org

Michael Auerbach/Editor

Automotive Technician

Snapshot

Career Cluster: Engineering; Maintenance & Repair; Technology

Interests: Automobiles, customer service, solving problems, working with machinery

Earnings (Yearly Average): $39,450

Employment & Outlook: Average Growth Expected

OVERVIEW

Sphere of Work

Automotive technicians maintain and repair cars and light trucks, using computers and other diagnostic tools to troubleshoot problems and a wide variety of hand and power tools to replace parts and make adjustments. They must be able to work with traditional tools and machinery while also keeping up with rapidly evolving technology, both in automobiles and in the diagnostic tools used to maintain and repair them.

Work Environment

Automotive technicians work in a variety of facilities, from single-bay garages attached to gas stations to large service bays at automobile dealerships. Some national automotive maintenance and repair chains offer consistent work environments, which tend to have standardized safety protocols and processes for carrying out routine work. Other facilities specialize in repairing one component of automobiles, such as brakes, mufflers, or transmissions. Repair shops can be very noisy, and technicians are frequently exposed to potentially hazardous substances such as grease, oil, and other system fluids. Because of the hazards inherent in the work, technicians must often wear safety equipment such as earplugs, safety glasses, and steel-reinforced boots.

Profile

Working Conditions: Work Indoors
Physical Strength: Medium Work
Education Needs: On-The-Job Training, High School Diploma with Technical Education, Technical/Community College
Licensure/Certification: Required
Physical Abilities Not Required: N/A
Opportunities For Experience: Apprenticeship, Military Service, Part-Time Work,
Holland Interest Score*: RCI, RES, RIE

* See Appendix A

Occupation Interest

Individuals drawn to the profession of automotive technician tend to be independent workers who enjoy solving problems and working with automobiles. As automotive technicians must at times interact with customers, particularly at smaller shops, they must be capable of providing excellent customer service and explaining mechanical concepts in a clear, understandable manner. Automotive technicians must be quick learners able to keep up with rapidly evolving technology, and they should enjoy the challenge of working with complex machinery.

A Day in the Life—Duties and Responsibilities

The daily duties of an automotive technician vary widely according to the type of shop in which he or she is employed. An automotive technician who works on only one automotive system may spend days performing routine tasks such as oil changes or brake work. Since the structure and components of an automotive system vary with the make, model, and age of the vehicle, however, a high degree of skill is still necessary to perform even routine maintenance and repair.

Automotive technicians with a wider range of responsibilities must master all aspects of automobile repair and maintenance and engage in a much greater variety of activities. Typically, an automotive technician first assesses a vehicle in order to determine the source of the damage or malfunction, using traditional and technological diagnostic tools, and provides an estimate for repair to the customer. In some cases, the automotive technician may test-drive the vehicle to gain a better understanding of the problem.

Once the scope of the required repair is determined, the automotive technician will begin working on the vehicle. Automobile repair shops often use lifts or work pits to provide access to the undercarriage of vehicles, so automotive technicians must also manage these lift or jacking systems. They may employ a variety of gauges and testing equipment to determine compression, alignment, and pressure and may repair or replace parts depending on the extent of the damage. Automotive technicians may also complete routine inspections to test for common mechanical and safety issues. Once a repair is completed or routine maintenance work has been performed, the automotive technician will log the time and expense of the work. In many cases, he or she will interact directly with the customer to offer information about current and upcoming work.

Duties and Responsibilities

- Examining vehicles and advising customers of their findings
- Planning work routines using charts and manuals
- Raising vehicles using a hydraulic jack or hoist
- Removing units such as engines and transmissions
- Rewiring ignition systems, lights and instrument panels
- Relining and adjusting brakes
- Aligning front ends

OCCUPATION SPECIALTIES

Air Conditioning Technicians

Air Conditioning Technicians install, repair and service air conditioners in automobiles.

Brake Repair Technicians

Brake Repair Technicians repair automotive brake systems. They replace brake pads and linings, repair hydraulic cylinders and turn discs and drums.

Front End Technicians

Front End Technicians repair steering mechanisms, suspension systems and align and balance wheels.

Transmission Technicians

Transmission Technicians work on gear trains, couplings, hydraulic pumps, and other parts of transmissions. Extensive knowledge of computer controls, the ability to diagnose electrical and hydraulic problems, and other specialized skills are needed to work on these complex components.

Tune-Up Technicians

Tune-Up Technicians, also known as Drivability Technicians, ensure efficient automotive engine performance using various testing machines to check overall performance capabilities.

WORK ENVIRONMENT

Physical Environment

Automotive technicians work in a range of environments, from large repair facilities and dealerships with state-of-the-art equipment to small garages. These environments present a number of hazards, including significant noise and fumes from industrial fluids, so technicians must follow safety procedures at all times. All automotive technicians must also be able to lift and maneuver heavy parts and have excellent visual and manual acuity.

Relevant Skills and Abilities

Research & Planning Skills
- Analyzing information
- Identifying problems

Technical Skills
- Working with machines, tools or other objects
- Working with your hands

Unclassified Skills
- Being physically active

Human Environment

Automotive technicians often work alongside other technicians, but they may have limited opportunities for interaction while work is being performed. Periodic contact may be made with others to ask for advice or direction. Some automotive technicians have extensive contact with the public, so customer-service and communication skills are needed.

Technological Environment

Automotive technicians work with a variety of testing and diagnostic equipment and should be familiar with project-management software. As automobile technology continues to develop, automotive technicians must keep abreast of the rapid advances in the field.

EDUCATION, TRAINING, AND ADVANCEMENT

High School/Secondary

Students interested in the field of automobile repair should take courses in mathematics and mechanics. Electronics or metal-shop classes, if offered, may also be beneficial. Many technical and vocational high schools offer courses in automobile repair, and students can gain additional experience through part-time work and personal automotive projects.

Suggested High School Subjects
- Applied Math
- Auto Collision Technology
- Auto Service Technology
- Blueprint Reading
- Electricity & Electronics
- English
- Machining Technology
- Metals Technology
- Shop Math
- Shop Mechanics
- Trade/Industrial Education
- Welding

Famous First

The first brake for a four-wheeled car (yes, there were three-wheeled vehicles early in the development of the automobile) was patented in 1908 as a "power applying mechanism" by Otto Zachow and William Besserdich of Clintonville, Wisconsin.

College/Postsecondary

Although postsecondary study is typically not required, some community and technical colleges offer courses in automobile technology as well as apprentice or work-study programs that allow students to gain hands-on experience. Such courses may be beneficial to aspiring technicians or working technicians seeking to gain additional skills.

Related College Majors
• Auto/Automotive Mechanics

Adult Job Seekers

Some experience in repairing automobiles or other machinery is typically required for those seeking to transition to the field of automobile repair, and adult job seekers hoping to advance to higher positions in the field may benefit from obtaining certification while on the job. Job seekers may obtain training in automobile repair through technical or vocational programs, military service, and in-house training programs and apprenticeships.

Professional Certification and Licensure

Though not required by law, certification is required by many employers. The National Institute for Automotive Service Excellence is the primary certification body in the industry, certifying automotive technicians in such areas as collision repair, diesel engine diagnosis, and school-bus repair. Each certification requires both a written test and work experience.

Additional Requirements

Automotive technicians often work forty or more hours per week. Strength and stamina are crucial, as is a strong interest in mechanics and automobiles. Customer-service skills and attention to detail are also very important.

Fun Fact

Car and Driver says the craziest car engine ever produced was in the original Volkswagen Bug. The magazine called the 8.0-liter engine with 64 valves and four turbochargers "the most powerful and complex production engine in history." Still, they were easy to work on. The VW Beetle was Hitler's idea, meant to be "the people's car."

Source: caranddriver.com/features/the-10-most-unusual-engines-of-all-time-feature

EARNINGS AND ADVANCEMENT

Automotive technicians in repair shops are often paid a percentage of the labor charges for repairs they make. Skilled automotive technicians usually earn between two and three times as much as inexperienced apprentices who are paid an hourly rate until they are skilled enough to work on commission.

Nationally, in 2013, mean annual earnings of automotive technicians were $39,450. The lowest ten percent earned less than $20,920, and the highest ten percent earned more than $61,210. Employers usually guarantee automotive technicians a minimum weekly salary.

Automotive technicians may receive paid vacations, holidays, and sick days; life and health insurance; and retirement benefits. These are usually paid by the employer. Some employers may provide uniforms and premium pay for overtime.

Metropolitan Areas with the Highest
Employment Level in this Occupation

Metropolitan area	Employment [1]	Employment per thousand jobs	Hourly mean wage
Chicago-Joliet-Naperville, IL	14,860	4.01	$20.80
New York-White Plains-Wayne, NY-NJ	14,010	2.67	$20.68
Los Angeles-Long Beach-Glendale, CA	13,070	3.29	$17.81
Atlanta-Sandy Springs-Marietta, GA	10,950	4.74	$19.69
Houston-Sugar Land-Baytown, TX	9,990	3.62	$19.17
Philadelphia, PA	9,670	5.25	$19.91
Washington-Arlington-Alexandria, DC-VA-MD-WV	9,570	4.04	$22.96
Phoenix-Mesa-Glendale, AZ	7,900	4.44	$20.60
Dallas-Plano-Irving, TX	7,450	3.47	$19.69
St. Louis, MO-IL	7,090	5.49	$19.87

[1]Does not include self-employ ed. Source: Bureau of Labor Statistics

EMPLOYMENT AND OUTLOOK

Automotive technicians held about 700,000 jobs in 2012. Employment is expected to grow about as fast as the average for all occupations through the year 2022, which means employment is projected to increase 7 percent to 12 percent. Population growth will boost demand for automobiles, which will require regular maintenance and service. In addition, replacements will be needed as experienced workers retire, move to other occupations, or stop working for other reasons.

Employment Trend, Projected 2012–22

Total, All Occupations: 11%

Installation, Maintenance, and Repair Occupations: 10%

Automotive Technicians: 9%

Note: "All Occupations" includes all occupations in the U.S. Economy. Source: U.S. Bureau of Labor Statistics, Employment Projections Program

Related Occupations
- Aircraft Mechanic
- Automotive Body Repairer
- Automotive Service Advisor
- Automotive Service Attendant
- Diesel Service Technician
- Farm Equipment Mechanic
- Heavy Equipment Service Technician
- Small Engine Mechanic

Related Military Occupations
- Automotive & Heavy Equipment Mechanic
- Heating & Cooling Mechanic

Conversation With . . .
BOGI LATEINER

Auto Repair Shop Owner
180 Automotive Degrees, Phoenix, AZ
Auto mechanic/technician, 14 years

1. What was your individual career path in terms of education/training, entry-level job, or other significant opportunity?

My path was a bit crooked. I had taken auto shop in high school in New Jersey, which was a tiny underfunded program. I was interested in auto shop specifically because I had a VW bug that I rebuilt from the ground up. I hated the way mechanics treated me as a woman. I went to Oberlin College in Ohio and studied pre-law and women's studies. When I graduated, I realized I didn't want to go into law. I moved to Arizona and enrolled in the Universal Technical Institute for automotive technology. From there, I had a very hard time getting a job. It's incredibly difficult to get that first job when you're young and inexperienced and female. Finally I got a job at an independent BMW shop. That introduced me to BMW and I did continuing education with them. Most of the manufacturers have dealership-level training and if you do that, you're pretty much guaranteed a job. I wanted to be taken seriously and to say I was a master BMW technician. Eventually, I got tired of dealership life. It just wasn't that satisfying. I was missing the bigger impact stuff. In academia, you're very much in your head. In college, I was a rape crisis counselor and domestic abuse counselor. That job is never done, whereas auto repair is tangible. A car is broken and you fix it. I liked that, but realized I was missing that other part. I decided to open my own shop. I have a five-bay shop with seven employees. Our entry-level job is pretty much reserved for a recent female graduate. I'm also on the show *All Girls Garage* on the Velocity channel. It's a lot of fun. I do customer service coaching and consulting through the Cecil Bullard Institute for Automotive Business Excellence and through WorldPac, a wholesale distributor of automotive equipment.

2. What are the most important skills and/or qualities for someone in your profession?

I think it's problem solving, the ability to follow processes and yet also think outside the box. For women in the industry, you have to have tenacity. It's still very much a man's world.

3. What do you wish you had known going into this profession?

I wish I had known how much personal investment you put into your tools. The average technician probably has a minimum of $50,000 worth of tools. I also wish I had less of a liberal arts background and more of a business background. You go into business for yourself because you love what you're doing, but once you do, you're not figuring out cars anymore or baking pies or whatever the case may be. You're building a business, and that looks very different.

4. Are there many job opportunities in your profession? In what specific areas?

Oh yes. There's a serious, serious lack of qualified automotive technicians. Once you get that first job and gain experience and show that you have good ethics and good skills, you will have no problem finding a job.

5. How do you see your profession changing in the next five years, what role will technology play in those changes, and what skills will be required?

Technology will continue to progress at a startling rate, from sound systems to GPS to automated parking and cars that drive themselves and hybrid cars and cars that activate the brakes for you. It used to be that you learned to be a mechanic and you were done. More and more, automotive techs have to make a commitment to continuing education. There's a perception that smart kids go to college and dumb kids go to wood shop or the automotive track. That needs to shift. This is a highly skilled trade that requires a lot of intelligence and deserves respect.

6. What do you enjoy most about your job? What do you enjoy least about your job?

The thing I enjoy most is when you find that solution to a problem that was a mystery and you see the car leaving and you say, "I did that. I solved the unsolvable." I love helping customers understand their vehicle and take better care of it.

What I like least sometimes are the hours. And it's hard work. You're bending over, you're using your body. It can be physically exhausting. And there are the customers who don't trust you, who want to bring in their own parts, who buy into the stereotypes about mechanics.

7. Can you suggest a valuable "try this" for students considering a career in your profession?

Take a basic automotive class in your high school if you're still at the high school level. Going to trade school is great; getting an apprenticeship is great. Be willing to start at the bottom. You might work in a shop cleaning windows and filling coolant levels. Don't be afraid to tinker with your own car, play around and see how things work.

SELECTED SCHOOLS

A college degree is not necessary in most cases to work as an automotive technician. For those interested in the field, however, a technical or community college is a good place to start. Many commercial trade schools are also available. Students are advised to consult with their school guidance counselor or research area post-secondary schools to find the right program.

MORE INFORMATION

Autocare Association
7101 Wisconsin Avenue
Suite 1300
Bethesda, MD 20814-3415
301.654.6664
www.autocare.org

Automotive Service Association
8190 Precinct Line Road
Suite 100
Colleyville, TX 76034
800.272.7467
www.asashop.org

Automotive Youth Education Services
101 Blue Seal Drive SE, Suite 101
Leesburg, VA 20175
703.669.6677
www.ayes.org

National Automotive Technicians Education Foundation
101 Blue Seal Drive, SE, Suite 101
Leesburg, VA 20175
703.669.6650
www.natef.org

National Institute for Automotive Service Excellence
101 Blue Seal Drive, SE, Suite 101
Leesburg, VA 20175
703.669.6600
www.ase.com

Bethany Groff/Editor

Biomedical Equipment Technician

Snapshot

Career Cluster: Electronics; Engineering; Maintenance & Repair; Technology

Interests: Mechanical work, precision work, sciences, solving problems, analyzing information

Earnings (Yearly Average): $47,120

Employment & Outlook: Faster than Average Growth Expected

OVERVIEW

Sphere of Work

Biomedical equipment technicians, also called service technicians or medical equipment repairers, are responsible for the inspection, maintenance, calibration, modification, and repair of a wide range of biomedical equipment. They may specialize in equipment needed for radiology, nuclear medicine, surgical operations, dialysis, intensive care, clinical laboratories, or dental medicine.

Work Environment

Biomedical equipment technicians may work in medical facilities or in equipment repair shops. They generally work forty-hour weeks. Their shifts may include days, evenings, weekends, or on-call hours to meet the medical community's need for functional, safe biomedical equipment. Biomedical equipment technicians are at risk for exposure to radiation, noxious fumes, and infection, and job-related injuries due to machine accidents and electric shock.

Profile

Working Conditions: Work Indoors
Physical Strength: Light Work
Education Needs:
  Technical/Community College,
  Bachelor's Degree
Licensure/Certification:
  Recommended
Physical Abilities Not Required: No
  Heavy Labor
Opportunities For Experience:
  Internship, Apprenticeship,Part-Time
  Work
Holland Interest Score*: RIE

* See Appendix A

Occupation Interest

Individuals drawn to the profession of biomedical equipment technician tend to be intelligent, analytical, and detail oriented. Those most successful as biomedical equipment technicians display traits such as physical strength, hand-eye coordination, focus, problem-solving abilities, manual dexterity, and reliability. Biomedical equipment technicians should enjoy mechanical work and thrive under pressure.

A Day in the Life—Duties and Responsibilities

A biomedical equipment technician inspects, services, repairs, and calibrates electrical, mechanical, hydraulic, and pneumatic equipment that medical personnel rely on for the diagnosis and treatment of patients. During the course of a given workday, the biomedical equipment technician may design or install new biomedical equipment, perform routine maintenance on equipment with motors and filters, or service devices such as electric and pneumatic drills, EKG machines, prosthetic devices, and X-ray machines. The biomedical equipment technician prepares and cleans the tools used for equipment repair and maintenance and follows manufacturers' manuals as guides for troubleshooting and fixing equipment. For a repair, he or she must assess the equipment's condition, locate the malfunctioning parts, replace or modify the necessary pieces, and correctly reassemble the equipment. Cleaning and calibration are common maintenance activities. The biomedical equipment technician also performs safety checks on all biomedical equipment and machines, particularly those emitting radiation for use in nuclear medicine, and makes recommendations regarding when to acquire new technologies and when to take medical equipment out of service due to obsolescence, age, or disrepair.

Biomedical equipment technicians are also responsible for all communication related to their work. They track supply inventories and record the type and date of all inspections, maintenance, services, repairs, and calibrations performed on medical equipment in equipment logs. Biomedical equipment technicians also make copies of all inspection certificates for equipment owners, medical office staff, or hospital personnel. Whenever necessary, they notify equipment manufacturers of faulty parts. Their most important duty may be teaching medical personnel such as physicians, laboratory technicians, nurses, scientists, and engineers how to care for and use biomedical equipment on a daily basis.

Duties and Responsibilities

- **Testing electronic circuits and components**
- **Soldering loose connections**
- **Using hand tools to replace tubes, transformers, resistors, condensers, and switches**
- **Disassembling equipment and repairing or replacing faulty mechanical parts**
- **Adjusting and repairing styluses, graphs and other recording devices**
- **Operating engine lathes**
- **Installing new equipment**
- **Keeping extensive records of equipment checks**
- **Instructing health-care professionals on how to operate new equipment properly and safely**

WORK ENVIRONMENT

Physical Environment

Biomedical equipment technicians generally spend their workdays in hospitals, medical clinics or offices, laboratories, medical instrument manufacturers and suppliers, or equipment repair shops. Travel to repair sites is sometimes required. Technicians must follow safety procedures and wear proper eye protection and masks in order to avoid job-related illness and injuries.

Relevant Skills and Abilities

Communication Skills
- Speaking effectively
- Writing concisely

Interpersonal/Social Skills
- Being flexible

Organization & Management Skills
- Making decisions
- Managing time
- Meeting goals and deadlines
- Paying attention to and handling details

Research & Planning Skills
- Using logical reasoning

Technical Skills
- Working with machines, tools or other objects

Human Environment

Biomedical equipment technicians should be comfortable interacting with biomedical engineers, hospital engineers, physicians, laboratory technicians, nurses, scientists, and patients. They are supervised by biomedical engineers and hospital engineers, and often provide instruction and training to other medical or laboratory personnel.

Technological Environment

Biomedical equipment technicians use a wide variety of tools and equipment to complete their work, including hand tools, power tools, soldering irons, and measuring devices such as voltage meters, precision levels, and pressure gauges. They are trained to disassemble, service, repair, and calibrate equipment such as X-ray machines, defibrillators, patient monitors, patient call systems, electrocardiographs, electroencephalographs, electric drills, pneumatic drills, blood-gas analyzers, anesthesia machines, pacemakers, blood-pressure transducers, sterilizers, and diathermy machines. In addition to Internet communication tools and standard office applications, biomedical equipment technicians may use maintenance management programs and medical equipment diagnostic software.

EDUCATION, TRAINING, AND ADVANCEMENT

High School/Secondary

High school classes in drafting, electronics, science, health, and mathematics will provide a strong foundation for work as a biomedical equipment technician or college-level study in the field. Students interested in this career path will benefit from seeking apprenticeships or part-time jobs that expose the students to machine repair or engineering.

Suggested High School Subjects
- Algebra
- Applied Communication
- Applied Math
- Biology
- Blueprint Reading
- Chemistry
- Electricity & Electronics
- English
- Geometry

Famous First

The first major breakthrough in biomedical equipment was the x-ray machine, developed by the German physicist Wilhelm Röntgen in 1895. The device quickly made its way into the medical world and continues, of course, to be used today (albeit in a more sophisticated form). For his efforts Röntgen was awarded the Nobel Prize in physics in 1901.

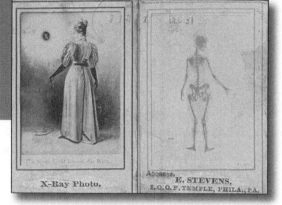

X-Ray Photo.

E. STEVENS,
I.O.O.F. TEMPLE, PHILA., PA.

College/Postsecondary

Although some positions do not require formal postsecondary training, aspiring biomedical equipment technicians should work toward an associate's or bachelor's degree in biomedical equipment engineering, electronics engineering, or a related field. These programs usually include coursework in mathematics, chemistry, physics, technical writing, circuitry, electronic devices, and drafting. Postsecondary students can gain work experience and potential advantage in their future job searches by securing internships or part-time employment in machine repair or engineering environments.

Related College Majors
• Biomedical Engineering-Related Technology

Adult Job Seekers

Adults seeking employment as biomedical equipment technicians should have, at a minimum, a high school diploma or an associate's degree. A bachelor's degree is typically required for more complex assignments and advancement to supervisory positions. Most employers provide supervised training for newly hired biomedical equipment technicians regardless of their level of education. Adult job seekers may benefit from joining professional associations, such as the International Society of Certified Electronics Technicians, which can help with networking and job searching.

Professional Certification and Licensure

Certification and licensure is not legally required for biomedical equipment technicians but may be required as a condition of employment or promotion. The Association for the Advancement of Medical Instrumentation provides the following options for voluntary biomedical equipment certification: Certified Biomedical Equipment Technician (CBET), Certified Radiology Equipment Specialist (CRES), and Certified Laboratory Equipment Specialist (CLES). These voluntary certifications are earned by passing a national written examination and by completing a combination of electronics technology or biomedical equipment technology training and minimum work experience requirements. Continuing education is required for ongoing certification.

Additional Requirements

Individuals who find satisfaction, success, and job security as biomedical equipment technicians will be knowledgeable about the profession's requirements, responsibilities, and opportunities. Membership in professional electronic engineering associations is encouraged among all biomedical equipment technicians as a means of building professional community and networking.

EARNINGS AND ADVANCEMENT

Earnings depend on the type, size, and geographic location of the employer, and the individual's education and experience. Mean annual earnings of biomedical equipment technicians were $47,120 in 2013. The lowest ten percent earned less than $26,930, and the highest ten percent earned more than $72,660.

Biomedical equipment technicians may receive paid vacations, holidays and sick days; life and health insurance; and retirement benefits. These are usually paid by the employer.

Metropolitan Areas with the Highest
Employment Level in this Occupation

Metropolitan area	Employment [1]	Employment per thousand jobs	Hourly mean wage
Chicago-Joliet-Naperville, IL	1,060	0.29	$22.62
Tampa-St. Petersburg-Clearwater, FL	820	0.71	$19.65
Seattle-Bellevue-Everett, WA	790	0.55	$24.87
St. Louis, MO-IL	770	0.60	$22.06
Philadelphia, PA	770	0.42	$24.49
Los Angeles-Long Beach-Glendale, CA	760	0.19	$24.58
New York-White Plains-Wayne, NY-NJ	750	0.14	$27.79
Indianapolis-Carmel, IN	750	0.82	$22.01
Minneapolis-St. Paul-Bloomington, MN-WI	720	0.40	$25.51
Denver-Aurora-Broomfield, CO	710	0.56	$22.60

[1]Does not include self-employ ed. Source: Bureau of Labor Statistics

EMPLOYMENT AND OUTLOOK

There were 42,000 biomedical equipment technicians employed nationally in 2012. Employment is expected to grow much faster than the average for all occupations through the year 2022, which means employment is projected to increase 29 percent or more. The rapidly expanding healthcare industry and elderly population should spark strong demand for biomedical equipment and, in turn, create good employment opportunities in this occupation.

Employment Trend, Projected 2012–22

Biomedical Equipment Technicians: 30%

Other Installation, Maintenance, and Repair Occupations: 12%

Total, All Occupations: 11%

Note: "All Occupations" includes all occupations in the U.S. Economy. Source: U.S. Bureau of Labor Statistics, Employment Projections Program

Related Occupations
- Electromechanical Equipment Assembler
- Electronic Equipment Repairer
- Telecommunications Equipment Repairer

Conversation With . . .
CHRIS WALTON, CBET

North Seattle College
Technical Advisory Committee Chairman
Biomedical Equipment Technician, 30-plus years

1. What was your individual career path in terms of education/training, entry-level job, or other significant opportunity?

I was fortunate to have participated in all areas of biomedical equipment technology. I volunteered at Children's Hospital in Oakland, CA, for two years while attending San Francisco State to get my bachelor's degree. That opened many doors. I became a biomed technician (BMET) at Children's while continuing my master's degree. After graduating with my master's, I became manager of the biomed department at Providence Hospital, also in Oakland. When Providence was sold to another hospital chain and I lost my job, I became an independent contractor installing major medical equipment systems for Hewlett Packard. Eventually I was hired as a full-time ultrasound field service technician for Hewlett Packard. Then I became a factory technical support engineer for HP and was promoted to Service Product Manager. My division became Agilent Technologies, which was bought by Philips Healthcare. Two years ago, I was recruited by Physio-Control to be their first Service Product Manager. I retired just recently. I'm treasurer of the Washington State Biomedical Association.

2. What are the most important skills and/or qualities for someone in your profession?

Strong interpersonal skills are required, including the ability to communicate well and to be a strong team player. You must be reliable and trustworthy, adaptable, and willing to constantly learn. You must be technically competent, with a good foundation in electronics, physics, chemistry, math, biology, and medical technologies and terminology. You need strong mechanical skills and computer skills, particularly working with networks. You need to be familiar with medical electrical safety. Being certified by the Association for the Advancement of Medical Instrumentation (AAMI) will typically result in higher pay. Some hospitals may require it. There are various specializations with this certification. In fact, it's one of the changing trends for the future.

3. What do you wish you had known going into this profession?

I wish I had known about this profession when I was in high school. I could have obtained free training in the military, and probably would have done that.

4. Are there many job opportunities in your profession? In what specific areas?

There are many opportunities. Many current biomedical technicians are older and leaving the field. Companies are finding it difficult to fill the gap. With increasing demands on the medical system due to aging baby boomers, the need to support medical equipment will continue to grow.

There are opportunities with third-party service providers (which are companies that don't manufacture equipment, but do service it, such as Aramark), manufacturer field representative positions, and in hospitals. Small community hospitals typically have very little turnover; there are more jobs in large metropolitan areas. People with both computer and medical equipment skills will be highly sought. Another high demand (and higher paying) area is medical imaging.

5. How do you see your profession changing in the next five years? What role will technology play in those changes, and what skills will be required?

Recently, our field changed its name and is now called Healthcare Technology Management, or HTM. HTM Professionals will need less component-level knowledge. Because most repairs today are at the board level, technicians must instead understand medical device integration. There will be increasing emphasis on patient data security; this impacts the BMET because these devices contain a lot of personal information. Successful technicians will need to communicate well with upper management and act as technical advisors to the hospital. I expect the relationship between HTM Departments and IT Departments to get closer. Also, there is increasing regulation in the medical environment, which biomed techs need to stay abreast of. Finally, we will see more equipment in the outpatient setting and for home care patients. This will probably lead to new areas of support that do not exist today—this is one of the reasons the term Healthcare Technology Management was created.

6. What do you enjoy most about your job? What do you enjoy least about your job?

The thing I liked most about the field was working with hospital staff. These people are dedicated and take their work very seriously. There's a lot of variety in this work—no two days are quite the same. What I enjoyed least about working in a hospital setting was the politics, especially with doctors who had a lot of influence.

7. Can you suggest a valuable "try this" for students considering a career in your profession?

Check the website for the Association for the Advancement of Medical Instrumentation (AAMI), specifically its student page. You can read biomedical magazines free online, such as 24X7 (www.24x7mag.com) or Tech Nation (www.1technation.com). You can attend meetings of your local HTM or biomedical technology association. Finally, volunteer in a hospital HTM/biomedical equipment department or for a medical device manufacturer, if possible.

SELECTED SCHOOLS

Many technical and community colleges offer programs in or related to medical equipment maintenance and repair. Commercial trade schools are also an option. Students are advised to consult with their school guidance counselor or research area post-secondary schools to find the right program.

MORE INFORMATION

Association for the Advancement of Medical Instrumentation
4301 North Fairfax Drive
Suite 301
Arlington, VA 22203
703.525.4890
www.aami.org

Biomedical Engineering Society
8201 Corporate Drive, Suite 1125
Landover, MD 20785
877.871.2637
www.bmes.org

Federation of Medical Equipment Support Associations
www.fmesa.org

Medical Equipment and Technology Association
www.mymeta.org

Simone Isadora Flynn/Editor

Computer Service Technician

Snapshot

Career Cluster: Electronics; Engineering; Maintenance & Repair; Technology

Interests: Computer maintenance and repair, solving problems, working with your hands

Earnings (Yearly Average): $38,310

Employment & Outlook: Slower than Average Growth Expected

OVERVIEW

Sphere of Work

Computer service technicians analyze, maintain, troubleshoot, and repair problems with computer systems. They may specialize in several different areas of computing, from personal computers such as notebooks and tablets to more complex business systems consisting of multiple servers, network technology, and workstations. Computer service technicians are employed by several different entities. Some work for private computer-repair firms, while others are members of larger organizations. Many service

techs are also employed by retail outlets specializing in computers and electronics.

Work Environment

Computer service technicians work primarily in repair shops, although those employed by large companies may work exclusively in administrative and office settings. Service techs who are employed by retail outlets may work remotely, traveling to businesses and residences in work vans and troubleshooting problems on-site. Computer service technicians who work remotely in homes and businesses must combine their technological savvy with deft customer-service skills to assist clients who are trying to address problems or work with systems they may be unfamiliar with.

Profile

Working Conditions: Work Indoors
Physical Strength: Light Work
Education Needs: On-The-Job Training, High School Diploma or G.E.D.
Licensure/Certification: Recommended
Physical Abilities Not Required: No Heavy Labor
Opportunities For Experience: Internship, Volunteer Work, Part-Time Work
Holland Interest Score*: RES

* See Appendix A

Occupation Interest

The field of computer service attracts a wide range of technically savvy professionals of all ages. Some are young professionals and students eager to gain experience in computer maintenance while planning a future career in another computer-related field, such as programming, software engineering, or hardware development. Other computer techs are longtime computer hobbyists who have decided to turn their passion for computing into a livelihood.

A Day in the Life—Duties and Responsibilities

Computer service technicians are tasked with a variety of duties and responsibilities each day. Many of their responsibilities vary depending on their particular arena of employment. The multitude of assignments and diverse workload presented to computer repair technicians require deft organization skills and the ability to prioritize and work on multiple projects simultaneously.

Those who are employed as team members in a large institution, such as a business, a university, or a government body, are often responsible for performing a variety of maintenance and upkeep tasks on organizational computer systems, ranging from cleaning out old files to updating antivirus and security software.

Service techs who are employed by computer-repair companies or who are self-employed spend their days evaluating machines in order to diagnose and solve the problems disrupting a computer's normal use. This can involve extensive interactions with customers, who may be contacted to initiate the course of repair best suited to their budget and needs.

Computer service technicians employed by computer stores and other retail electronic outlets perform a variety of tasks outside of maintenance and repair. They may be called upon to set up residential home-computing systems on-site, or they may travel to residences and businesses to assist with computer maintenance and repair.

Duties and Responsibilities

- Keeping maintenance records and repair reports
- Maintaining inventory of parts
- Ordering repair parts and selling supplies
- Advising customers concerning operation, maintenance and programming
- Installing equipment according to manufacturer's specifications
- Repairing equipment and instructing others on service and repair
- Preparing machines for customer use
- Consulting with supervisor to plan layout of equipment
- Running special diagnostic programs through computer equipment to help pinpoint problems

WORK ENVIRONMENT

Physical Environment

Service techs work primarily in office and workshop settings. Computer service technicians may also be required to visit homes and businesses.

Relevant Skills and Abilities

Technical Skills
- Performing technical work
- Working with machines, tools or other objects

Human Environment

Computer repair is both solitary and collaborative. Many computer technicians work individually, while others are required to interact with other professionals and home-computer owners. Technicians who work with clients are often charged with explaining complex concepts in terms novice users can understand.

Technological Environment

Computer service technicians must be very well versed in the common elements of contemporary computer technology, ranging from both personal computer and Mac OS systems to peripherals such as printers, scanners, and mobile technology. Knowledge of networks, system administration, and computer-security apparatuses is also beneficial.

EDUCATION, TRAINING, AND ADVANCEMENT

High School/Secondary

High school students can best prepare for a career in computer service by completing courses in algebra, calculus, geometry, trigonometry, introductory programming, desktop publishing, and introductory computer science. Participation in any available advanced placement (AP) classes in computing and technology are especially recommended, but these courses may not be offered at every school. Science and technology fairs are a good opportunity for students to immerse themselves in computer technology by conceptualizing and creating computer-related projects, while summer volunteer programs and internships at computer-related organizations can provide crucial reinforcement of the fundamentals of computer service.

Suggested High School Subjects
- Algebra
- Applied Communication
- Applied Math
- Blueprint Reading
- Computer Science
- Electricity & Electronics
- English
- Mechanical Drawing
- Shop Mechanics
- Trade/Industrial Education
- Welding

Famous First

The first computer bug was an actual bug—that is, a moth that got inside a Mark II computer at Harvard University, pictured, in 1945. Computer pioneer Grace Hopper removed the moth with a pair of tweezers. It was later preserved at the naval museum at Dahlgren, Virginia (now called the Dahlgren Heritage Museum). The terms "bug" and "debug" as used by computer technicians do not derive from the moth incident, however. Rather, the term "bug" was in use in the 19th century meaning a defect in a piece of equipment.

College/Postsecondary

Possession of a postsecondary degree is not a strict requirement for all computer service technician jobs, particularly those at the entry level. Many applicants who have amateur and hobbyist backgrounds in computers and are able to demonstrate their knowledge can often land entry-level positions. Managerial roles in computer service, however, almost exclusively require some kind of postsecondary study in computer science, computer programming, network administration, or the like, as do positions involving work with larger and more complex computer systems, networks, and databases.

Many US colleges and universities offer certification programs in computer technology in addition to more traditional undergraduate-level course work in information technology, computer service, and network administration. Certificate-level course work in computer repair trains students to address all major computer malfunctions and perform routine maintenance, basic hardware upgrades, and systematic troubleshooting.

Related College Majors
- Computer Engineering Technology
- Computer Installation & Repair
- Computer Maintenance Technology

Adult Job Seekers

Computer service is a popular realm of employment for adult job seekers, given its standard hours and localized nature. There is a growing need for technicians as computers and computer-aided technology become more commonplace worldwide. Individuals with personal or professional experience in computer science and technology are traditionally given preference for open positions, particularly when that experience is bolstered by formal education.

Professional Certification and Licensure

Although no specific certification or licensure is required, becoming a certified computer service technician increases an applicant's job opportunities. Membership in one of numerous professional organizations can help computer service technicians stay in tune with emerging trends and technologies related to the field.

Additional Requirements

Computer service technicians must be able to work independently and with little direction or guidance. Service techs must also be willing to regularly update their knowledge of computer hardware and software as the technology evolves.

Fun Fact

In 2012, households in the U.S. had an average of three computers—not including smart phones. That number was far surpassed by Bahrain, which averaged 7.23 computers per household, according to TekCarta. At the other end of the spectrum was Tanzania, with just .11 computers per household.

Source: generatorresearch.com/tekcarta/databank/personal-computers-per-household/

EARNINGS AND ADVANCEMENT

Mean annual earnings of computer service technicians were $38,310 in 2013. The lowest ten percent earned less than $21,890, and the highest ten percent earned more than $57,880.

Computer service technicians may receive paid vacations, holidays, and sick days; life and health insurance; and retirement benefits. These are usually paid by the employer.

Metropolitan Areas with the Highest
Employment Level in this Occupation

Metropolitan area	Employment [1]	Employment per thousand jobs	Hourly mean wage
Dallas-Plano-Irving, TX	4,280	1.99	$16.82
New York-White Plains-Wayne, NY-NJ	3,570	0.68	$19.97
Atlanta-Sandy Springs-Marietta, GA	2,850	1.24	$18.01
Houston-Sugar Land-Baytown, TX	2,670	0.97	$17.93
Chicago-Joliet-Naperville, IL	2,660	0.72	$19.13
Los Angeles-Long Beach-Glendale, CA	2,530	0.64	$21.26
Philadelphia, PA	2,260	1.23	$19.77
Minneapolis-St. Paul-Bloomington, MN-WI	2,100	1.17	$18.66
Fort Worth-Arlington, TX	1,910	2.10	$13.65
Santa Ana-Anaheim-Irvine, CA	1,720	1.19	$22.36

[1]Does not include self-employ ed. Source: Bureau of Labor Statistics

EMPLOYMENT AND OUTLOOK

There were approximately 133,000 computer, automated teller, and office machine repairers employed nationally in 2012. Employment is expected to grow slower than the average for all occupations through the year 2022, which means employment is projected to increase 1 percent to 7 percent. Although computer equipment continues to become less expensive and more reliable, malfunctions still occur and can cause severe problems for users, most of whom lack the knowledge to make repairs.

Employment Trend, Projected 2012–22

Total, All Occupations: 11%

Installation, Maintenance, and Repair Occupations: 10%

Computer Service Technicians: 4%

Note: "All Occupations" includes all occupations in the U.S. Economy. Source: U.S. Bureau of Labor Statistics, Employment Projections Program

Related Occupations
- Computer Network Architect
- Computer Support Specialist
- Electronic Equipment Repairer
- Home entertainment equipment technician
- Office Machine Repairer
- Robotics Technician
- Telecommunications Equipment Repairer
- Television & Radio Repairer

Conversation With . . .
JAMES KERR

Founder & Chief Geek
Super Geeks, Hawaii
Computer Service Technician, 25-plus years

1. What was your individual career path in terms of education/training, entry-level job, or other significant opportunity?

It all started in high school. At the time, there were no computers in schools. You could get one at Radio Shack for a few thousand dollars. It didn't really do much. But my school had one computer connected to the local university. We would play Star Wars on that machine. It had no screen—just reams and reams of paper flying through a high-speed printer. My lunch time was spent on that thing. It was true love!

In college, I was pre-med, hoping to be a physician. In addition to all the biology and chemistry classes, I majored in mechanical engineering. One day I realized I could skip medical school, do engineering instead, and be just as happy. So that's what I did.

After graduating, I worked for Sony in Tokyo, Japan. It was the height of the Japanese bubble economy and Sony was at the top of its game at the time. I started in the Corporate Strategy and Research & Development Planning departments, and eventually followed a "bleeding edge" technology— that is, one so new that it's considered high risk—into a business group. That technology was called digital still imaging. We built $30,000 digital cameras by hand and sold only 15 per month— mostly to competitors wanting to take them apart. Well, that CCD (or semiconductor imager) is the great-great-grandparent of the imager in your iPhone. Except that imager now costs only $8.

In 1997, I founded SuperGeeks, a company that fixes computers, builds websites and apps, creates online stores, and more. We provide tech services and products to consumers and businesses. I have 20 "geeks" working for me, and five locations, three of which are franchises.

2. What are the most important skills and/or qualities for someone in your profession?

You have to thrive on both learning and change. The tech industry continues to change daily. You need to stay abreast of those changes and be willing and able to master new technologies. What was unimaginable just five years ago is now commonplace.

3. What do you wish you had known going into this profession?

I am a business owner now. I wish I had delegated more from the get-go. If someone can do something at least equally as well as you, it's wiser to pay that person to do it so you can work on higher level things. If you want to go fast, go by yourself. If you want to go far, go together.

4. Are there many job opportunities in your profession? In what specific areas?

Yes, there are tremendous opportunities. We are just in the first few seconds of the first few minutes of this thing call the Internet. Find an area that interests you and dive deep into it. Ten years ago, it was all about servers and workstations. These days it's software and data. For example, learn how to mine business analytics and companies will pay you handsomely for your expertise.

5. How do you see your profession changing in the next five years? What role will technology play in those changes, and what skills will be required?

The cost of app development will drop. Just like globalization reduced the cost of manufacturing, geeks overseas will produce even more code. The rest of the world will be connected to the Internet. Anyone, anywhere will be able to access knowledge, goods, and services.

Ordinary things in our lives will become "smart" and connected to the Internet. Privacy will disappear. And eventually software will emulate my personality and follow me around like a happy little cloud of data.

6. What do you enjoy most about your job? What do you enjoy least about your job?

I enjoy learning new things and helping my clients harness computing. What do I enjoy least? A slow Internet connection?

7. Can you suggest a valuable "try this" for students considering a career in your pro-fession?

Try selling something—anything—online. It could be an information product, like *5 Tips on How to Make Old Dog Do New Tricks*, or some kind of widget. Create a website using SquareSpace, learn how to code at Scratch, and play with Canva.com.

SELECTED SCHOOLS

Many technical and community colleges offer programs in computer technology and repair. Commercial trade schools are also an option. For advanced positions a bachelor's degree is sometimes expected. Students are advised to consult with their school guidance counselor or research area post-secondary schools to find the right program.

MORE INFORMATION

Association for Computing Machinery
2 Penn Plaza, Suite 701
New York, NY 10121-0701
800.342.6626
www.acm.org

Association of Computer Repair Business Owners
2215 Jefferson Davis Highway
Suite 201
Fredericksburg, VA 22401
888.710.9006
www.acrbo.com

Computing Technology Industry Association
1815 South Meyers Road, Suite 300
Oakbrook Terrace, IL 60181-5228
630.678.8300
www.comptia.org

Electronics Technicians Association International
5 Depot Street
Greencastle IN 46135
800.288.3824
www.eta-i.org

Information Technology Association of America
601 Pennsylvania Avenue, NW
North Building
Washington, DC 20004
202.682.9110
www.techamerica.org

John Pritchard/Editor

Diesel Service Technician

Snapshot

Career Cluster: Engineering; Maintenance & Repair

Interests: Engineering, engine mechanics, machinery, solving problems, working with your hands

Earnings (Yearly Average): $44,120

Employment & Outlook: Average Growth Expected

OVERVIEW

Sphere of Work

Diesel service technicians maintain and repair vehicles with diesel engines. Diesel engines are similar to gasoline engines; however, gasoline engines are spark-ignition engines, whereas diesel engines are compression-ignition engines. Buses and trucks commonly have diesel engines.

Diesel engines are more efficient and durable than gasoline engines and therefore more practical for heavy-duty jobs. Construction equipment and industrial vehicles such as cranes, bulldozers, tractors, locomotives, and commercial boats all use diesel engines. A diesel service technician is responsible for understanding the inner workings of these different machines, though they often specialize in a particular type of vehicle.

Work Environment

Diesel service technicians work in repair shops where customers or colleagues bring their vehicles to be serviced. On occasion, diesel service technicians travel to their customers, meeting them at their workplace or at a location where their vehicle or equipment has broken down.

Profile

Working Conditions: Work both Indoors and Outdoors

Physical Strength: Medium to Heavy Work

Education Needs: On-The-Job Training, High School Diploma with Technical Education, Technical/Community College

Licensure/Certification: Recommended

Physical Abilities Not Required: N/A

Opportunities For Experience: Apprenticeship, Military Service, Part-Time Work

Holland Interest Score*: REI

* See Appendix A

Occupation Interest

Diesel service technicians are problem solvers who have the patience and ability to take machines apart, diagnose their problems, and rebuild them. Technicians are interested in engineering, engine mechanics, and machinery. They enjoy facing new challenges and are open to working in dynamic circumstances.

A Day in the Life—Duties and Responsibilities

Most diesel service technicians work in a repair shop. Some work for companies and service a particular fleet of vehicles, while others perform repairs on a per-customer basis. Diesel service technicians often work irregular hours. Overtime, weekend, and evening shifts are common, as some shops offer twenty-four-hour service.

Technicians associated with a company or a specific organization that owns a number of vehicles or machines spend most of their time maintaining those vehicles or machines to prevent them from breaking down. Diesel service technicians who work in a repair shop predominantly identify and respond to problems with broken machines as they come into the shop.

Diesel service technicians must adhere to a checklist of requirements when they are performing an inspection. They test vehicles and engines and analyze the results in order to diagnose problems. They are trained in using hand tools as well as computerized testing equipment. The work can be strenuous and intricate; technicians often perform routine checkups, but they must also be able to take a machine apart and put it back together again if required. Technicians are also responsible for making sure that a vehicle is compliant with federal emissions standards. Working with heavy-duty machines can be dangerous, but technicians are trained in safety procedures.

Duties and Responsibilities

- Test driving trucks and buses
- Performing preventive maintenance to assure safe vehicle operation and to prevent wear and damage to parts
- Repairing, replacing or overhauling parts such as pistons, valves, rods, carburetors, pumps and generators
- Rewiring ignition systems, lights and instrument panels
- Relining and adjusting brakes and front ends
- Installing and repairing accessories such as radios, heaters, mirrors and windshield wipers
- Examining protective guards, loose bolts and specified safety devices and making adjustments

WORK ENVIRONMENT

Physical Environment

Most diesel service technicians work in a repair shop. Shops are often noisy due to the use of equipment, ventilators, and other machines and the activity of technicians and customers. The work of a technician is often dirty, physically demanding, and dangerous. Technicians take precautions to ensure their safety while working with power tools and heavy equipment.

Relevant Skills and Abilities

Interpersonal/Social Skills
- Being able to work independently

Organization & Management Skills
- Performing duties that change frequently

Technical Skills
- Working with machines, tools or other objects

Unclassified Skills
- Using set methods and standards in your work

Human Environment

Diesel service technicians interact with customers and colleagues on a daily basis. They need to be effective communicators in order to ascertain and explain problems and solutions. Technicians should be comfortable working either individually or as members of a team.

Technological Environment

Diesel service technicians work in a complex technological environment. Technicians typically use both handheld and laptop computers on the job. They use computer-based testing equipment to check emissions, fuel efficiency, and other engine components. They also work with electronic systems that are incorporated into engines.

EDUCATION, TRAINING, AND ADVANCEMENT

High School/Secondary

An aspiring diesel service technician should take classes in English, mathematics, and physics. He or she should also study electronics and automotive repair. Most employers require that employees finish high school or pass a general educational development (GED) test. Many companies and repair shops also require that applicants be at least eighteen years of age.

Suggested High School Subjects
- Applied Math
- Applied Physics
- Auto Collision Technology
- Auto Service Technology
- Diesel Maintenance Technology
- English
- Machining Technology
- Shop Math
- Shop Mechanics
- Welding

Famous First

The first diesel-engine automobiles were produced on a small scale in the 1930s by the European car makers Citroen and Mercedes-Benz. European brands, including Peugeot and Volkswagen, continued to dominate the field through the late 1970s, when American manufacturers began introducing diesel models.

College/Postsecondary

Most diesel service technicians attend a technical school or community college. Programs last from six months to two years and culminate in an associate's degree or certificate in diesel engine repair. The programs themselves vary in focus. Some programs emphasize hands-on work, while others spend more time in a lab or classroom

Though most technicians receive some kind of formal training, some are trained entirely on the job. These technicians usually start their careers by doing smaller jobs in repair shops, such as cleaning machines or moving vehicles and equipment, and are promoted as they acquire and master new skills.

Related College Majors
* Diesel Engine Mechanics & Repair

Adult Job Seekers

A career as a diesel service technician is a good choice for adult job seekers because the field draws on a number of skills. A working knowledge of cars and engines, military service, and experience in sales are all valuable transferable skills. The paths to success for a diesel service technician are varied and flexible.

Professional Certification and Licensure

Most aspiring technicians, whether formally trained or trained in the field, take tests to earn national certification. While national certification through the National Institute for Automotive Service Excellence (ASE) is not an official requirement, most successful technicians have ASE certification, as it increases one's chances for employment and promotion. A technician can be certified in over forty specializations pertaining to different types of vehicles (school bus, light truck), machinery (electronic diesel engine, parts specialist), and repairs (collision damage, light repair, refinishing). Technicians must retake tests every five years to maintain certification. By taking multiple related tests, a technician can be certified as a master technician in a particular field of vehicle repair. Technicians must also have a state driver's license that qualifies them to test-drive the vehicles they repair, including trucks and buses.

Additional Requirements

Skills in sales, management, and leadership are valued in a repair shop. A successful diesel service technician is not only technically skilled but also good at dealing with customers and other technicians. Technicians should be willing to learn new skills when it is required of them.

EARNINGS AND ADVANCEMENT

Experience is the major factor affecting earnings of diesel service technicians. Beginning workers usually earned from 50 percent to 75 percent of the rate of skilled workers and received increases as they became more experienced. Mean annual earnings of diesel service technicians were $44,120 in 2013. The lowest ten percent earned less than $27,270, and the highest ten percent earned more than $63,760. Many diesel service technicians also received a commission.

Diesel service technicians may receive paid vacations, holidays, and sick days; life and health insurance; and retirement benefits. These are usually paid by the employer. Most employers also provide uniforms.

Metropolitan Areas with the Highest
Employment Level in this Occupation

Metropolitan area	Employment [1]	Employment per thousand jobs	Hourly mean wage
New York-White Plains-Wayne, NY-NJ	5,940	1.13	$27.71
Chicago-Joliet-Naperville, IL	5,790	1.57	$23.22
Houston-Sugar Land-Baytown, TX	5,450	1.98	$20.32
Los Angeles-Long Beach-Glendale, CA	5,010	1.26	$24.21
Atlanta-Sandy Springs-Marietta, GA	3,940	1.71	$21.53
Dallas-Plano-Irving, TX	3,600	1.67	$21.40
Minneapolis-St. Paul-Bloomington, MN-WI	3,480	1.94	$22.53
Riverside-San Bernardino-Ontario, CA	3,370	2.81	$21.48
Denver-Aurora-Broomfield, CO	2,960	2.31	$21.70
Indianapolis-Carmel, IN	2,580	2.83	$20.17

[1]Does not include self-employ ed. Source: Bureau of Labor Statistics

EMPLOYMENT AND OUTLOOK

Diesel service technicians held about 250,000 jobs in 2012. They were employed by almost every industry; in particular, those that use trucks, buses, and equipment to haul, deliver, and transport materials, goods, and people.

Employment is expected to grow about as fast as the average for all occupations through the year 2022, which means employment is projected to increase 7 percent to 11 percent. Job opportunities created by the continued growth of freight being transported by trucks will be slightly diminished due to the increasing durability of new vehicles.

Employment Trend, Projected 2012–22

Total, All Occupations: 11%

Installation, Maintenance, and Repair Occupations: 10%

Diesel Service Technicians : 9%

Note: "All Occupations" includes all occupations in the U.S. Economy. Source: U.S. Bureau of Labor Statistics, Employment Projections Program

Related Occupations
- Aircraft Mechanic
- Automotive Body Repairer
- Automotive Technician
- Farm Equipment Mechanic
- Heavy Equipment Service Technician
- Industrial Machinery Mechanic
- Small Engine Mechanic

Related Military Occupations
- Automotive & Heavy Equipment Mechanic
- Marine Engine Mechanic

Conversation With . . .
DAVID GREGORY

Diesel Service Technician, 38+ years
Co-owner of family diesel service business
Southern Oregon Diesel, Roseburg, Oregon

1. What was your individual career path in terms of education/training, entry-level job, or other significant opportunity?

My father started the business in 1954 and I had to work in it when I was young. I had to do things like steam-clean diesel engines and, let me tell you, when you had to do that in the summer, it was super-hot.

After high school, I ended up running a concrete plant. I didn't plan to go back to work in my dad's business. But he got sick and couldn't keep it up and I got with my younger brother and we decided we had to pull together to keep it going to support him and my mom. We've run the business ever since. That was 38 years ago.

It's been tough. At times, we've had to work as much as seven days a week to keep afloat. We've had to change directions and reinvent ourselves to deal with a changing economy. Originally, our key business was logging trucks and logging machinery. Then we worked on trucking fleets. We're now seguing to a focus on servicing pickup trucks, RVs and passenger cars. I still work on engines in between my responsibilities as an owner. I also have two full-time mechanics.

2. What are the most important skills and/or qualities for someone in your profession?

You have to be mechanically inclined. That's one key. But you have to be willing to learn and be responsible. That is, show up and be on time. Do your best and focus on the job. Don't short-change the customer or your employer when you're on the clock by pulling out your cellphone to go on Facebook or answer a text. Save that for a break. If you've got all that, you can learn what you need to do and be successful. I'm willing to train kids if they have a knack for mechanics, a good personality, aren't a smart aleck and show up.

3. What do you wish you had known going into this profession?

There wasn't much I could have done about it, given my circumstances. For young people considering this profession, I'd tell them to go for it as long as they're willing to be responsible and give a good day's work for a good day's pay.

4. Are there many job opportunities in your profession? In what specific areas?

There are many, many job opportunities. Diesel engines are being used in more consumer applications around the world as well as by commercial and industrial customers. For example, we'll be using more engines that run mostly on natural gas but use diesel to start and again on large hills and the like.

5. How do you see your profession changing in the next five years, what role will technology play in those changes, and what skills will be required?

Diesel engines aren't simple and will only get more complex. Mechanics who are trained in electronics and computers and who keep themselves current on changes will do best. People can acquire some skills at trade schools and community colleges. But you have to take the right courses. Focus on the basics and on electronics. Don't take courses in subjects like race-car engines. That's not going to help you get a job at a repair shop or with a big diesel-engine maker like Caterpillar or Cummins. And you'll always need a solid work ethic.

6. What do you enjoy most about your job? What do you enjoy least about your job?

I enjoy the people the most. I love our customers and want to give them excellent service so they'll come back and so they'll tell other people about us. We have a great reputation and I want to keep it.

I least like employees who are irresponsible and don't focus on their jobs.

7. Can you suggest a valuable "try this" for students considering a career in your profession?

I suggest they look for an internship. I have had lots of interns over the years. It gives me an opportunity to immerse them in the business. They start at the bottom pushing a broom and work up and that's how they learn and earn the right to be a diesel mechanic. Often they appreciate it more and actually learn more than those who go to technical schools.

SELECTED SCHOOLS

Many technical and community colleges offer programs in diesel engine technology and repair. Commercial trade schools are also an option. Students are advised to consult with their school guidance counselor or research area post-secondary schools to find the right program.

MORE INFORMATION

Association of Diesel Specialists
400 Admiral Boulevard
Kansas City, MO 64106
816.285.0810
www.diesel.org

Automotive Service Association
8190 Precinct Line Road, Suite 100
Colleyville, TX 76034
800.272.7467
www.asashop.org

Diesel Technician Society
P.O. Box 298
Flanders, NJ 07836
www.forddoctorsdts.com

National Automotive Technicians Education Foundation
101 Blue Seal Drive, SE, Suite 101
Leesburg, VA 20175
703.669.6650
www.natef.org

National Institute for Automotive Service Excellence
101 Blue Seal Drive SE, Suite 101
Leesburg, VA 20175
703.669.6600
www.ase.com

National Truck Equipment Association
37400 Hills Tech Drive
Farmington Hills, MI 48331-3414
800.441.6832
www.ntea.com

Molly Hagan/Editor

Electronics Engineering Technician

Snapshot

Career Cluster: Electronics; Engineering; Maintenance & Repair; Manufacturing; Technology

Interests: Electronics, solving problems, analyzing information

Earnings (Yearly Average): $58,770

Employment & Outlook: Slower than Average Growth Expected

OVERVIEW

Sphere of Work

Electronics engineering technicians are paid to test, maintain, assemble, and repair electronic equipment and electronic systems. Technicians work in a variety of industries. Some assemble electronics in-house, while other work in the field. Repair technicians apply their training and knowledge to troubleshoot and diagnose faulty equipment. If electronic equipment is beyond their repair, technicians will typically bring the equipment to a shop or

install replacement equipment. Electronics engineering technicians work closely with electronics engineers to make sure that electronic equipment has optimal design and function.

Work Environment

Electronics engineering technicians work in an assortment of locations that vary depending on the industry. These environments include offices, laboratories, and manufacturing locations. Some technicians work on assembly lines, where they build electronic components. Given the variety of equipment, tools, and materials used in the assembly of electronic products and systems, technicians may be exposed to hazards. In order to avoid injury and exposure to harmful materials, proper safety procedures must be followed at all times.

Profile

Working Conditions: Work Indoors
Physical Strength: Light Work
Education Needs: High School Diploma with Technical Education, Technical/Community College
Licensure/Certification: Recommended
Physical Abilities Not Required: No Heavy Labor
Opportunities For Experience: Apprenticeship, Military Service
Holland Interest Score*: IRE

* See Appendix A

Occupation Interest

Electronics engineering technicians apply a variety of skills and knowledge to the testing, repair, and production of electronic equipment. Individuals who choose this profession have strong backgrounds in electronics or electronics engineering technology. The work of an electronics engineering technician requires excellent attention to detail and the ability to work with complex electrical components. Technicians are problem solvers who are able to work cooperatively. They have keen minds for analysis and troubleshooting.

A Day in the Life—Duties and Responsibilities

Throughout their workday, technicians work closely with engineers in the design and development of a wide range of electronics-based equipment, including communication devices, machine controls, and computer equipment. They use their knowledge of electronics principles and theory to assist in the design and assembly of equipment. Technicians can also work in the research-and-development field, where they test and evaluate electronic components and systems.

Electronics engineering technicians use engineering specifications, systems manuals, and their knowledge of electronics to assemble prototype models. During the assembly process, technicians will identify design flaws and recommend adjustments. In order to test equipment, electronics engineering technicians develop test apparatuses and devices, then analyze and interpret the resulting data. They communicate regularly with electronics engineers, supervisors, and other technicians.

When a technician is called in to perform repairs, he or she will first troubleshoot the problem. Repairs can involve adjustments, calibrations, or modifications to circuitry and components. If a technician in the field is unable to repair a machine or electronic system, he or she brings the machine to the shop or calls for assistance.

Technicians are responsible for writing technical reports, drawing schematics, and assembling other information in order to detail the performance, limitations, and other characteristics of electronic systems. Their work also involves inspecting newly installed equipment in order to ensure that it is working properly.

Duties and Responsibilities

- **Verifying that set standards and specifications have been met**
- **Inspecting and repairing equipment**
- **Designing equipment and testing for defects**
- **Developing, manufacturing and servicing electronic equipment**

WORK ENVIRONMENT

Physical Environment

The immediate physical environment of an electronics engineering technician varies depending on the industry he or she works in. Potential environments include offices, laboratories, manufacturing facilities, and factory assembly lines. Electronic engineering technicians may also work on military bases.

Relevant Skills and Abilities

Interpersonal/Social Skills
- Being able to work independently

Organization & Management Skills
- Paying attention to and handling details

Technical Skills
- Performing scientific, mathematical and technical work
- Working with data or numbers
- Working with machines, tools or other objects
- Working with your hands

Plant Environment

Some electronics engineering technicians work in manufacturing facilities and factories. These environments often utilize heavy machinery and dangerous chemicals that can present a variety of health and safety hazards. Technicians must be sure to follow established safety procedures.

Human Environment

Electronics engineering technicians work with a variety of other professionals, including electronics engineers, supervisors, and other technicians. They also communicate regularly with clients.

Technological Environment

Electronics engineering technicians use a wide range of tools, including pliers, screwdrivers, drills, and bench lathes, in order to fabricate parts. They also use a wide variety of computer equipment.

EDUCATION, TRAINING, AND ADVANCEMENT

High School/Secondary

Employers normally require an electronics engineering technician to have a high school diploma or an equivalent general educational development (GED) certificate. Typically, a high school curriculum offers several basic and advanced courses that an individual interested in becoming a technician will benefit from, including mathematics, engineering, and physics. Some high schools have workshops that instruct students in the fundamentals of electronics.

Suggested High School Subjects
- Applied Math
- Blueprint Reading
- Electricity & Electronics
- English
- Shop Math
- Shop Mechanics
- Welding

Famous First

The first electronic pocket calculator was introduced by Texas Instruments of Dallas, Texas, in 1971. The unit was battery powered, weighed a full 2.5 pounds, and cost $149. It could only perform basic mathematical functions such as addition, subtraction, multiplication, and division. The results were displayed on an LED (light-emitting diode) window. Later models were lighter and more powerful.

College/Postsecondary

Most employers require applicants to have at least an associate's degree in electrical or electronics engineering technology. Some four-year and community colleges offer these programs, and those interested in the profession should look for reputable ones in their area. College curriculums often place more focus on theory than hands-on training.

Many technical schools have two-year programs in relevant fields. These programs normally emphasize hands-on training. Electronics technicians gain strong skills and knowledge by taking courses in programming, physics, circuitry, and other related areas.

While researching educational opportunities, an individual should look for programs and schools accredited by the Technology Accreditation Commission (TAC) of the Accreditation Board for Engineering and Technology (ABET). Technical schools usually work with local employers in the industry, which makes them a great place for job seekers to network. Many schools also offer job-placement programs. Some applicants enter the field through the military.

Related College Majors
- Computer Engineering Technology
- Electrical, Electronics & Communications Engineering
- Robotics Technology

Adult Job Seekers

Those interested in employment as an electronics technician should first research the average annual income, required hours, and advancement opportunities to be sure that these factors suit their interests. Individuals without any background or experience in electronics or engineering should enter a program at a technical school or a college. Local unions, trade organizations, and schools are great places to go with any questions.

Professional Certification and Licensure

Although certification is not required by all employers, an electronics technician who has acquired certification is more likely to be hired. Technicians can seek certification through the Electronics Technicians

Association (ETA) International. Becoming certified through the ETA will provide job seekers with more opportunities for career advancement and recognition in the industry. Certification programs are offered in a variety of specialized areas, including communications, information technology, and renewable energy. Certification tests through the ETA can be taken online or at designated test sites. A fee is required.

Most electronics technicians start out in the role of apprentice. After a certain amount of hands-on training and instruction is acquired, they become experienced enough to work with little or no supervision. Experienced workers can go on to become supervisors or own their own shops.

Additional Requirements

Electronics technicians must possess great reasoning skills in order to properly and quickly identify problems in malfunctioning or defective equipment. The inability to identify problems quickly can lead to more problems and profit loss. Technicians need to pay close attention to detail when working with specifications, machine and product manuals, and other detailed information regarding equipment and components. Problem-solving skills are also essential to the design, production, and testing of electronic equipment.

Fun Fact

"Moore's Law," says that the number of components per microchip doubles every 12 months. Named for Gordon Moore, Fairchild Semiconductor's Director of R&D (later with Intel), who suggested this fact in 1965.

Source: http://www.computerhistory.org/semiconductor/timeline/1965-Moore.html

EARNINGS AND ADVANCEMENT

Electronic engineering technicians usually begin by doing routine work under the close supervision of an experienced technician, engineer or scientist. As they gain experience, they are given more difficult assignments with only general supervision. Some electronic engineering technicians eventually become supervisors.

Mean annual earnings of electronic engineering technicians were $58,770 in 2013. The lowest ten percent earned less than $34,570, and the highest ten percent earned more than $85,350.

Electronic engineering technicians may receive paid vacations, holidays, and sick days; life and health insurance; and retirement benefits. These are usually paid by the employer.

Metropolitan Areas with the Highest
Employment Level in this Occupation

Metropolitan area	Employment [1]	Employment per thousand jobs	Hourly mean wage
Austin-Round Rock-San Marcos, TX	4,580	5.36	$31.54
San Jose-Sunnyvale-Santa Clara, CA	4,240	4.56	$31.37
Phoenix-Mesa-Glendale, AZ	3,740	2.10	$26.64
Houston-Sugar Land-Baytown, TX	3,620	1.31	$31.02
Los Angeles-Long Beach-Glendale, CA	3,510	0.88	$29.58
Dallas-Plano-Irving, TX	3,290	1.53	$24.82
Atlanta-Sandy Springs-Marietta, GA	3,130	1.36	$27.60
Washington-Arlington-Alexandria, DC-VA-MD-WV	3,090	1.30	$34.26
San Diego-Carlsbad-San Marcos, CA	3,020	2.34	$29.63
Portland-Vancouver-Hillsboro, OR-WA	2,830	2.76	$28.35

[1]Does not include self-employ ed. Source: Bureau of Labor Statistics

EMPLOYMENT AND OUTLOOK

Electronic engineering technicians held about 147,000 jobs nationally in 2012. Employment is expected to grow slower than the average for all occupations through the year 2022, which means employment is projected to increase 0 percent to 4 percent. Although there is still rising demand for electronic goods, foreign competition in design and manufacturing will limit employment growth. Employers will continue to look for electronic engineering technicians who are skilled in new technology and require a minimum of additional job training. Many job openings will be to replace workers who transfer to other occupations or retire.

Employment Trend, Projected 2012–22

Total, All Occupations: 11%

Engineering Technicians (All): 1%

Electronics Engineering Technicians: 0%

Note: "All Occupations" includes all occupations in the U.S. Economy. Source: U.S. Bureau of Labor Statistics, Employment Projections Program

Related Occupations
- Broadcast Technician
- Electronic Equipment Repairer
- Engineering Technician
- Home entertainment equipment technician

Conversation With . . .
CHARLES KELLER

Senior Curriculum Manager
APT College, Carlsbad, CA, 4 ½ years
Electronics and Telecommunications Industry
30+ years

1. What was your individual career path in terms of education/training, entry-level job, or other significant opportunity?

I started in electronics at 12 years of age when I became a ham radio operator. From there, I obtained some amateur radio licenses. After I left high school, I joined the Navy, where I received additional electronics training. I started as a radio technician and worked on radios, transmitters, and antennae. When I retired from the Navy after 21 years, I was a lieutenant junior grade officer and managed electronics departments. After I left the Navy, I got my bachelor's degree in liberal arts, and also went to work for San Diego Gas and Electric. There, I had various roles, from technician to management, in electronics and telecommunications. I retired from that company to come here, where I develop new courses and update older courses in electronics, telecommunications, wireless, and fiber optics.

A field engineering technician in electronics would assist an engineer in designing and field-testing equipment. When I was at San Diego Gas and Electric, for instance, I designed and installed two-way radio systems—similar to police radios—and also worked on microwave radios, fiber optics equipment, and telephone systems.

2. What are the most important skills and/or qualities for someone in your profession?

You have to be motivated to learn the technology because sometimes there's not a course that you can take. You have to study on your own and continuously improve your skills. It's also critical to have some basic background in science and math.

3. What do you wish you had known going into this profession?

It would have been nice to have had the money for extra training prior to going into the military, where I received my formal training.

4. Are there many job opportunities in your profession? In what specific areas?

You can be quite successful with an electronics background in many fields. City, state and federal governments need engineering technicians, including wireless technicians. Other areas include electric utilities across the country, telephone companies, the military, avionics, and automotive electronics. Any large company needs engineering technicians. Cellular and cable companies have extensive groups of engineering technicians. Specialty technologies you might want to look into include microwave, two-way radio systems, fiber optics, and power systems, including UPS systems—or uninterruptible power systems, which are backup systems.

5. How do you see your profession changing in the next five years, what role will technology play in those changes, and what skills will be required?

Obviously, the technology is changing all the time. The electronics are still the same, but there will be newer applications for technology. Think of the phone you carry with you. You can see that it's changing all the time.

As far as skills, a successful engineering technician has to have strong interpersonal skills. Say you're designing a wireless system. You have to interface with different work groups, such as IT work groups, possibly construction groups, and accounting and business people. There's a cost to all of this, so you need to be able to relate to the person who is controlling the money. All of these people have different skill sets and you have to talk in a language they can all understand.

6. What do you enjoy most about your job? What do you enjoy least about your job?

What I'm doing now is taking all of my prior knowledge and creating and updating courses based on new technology. Then I get to try it out through teaching, so I get the best of both worlds, and that's why I enjoy doing it. I've been very fortunate because I knew what I wanted to do from an early age, so I can't think of much in my career I haven't enjoyed.

7. Can you suggest a valuable "try this" for students considering a career in your profession?

Attend a seminar on a specialty that interests you, such as wireless telecommunications. Some of these seminars are inexpensive, or even free. Organizations that specialize in electronics and might offer such seminars include the International Wireless Communications Exposition, the Building Industry Consulting Services International, and the Electronics Technicians Associated, International.

SELECTED SCHOOLS

Many technical and community colleges offer programs in electrical and electronic engineering technology. Commercial trade schools are also an option. Students are advised to consult with their school guidance counselor or research area post-secondary schools to find the right program.

MORE INFORMATION

Accreditation Board for Engineering and Technology
111 Market Place, Suite 1050
Baltimore, MD 21202
410.347.7700
www.abet.org

American Society for Engineering Education
1818 N Street NW, Suite 600
Washington, DC 20036
202.331.3500
www.asee.org

Electronics Technicians Association International
5 Depot Street
Greencastle, IN 46135
800.288.3824
www.eta-i.org

International Society of Certified Electronics Technicians
3608 Pershing Avenue
Fort Worth, TX 76107
800.946.0201
www.iscet.org

Patrick Cooper/Editor

Electronic Equipment Repairer

Snapshot

Career Cluster: Electronics; Engineering; Maintenance & Repair; Technology

Interests: Electronics, mechanics, solving problems, working with your hands

Earnings (Yearly Average): $51,220

Employment & Outlook: Slower than Average Growth Expected

OVERVIEW

Sphere of Work

Electronic equipment repairers work within the service industry. They work on various types of electronic equipment with a range of applications. Often, they specialize in a particular field, such as repair of commercial and industrial equipment in the manufacturing or telecommunications industry or repair of electronic equipment in the power or other utilities industry. Repair of electronic equipment in the transportation sector primarily covers the electronic components of boats,

ships, and locomotive engines, with repair of electronic equipment of motor vehicles as a separate specialty. Repair of avionics is not part of this occupation.

Work Environment

Electronic equipment repairers work either in the field at customers' locations or in repair shops. Field sites vary greatly, depending on the type of electronic equipment needing repair. They include factories, powerhouses and substations, railroad yards, harbors, offices, and commercial shops.

Repair shops are generally indoors, designed for customers to bring in their malfunctioning electronic equipment. These include places where electronic equipment for whole motor vehicles can be repaired. Some repair shops specialize in working on broken equipment sent in after it has been removed and replaced by customers.

Profile

Working Conditions: Work Indoors
Physical Strength: Light to Medium Work
Education Needs: On-The-Job Training, High School Diploma with Technical Education, Technical/Community College
Licensure/Certification: Recommended
Physical Abilities Not Required: No Heavy Labor
Opportunities For Experience: Apprenticeship, Military Service, Part-Time Work
Holland Interest Score*: REI

* See Appendix A

Occupation Interest

Electronic equipment repair can appeal to a person who likes to tinker with equipment and takes pride in fixing things. Mechanical and troubleshooting skills are essential. Repair work tends to be varied, and fieldwork combines travel with working indoors. Educational training focuses on practical skills. Earnings in the field have been attractive, too, especially for repairing industrial and commercial electronic equipment.

A Day in the Life—Duties and Responsibilities

The workday of an electronic equipment repairer generally begins either at the site of a customer's malfunctioning equipment or in a repair shop. Many repairers work independently with little direct supervision, especially in the field.

Initial fault assessment demands good skills in troubleshooting, testing, and common sense. It is important to determine whether the problem is due to technical reasons, human error, or even outside influences such as a loose or frayed wire connection. For inspection and testing, an electronic equipment repairer will use sophisticated electronic diagnostic tools. Repairers must be knowledgeable about the operation processes and composition of the electronic equipment they are examining.

Before agreeing to repair work, some customers will want a cost estimate, which is often calculated by the repairers themselves. To repair certain key electronic equipment at a power house or on a factory floor, for example, a plant has to be shut down for a scheduled period of time.

Actual repair work depends on the type of electronic equipment and the cause of its breakdown. For repairs, an electronic equipment repairer relies on fine mechanical hand tools, the handling of which requires considerable mechanical skills and the ability to perform precision work.

After repairs are completed, the repaired equipment is reassembled and tested. In the field, the equipment is reconnected and its operations tested. By the end of the workday or upon completion of a task, electronic equipment repairers are generally required to log the details of their work, including parts used and labor time expended.

Duties and Responsibilities

- Conducting routine checks for defective parts, faulty circuits or poor connections
- Referring to wiring diagrams and service manuals
- Using testing equipment, such as voltmeters, oscilloscopes, signal generators, and frequency counters
- Replacing parts and making necessary adjustments
- Communicating with customers to identify the problem
- Making service calls to customer premises

OCCUPATION SPECIALTIES

Field Technicians

Field Technicians often travel to factories or a customer's site to repair broken down equipment. Because repairing components is a complex activity, workers in factories usually remove and replace defective units, such as circuit boards, instead of fixing them. Defective units are discarded or returned to the manufacturer or a specialized shop for repair.

Bench Technicians

Bench Technicians work in repair shops in factories and service centers, fixing components that cannot be repaired on a factory floor. These workers also locate and repair circuit defects, such as poorly soldered joints, blown fuses, or malfunctioning transistors.

WORK ENVIRONMENT

Physical Environment

Electronic equipment repair work is commonly done at a customer's location by a field technician or in a repair shop by a bench technician. Typically, field locations are industrial or commercial settings. They can range from large installations such as power plants to office suites with broken electronic security systems. Repair shops vary in size and specialization but are generally well lit and comfortable to work in.

Human Environment

Many electronic equipment repairers work alone on field assignments. In a repair shop, they usually have colleagues and supervisors. Work is done either during business hours or at any time when electronic equipment repairers are called on to perform emergency repairs.

Relevant Skills and Abilities

Interpersonal/Social Skills
- Being able to work independently

Organization & Management Skills
- Making decisions
- Paying attention to and handling details
- Performing duties that change frequently

Research & Planning Skills
- Developing evaluation strategies

Technical Skills
- Performing scientific, mathematical and technical work
- Working with machines, tools or other objects

Technological Environment

The work involves both sophisticated electronic diagnostic tools, such as testing software, advanced electronic multimeters, signal generators, and oscilloscopes, and mechanical precision instruments for repairs. The electronic equipment subject to repair is increasingly technologically complex.

EDUCATION, TRAINING, AND ADVANCEMENT

High School/Secondary

High school students should take classes in electricity and electronics, at the advanced placement (AP) level if offered. Other useful classes include applied mathematics, general mathematics, computer science, science, and English. To earn a high school diploma with technical education, classes in blueprint reading, shop mathematics and mechanics, and welding should be taken. Students should also join a high school or community electronics club if one is available and look for summer or part-time work as an assistant in an electronics repair shop.

Suggested High School Subjects
- Applied Math
- Blueprint Reading

- Electricity & Electronics
- English
- Shop Math
- Shop Mechanics
- Welding

Famous First

The first power plant to use alternating current was built in Great Barrington, Massachusetts, in 1886. The transformers were developed by William Stanley, Jr., under contract with Westinghouse Electric Company. The generator was used to light stores and offices in Great Barrington, pictured. Many electrical engineers came to the plant to study and learn from Stanley's achievement. The generator operated through the spring and early summer of that year, but was destroyed when a technician accidentally dropped a screwdriver into it.

College/Postsecondary

It is possible to obtain a job with just a high school degree, and the field has a strong focus on on-the-job training. However, initial employment chances are helped greatly if the applicant has received some specialized formal training in electronic equipment repair at a community college, technical college, or vocational school. Courses should include electronics and electronic equipment repair. An associate's degree in the field is useful both for obtaining initial employment and for professional advancement.

Completing at least some college work is advantageous, and it is required sometimes for positions in the best-paying specializations, such as repairing commercial and industrial electronic equipment or equipment at powerhouses, power substations, and relay stations. A baccalaureate degree in electronics, for example, qualifies a person for top positions in the field after gaining on-the-job experience. The U.S. Department of Labor Office of Apprenticeship Training recognizes six apprenticeships suitable for work in this occupation, including field service engineer, electronic sales and service technician, and specialization in meteorological equipment repair.

Related College Majors
- Electrical & Electronics Equipment Installation & Repair

Adult Job Seekers

An adult job seeker wishing to find employment as an electronic equipment repairer should have at least a high school degree or GED certificate. He or she should have taken some recent courses in electronics at an accredited postsecondary institution such as a community college. Having passed such a course shows potential employers that an applicant is familiar with the current developments in the field and has made a serious effort to prepare for work in this occupation.

If an adult job seeker is a recent military veteran, having worked on electronic equipment in the military is beneficial to finding employment. An adult job seeker may also prepare by working as an assistant in an electronic equipment repair shop.

Professional Certification and Licensure

Certification is offered by different organizations. In particular, as of 2013, the Electronics Technicians Association International offers more than fifty certification programs for specializations in this occupation. The International Society of Certified Electronics Technicians offers a similar array of certifications. To become certified, applicants have to meet professional requirements and pass a comprehensive exam. Licensing is not generally required.

Additional Requirements

An electronic equipment repairer should have a good service mentality and enjoy tinkering with and fixing electronic equipment. Because field technicians often travel to customers on their own, they need to have a certain sense of self-reliance and good troubleshooting skills and be able to solve problems by themselves.

Fun Fact

Commodities that can be extracted from recycled electronic equipment includes steel, aluminum, gold, silver, titanium, copper, nickel, plastic, and glass.

Source: Amy Neumann, "Interesting Facts on Electronics Recycling and Sustainability," Nov. 11, 2012; http://www.huffingtonpost.com/amy-neumann/interesting-facts-on-recy_b_2132923.html

EARNINGS AND ADVANCEMENT

Earnings depend on the type and geographic location of the employer, the skill level of the employee, and the type of equipment repaired. Median annual earnings of repairers of different types of electronic equipment in 2013 were: powerhouse, $69,720; commercial and industrial equipment, $53,400; transportation equipment, $52,830; electric motor and power tools, $38030; and motor vehicles, $31,230.

Benefits vary widely, depending on the employer and whether or not the employee belongs to the International Brotherhood of Electrical Workers.

Metropolitan Areas with the Highest
Employment Level in this Occupation
(Commercial & Industrial Equipment)

Metropolitan area	Employment [1]	Employment per thousand jobs	Hourly mean wage
Houston-Sugar Land-Baytown, TX	2,390	0.87	n/a
Dallas-Plano-Irving, TX	1,360	0.63	$23.59
Atlanta-Sandy Springs-Marietta, GA	1,290	0.56	$26.12
Chicago-Joliet-Naperville, IL	1,230	0.33	$25.19
Santa Ana-Anaheim-Irvine, CA	1,180	0.81	$29.26
Warner Robins, GA	1,160	20.43	$25.00
San Diego-Carlsbad-San Marcos, CA	1,000	0.77	$24.17
Orlando-Kissimmee-Sanford, FL	970	0.93	$25.01
Washington-Arlington-Alexandria, DC-VA-MD-WV	850	0.36	$30.26
Philadelphia, PA	800	0.44	$22.95

[1]Does not include self-employ ed. Source: Bureau of Labor Statistics

EMPLOYMENT AND OUTLOOK

There were about 145,000 electronic equipment repairers employed nationally in 2013. Employment is expected to grow slower than the average for all occupations through the year 2022, which means employment is projected to increase 0 percent to 6 percent. Equipment that is more reliable and requires less maintenance, including the increased use of disposable parts, will limit job growth. Job openings should result from the need to replace workers who transfer to other occupations or leave the work force.

Employment Trend, Projected 2012–22

Total, All Occupations: 11%

Electrical and Electronic Equipment Mechanics, Installers, and Repairers Electronic Equipment Repairers: 4%

Electronic Equipment Repairers: 1%

Note: "All Occupations" includes all occupations in the U.S. Economy. Source: U.S. Bureau of Labor Statistics, Employment Projections Program

Related Occupations
- Biomedical Equipment Technician
- Computer Network Architect
- Computer Service Technician
- Computer Support Specialist
- Electronic Engineering Technician
- Home entertainment equipment technician
- Musical Instrument Repairer
- Office Machine Repairer
- Telecommunications Equipment Repairer
- Telephone Installer & Repairer
- Television & Radio Repairer
- Vending Machine Repairer

Conversation With . . .
JOHN BALDWIN

Vice Chairman
Electronics Technicians Association International
Retired college educator, Faribault, MN, 39 years

1. What was your individual career path in terms of education/training, entry-level job, or other significant opportunity?

My interest in electronics started at a young age when I received a motor building kit and a radio kit as Christmas presents from relatives. I went on to build a few ham radios in junior high and took all the electronic shop classes, science and math classes I could in high school. I entered the University of Minnesota as an engineering student, and even obtained a 1st Class General Radiotelephone FCC license at the age of 19. I graduated with a BS in Industrial Education and taught high school electronics shop classes for one year before entering the US Air Force. I was given a direct duty assignment as a Communications Specialist working on all types of audio, video, RF, HF, VHF and UHF radios for B52 communications for four years. After my military service, I worked in tech support and tech training departments for EF Johnson for five years, and then I returned to education at South Central College in Mankato, MN, and Riverland Technical College in Faribault, MN. I taught basic electronics and business equipment repair, including computer servicing and local area networking. Then I headed up a wireless cellular communications AAS degree program for an AT&T cell tech training program.

2. What are the most important skills and/or qualities for someone in your profession?

Persistence, interest in how stuff works, and being able to work with people.

3. What do you wish you had known going into this profession?

How fast the pace of technology would change over the course of my career, and that you get to work with some very smart people.

4. Are there many job opportunities in your profession? In what specific areas?

Tons, in many areas. My favorite is wireless cellular, where rapid technological developments provide many opportunities to move to better positions. I loved learning about the engineering standards that made systems work together, such as FDMA, TDMA and CMDA wireless air interface access technologies. I worked on first generation cellular, which became 2G digital, then 3G and now 4G LTE. Manufacturing is making a comeback to the U.S, and will provide many new opportunities.

5. How do you see your profession changing in the next five years, what role will technology play in those changes, and what skills will be required?

More remote controlled functions via Internet and motion-controlled devices like drones will be developed, as will touch screen display technology, and interface devices embedded directly into humans. A combination of skills will be required because some people are book learners and some like hands-on. It takes both to learn electronics occupations and skills well. I've seen engineers and designers who can't make things work in the lab, only on paper or in ideas where technicians get to build and test those ideas in practical applications.

6. What do you enjoy most about your job? What do you enjoy least about your job?

Learning. It does not stop just because you get older. I least enjoy not having enough time to do what is required to understand completely how things work or function.

7. Can you suggest a valuable "try this" for students considering a career in your profession?

Get down to the basics of how things work vs. playing video games on the surface. Read parts catalogs, watch YouTube "how to" videos, take a few complicated things apart and reassemble them again and again until they work correctly. Understand electrical power and how energy is transferred efficiently. Look at cabling and connectors that are used in everyday devices such as, USB cables, video and power cables. Learn about the physical standards we deal with every day. PC file management is confusing to most people; figure out where files are stored on your device, phone, tablet, laptop, or PC. Don't give up until you understand how something works, where it can be used, and how it functions.

SELECTED SCHOOLS

A college degree is not always necessary to work as an electronic equipment repairer. For those interested in the field, however, a technical or community college is a good place to start. Many commercial trade schools are also available. Students are advised to consult with their school guidance counselor or research area post-secondary schools to find the right program

MORE INFORMATION

Armed Forces Communications & Electronics Association
4400 Fair Lakes Court
Fairfax, VA 22033-3899
800.336.4583
www.afcea.org

Electronic Technicians Association International
5 Depot Street
Greencastle, IN 46135
765.653.8262
www.eta-i.org

International Society of Certified Electronics Technicians
3608 Pershing Avenue
Fort Worth, TX 76107-4527
800.946.0201
www.iscet.org

National Electronics Service Dealers Association
3608 Pershing Avenue
Fort Worth, TX 76107-4527
817.921.9061
www.nesda.com

R. C. Lutz/Editor

Engineering Technician

Snapshot

Career Cluster: Engineering; Maintenance & Repair; Technology
Interests: Mechanics, analyzing information, working with your hands
Earnings (Yearly Average): $52,322
Employment & Outlook: Slower than Average Growth Expected

OVERVIEW

Sphere of Work

Engineering technicians work in careers spanning the broad spectrum of the engineering field. These include mechanical engineering, industrial engineering, civil engineering, environmental engineering, and electrical engineering.
As technicians, they work alongside engineers to apply the theories and principles of mathematics and science.

Engineering technicians create and modify designs and concepts used in various engineering systems. Technicians working in construction test and analyze building systems. Other technicians work in road construction, comparing and analyzing highway systems and traffic data. Engineering technicians also work in product design and development, helping to produce machine parts, engines, and other industrial systems.

Work Environment

Engineering technicians work in laboratories, offices, or construction settings. They transition from testing in the lab to on-site assistance as needed, and they work with others to implement the vision of the engineer using a variety of technologies.

Profile

Working Conditions: Work Inside
Physical Strength: Light Work
Education Needs:
Technical/Community College
Licensure/Certification:
Recommended
Physical Abilities Not Required: No
Heavy Labor
Opportunities For Experience:
Apprenticeship, Military Service
Holland Interest Score*: RIC

* See Appendix A

Occupation Interest

An engineering technician should be interested in how things work and run. Technicians enjoy observing and analyzing complex systems. They like working with their hands, taking things apart and putting them back together again. They are precise and attentive to detail, and they enjoy running tests to perfect a project or machine. They have no trouble applying abstract concepts to models and tangible objects.

A Day in the Life —Duties and Responsibilities

An engineering technician's typical workday varies depending on the field of engineering in which they specialize. For example, civil engineering technicians assist and performs tasks for civil engineers in a number of capacities related to construction. They work for city governments or corporations, estimating construction costs, mapping traffic patterns, reviewing blueprints, inspecting projects sites, preparing reports, determining building materials, and drafting plans using computer software. They spend most of their days performing these activities in an office, working regular hours. Sometimes they visit the site of a project to monitor its progress.

A mechanical engineering technician may work on any number of product design projects, including designs for toys, automobile parts, engine parts, medical devices, and household appliances. Technicians assist mechanical engineers in the design, development, testing, and manufacturing of a product or machine. They work in laboratories and offices and may work in machine shops. The daily responsibilities of a mechanical engineering technician include preparing sketches and drafts, testing components, recording data, calculating costs, and creating prototypes. In some cases, technicians operate computer systems or heavy machinery while creating or modifying a product.

Industrial engineering technicians work in a variety of industries. They assist industrial engineers in helping businesses to manage their resources and personnel more effectively. Working in teams, industrial engineering technicians spend their days in an office or observing workers in the field. They help companies revise their methods of operation, preparing charts and presentations to help implement those revisions.

Duties and Responsibilities

- Building or setting up equipment
- Preparing experiments
- Calculating and recording results
- Making prototype versions of newly designed equipment
- Assisting in routine design work
- Preparing materials' specifications
- Devising and running tests to ensure product quality
- Studying ways to improve manufacturing efficiency
- Supervising production workers
- Serving as field representatives of manufacturers, retailers, or wholesalers
- Helping customers install, operate and maintain complex technical equipment
- Writing repair or operating manuals

OCCUPATION SPECIALTIES

Electrical Technicians

Electrical Technicians apply electrical theory and related knowledge to test and modify developmental or operational electrical machinery and electrical control equipment and circuitry in industrial or commercial plants and laboratories.

Industrial Engineering Technicians

Industrial Engineering Technicians study and record time, motion, methods, and speed of maintenance, production, clerical and other work operations to establish standard production rates and improve efficiency.

Civil Engineering Technicians

Civil Engineering Technicians help civil engineers plan and build highways, buildings, bridges, dams, wastewater treatment systems, and other structures; they also do related surveys and studies. Some inspect water and wastewater treatment systems to insure that pollution control requirements are met. Others estimate construction costs and specify materials to be used.

Mechanical Engineering Technicians

Mechanical Engineering Technicians help engineers design, develop, test and manufacture industrial machinery, consumer products and other equipment.

WORK ENVIRONMENT

Physical Environment

Most engineering technicians work in an office setting, although some work in manufacturing areas or laboratories. Many engineering technicians also conduct work in the field. Depending on their area of specialty, the work of some technicians may involve heavy equipment, electrical equipment, or hazardous chemicals.

Relevant Skills and Abilities

Interpersonal/Social Skills
- Cooperating with others
- Working as a member of a team

Organization & Management Skills
- Coordinating tasks
- Making decisions
- Managing people/groups
- Paying attention to and handling details
- Performing duties which change frequently

Research & Planning Skills
- Developing evaluation strategies

Technical Skills
- Performing scientific, mathematical and technical work
- Working with machines, tools or other objects

Human Environment

Engineering technicians work with engineers, scientists, construction workers, draftspeople, and businesspeople on a daily basis. Technicians must be able to communicate their ideas effectively and take instruction from their colleagues.

Technological Environment

Regardless of specialization, the work of an engineering technician relies heavily on technology. Civil engineering technicians, for instance, use computers to draft architectural and construction designs. Mechanical engineers sometimes operate heavy and complex machinery. Industrial engineers use computer software to draft office layouts and map work-flow processes.

EDUCATION, TRAINING, AND ADVANCEMENT

High School/Secondary

Aspiring engineering technicians should enroll in classes related to mathematics, science, and computer science. They must be comfortable with visualizing data using charts and graphs. It is important that individuals interested in become engineering technicians familiarize themselves with laboratory science and the scientific method. A working knowledge of engineering, mechanics, and machinery is also helpful.

Suggested High School Subjects
- Algebra
- Applied Communication
- Applied Math
- Applied Physics
- Biology
- Chemistry
- Earth Science
- English
- Geometry
- Mathematics
- Physical Science
- Physics
- Science

Famous First

The first industrial research laboratory was the General Electric Research Laboratory, in Schenectady, New York, in September 1900. The lab, pictured, was supervised by Willis Rodney Whitney, a specialist in electrochemistry. By 1915 the lab had 250 researchers and assistants.

College/Postsecondary

Most engineering technician jobs require only an associate's degree; unlike engineers, an engineering technician is not required to complete a bachelor's degree. Individuals who pursue a bachelor's degree more often go on to become engineering technologists. Most employers require a two-year associate's degree from a school accredited by the Accreditation Board for Engineering and Technology (ABET). Some fields require only a certificate from an ABET-accredited vocational school or training program

Postsecondary training for engineering technicians focuses on skills related to math and science, though specifics vary from field to field. For example, an industrial engineering technician will take courses in computer-aided design and drafting (CADD) and computer-aided manufacturing (CAM) software.

Related College Majors
- Computer Engineering Technology
- Construction/Building Technology
- Electrical, Electronic & Communications Engineering Technology
- Engineering Technology, General
- Industrial/Manufacturing Technology
- Robotics Technology

Adult Job Seekers

Adult job seekers in this field can increase their chances of finding work by earning certification prior to applying for positions. Training and certification are available through various industry-affiliated educational programs and vocational study. Additionally, the military provides training programs for engineering technicians.

Professional Certification and Licensure

Not all employers require engineering technicians to have a license. However, many organizations offer licensure and certification programs that are specific to a particular industry or engineering sector. For instance, civil engineering technicians and electrical and mechanical systems engineering technicians can seek certification through the National Institute for Certification in Engineering Technologies (NICET), a nonprofit organization created by the

National Society of Professional Engineers. To acquire NICET certification, candidates must take a two-part exam.

Additional Requirements

Engineering technicians must be critical thinkers who are eager to identify and solve complex problems on a daily basis. They should enjoy working with others and have a stringent attention to detail. Though careers in engineering are focused on math and science, creative thinking skills are also important.

EARNINGS AND ADVANCEMENT

Earnings depend on the education, experience and specialty of the employee and whether the employer is in the private sector or the federal government. Engineering technicians advance by successful on-the-job experience and by obtaining the necessary special training. They may move from routine work to more difficult assignments and some may even become supervisors or engineers.

Median annual earnings of various specialties of engineering technology in 2013 were: electrical and electronics engineering technology, $58,770; mechanical engineering technology, $54,280; industrial engineering technology, $54,170; and civil engineering technology, $49,380.

Engineering technicians may receive paid vacations, holidays, and sick days; life and health insurance; and retirement benefits. These are usually paid by the employer.

Metropolitan Areas with the Highest
Employment Level in this Occupation
(Industrial Engineering Technician)

Metropolitan area	Employment [1]	Employment per thousand jobs	Hourly mean wage
Phoenix-Mesa-Glendale, AZ	3,620	2.03	$26.97
Seattle-Bellevue-Everett, WA	2,510	1.73	(8)
Warren-Troy-Farmington Hills, MI	1,940	1.74	$21.73
Minneapolis-St. Paul-Bloomington, MN-WI	1,870	1.05	$26.14
Los Angeles-Long Beach-Glendale, CA	1,300	0.33	$29.76
Detroit-Livonia-Dearborn, MI	1,290	1.85	$23.53
Houston-Sugar Land-Baytown, TX	1,070	0.39	$37.53
Boston-Cambridge-Quincy, MA	1,020	0.58	$29.67
Cleveland-Elyria-Mentor, OH	860	0.85	$22.59
Chicago-Joliet-Naperville, IL	730	0.20	$24.50

[1]Does not include self-employ ed. Source: Bureau of Labor Statistics

EMPLOYMENT AND OUTLOOK

Engineering technicians held about 350,000 jobs in 2012. About one-third of all engineering technicians worked in manufacturing, mainly in the computer and electronic equipment, transportation equipment, and machinery manufacturing industries. Another one-fourth worked in professional, scientific, and technical service industries, mostly in engineering or business services companies that do engineering work on contract for government, manufacturing firms, or other organizations.

Employment of engineering technicians is expected to grow slower than the average for all occupations through the year 2022, which means employment is projected to increase 3 percent to 9 percent. As technology becomes more sophisticated, employers will continue to look for engineering technicians who are skilled in new technology and require a minimum of additional job training. In addition, competitive pressures will force companies to improve and update manufacturing facilities and product designs, resulting in jobs for engineering technicians.

Employment Trend, Projected 2012–22

Total, All Occupations: 11%

Mechanical Engineering Technicians: 5%

Engineering Technicians (All): 2%

Note: "All Occupations" includes all occupations in the U.S. Economy. Source: U.S. Bureau of Labor Statistics, Employment Projections Program

Related Occupations
- Drafter
- Electronic Engineering Technician
- Energy Conservation & Use Technician
- Robotics Technician
- Science Technician
- Surveyor & Cartographer

Conversation With . . .
LARRY STEPHENS

Electrical Engineering Technician,
Fawn Engineering, Clive, Iowa, 2 years

1. What was your individual career path in terms of education/training, entry-level job, or other significant opportunity?

I took the long route to the position I hold today. Right out of high school I had a manual labor job at a recycling center. There was a lot of equipment that needed constant maintenance and my boss had an electrical engineering degree, but he had hand injuries and noticed that I was interested in helping. So he would look at the schematics, tell me what to do, and slowly I learned some basic repair skills.

From there I moved on to a company that was like an old time hardware store. I started out in the warehouse, but, since I liked working on equipment, wanted to transfer to the construction equipment rental and repair center. I was successful making that change because I was willing to come in on Saturdays and work for free during an eight-week period. During that time, I trained as a mechanic and learned to work on everything from a little hand drill to a concrete mixer. I got the full-time job, and learned much that helped me in the future.

Then I became a repair shop service manager with another company for about 10 years, and had a smaller variety of equipment to repair. The pay was better, but I missed learning from working on a wide variety of equipment.

Eventually, I started working at a vending machine company, became their senior field service technician, and traveled the United States and even a few foreign countries. Primarily, I repaired the machines and did training sessions for vending companies. The thing that really changed my life was working closely with my company's engineering department. I realized that engineering was my first love. So I transferred and became an engineering technician. My current job is interesting and rewarding in ways that my previous jobs weren't. I see and test everything new that my company makes and spend my time working with the engineers helping to solve problems. Recently I've worked on testing credit card readers – which are a major new addition to vending machines – and on assembly issues related to a newly-designed machine.

Looking back, the key moments to getting to where I am now were: helping an engineer back at the beginning, my willingness to work for free to get where I wanted to go, getting experience working on almost anything you can think of and, finally, working with an engineering department at a manufacturing company.

2. What are the most important skills and/or qualities for someone in your profession?

The single most important thing is to be interested in how and why things work.

3. What do you wish you had known going into this profession?

I wish I'd known about the profession of engineering technician! I've recently gone back to college for my engineering degree, which I would have done years ago had I understood what engineers do.

4. Are there many job opportunities in your profession? In what specific areas?

There will always be opportunities for people who like to solve problems. As far as a specific area, ask yourself: what interests you? Engineers design almost everything around us, so somewhere there is team of engineers working on whatever it is you are interested in, and you can be sure they need engineering technicians to help them.

5. How do you see your profession changing in the next five years, what role will technology play in those changes, and what skills will be required?

In the next five years everything will become even more tightly connected to the Internet. Information streaming over the web about the current status of equipment in the field will become the norm; reports will be generated and sent to phones and tablets. The main skill, as always, will be the desire to constantly learn and keep up with these changes.

6. What do you enjoy most about your job? What do you enjoy least about your job?

I enjoy finding and solving problems the most. I least enjoy doing the repetitive housekeeping tasks that every job has.

7. Can you suggest a valuable "try this" for students considering a career in your profession?

Look around your home, find something that is either old or broken, and take it apart. Try to understand how it works. If it is broken, try to fix it. If it is working, does it still work when you put it back together? If not, figure out why. Look at the individual components used inside and research them; try to figure out what they do and why they were used. If you find this exercise fascinating, a career as an engineering technician may be right for you.

SELECTED SCHOOLS

Many technical and community colleges offer programs in engineering technology. Commercial trade schools are also an option. Students are advised to consult with their school guidance counselor or research area post-secondary schools to find the right program.

MORE INFORMATION

Accreditation Board for Engineering and Technology
111 Market Place, Suite 1050
Baltimore, MD 21202-4012
410.347.7700
www.abet.org

American Society for Engineering Education
1818 N Street NW, Suite 600
Washington, DC 20036
202.331.3500
www.asee.org

American Society of Certified Engineering Technicians
P.O. Box 1536
Brandon, MS 39043
601.824.8991
www.ascet.org

Electronics Technicians Association, International
5 Depot Street
Greencastle, IN 46135
800.288.3824
www.eta-i.org

International Society of Certified Electronics Technicians
3608 Pershing Avenue
Fort Worth, TX 76107-4527
800.946.0201
www.iscet.org

International Union of Operating Engineers
Director of Research and Education
1125 17th Street, NW
Washington, DC 20036
202.429.9100
www.iuoe.org

National Institute for Certification in Engineering Technologies
1420 King Street
Alexandria, VA 22314-2794
888.476.4238
www.nicet.org

Molly Hagan/Editor

Farm Equipment Mechanic

Snapshot

Career Cluster: Engineering; Maintenance & Repair

Interests: Agriculture, mechanics, physical labor, solving problems

Earnings (Yearly Average): $36,390

Employment & Outlook: Average Growth Expected

OVERVIEW

Sphere of Work

Farm equipment mechanics, also referred to as agricultural mechanics and agricultural technicians, are responsible for the proper functioning of farm machinery, equipment, and vehicles used at farms, nurseries, ranches, slaughterhouses, and greenhouses. Farm equipment mechanics need very specialized mechanical knowledge and experience to assess, repair, maintain, and in some instances, fabricate or rebuild farm machinery.

Work Environment

Farms, nurseries, ranches, slaughterhouses, and greenhouses employ farm equipment

mechanics. Others work independently or for manufacturers and retail dealers. Farm equipment mechanics may have a dedicated mechanic repair shop or may exclusively service and repair equipment on-site in barns or equipment sheds. Farm equipment mechanics tend to be busier during planting and harvesting times when farm machinery is in near constant use.

Profile

Working Conditions: Work both Indoors and Outdoors
Physical Strength: Medium Work
Education Needs: On-The-Job Training, Technical/Community College, Apprenticeship
Licensure/Certification: Usually Not Required
Physical Abilities Not Required: N/A
Opportunities For Experience: Internship, Apprenticeship, Volunteer Work, Part-Time Work
Holland Interest Score*: RES, RSC

* See Appendix A

Occupation Interest

Farm equipment mechanics tend to be physically strong and intelligent individuals who possess strong problem-solving skills, physical stamina, ingenuity, and resourcefulness. They must be precise and able to understand and follow instruction manuals, mechanical blueprints, and circuit diagrams. Familiarity with computer technologies is advantageous. Farm equipment mechanics should enjoy physical labor and have a background in both agriculture and mechanics.

A Day in the Life—Duties and Responsibilities

The daily occupational duties and responsibilities of farm equipment mechanics vary by employer and specialty area. Farm equipment mechanics diagnose, repair, and maintain machinery, vehicles, equipment, wiring, and plumbing used for producing crops, beef, poultry, pork, dairy, or aquaculture. They may also install systems or system components, assemble parts, and clean and lubricate equipment. In shops with large staff, farm equipment mechanics may specialize in one type of repair or assembly or in specific machines. For example, some mechanics focus on hydraulics or transmissions while others only service tractors.

Farm equipment mechanics who support crop farm production work primarily with tractors, planting machines, harvesting machines, hay balers, irrigation systems, pesticide sprayers, and trucks used to transport crops to market. Those supporting meat production troubleshoot and service feeding systems, trucks, slaughtering technology, scales, and vehicles used to transport livestock. Farm equipment mechanics also maintain egg hatcheries, lighting and heating systems in poultry production facilities, and piglet warming systems for pork producers, as well as the milking machinery, refrigeration, and storage areas in dairy operations. Aquaculture producers rely on farm equipment mechanics to examine, fix, and service the floating net systems and the temperature systems and filters on stocking ponds.

All farm equipment mechanics are responsible for documenting all repairs and associated costs. Self-employed farm equipment mechanics have additional administrative and business responsibilities.

Duties and Responsibilities

- Doing preventive maintenance
- Assembling implements for dealers
- Installing or repairing wiring or motors on electrically driven machinery
- Repairing damaged sheet metal
- Diagnosing and repairing diesel and gasoline tractors and other equipment
- Welding defective body or frame parts
- Traveling to farms to make repairs on equipment
- Repairing air-conditioning units on cabs of combines and tractors

WORK ENVIRONMENT

Physical Environment

Farm equipment mechanics work in mechanic workshops or in barns or equipment sheds on farms, nurseries, ranches, slaughterhouses, and greenhouses. The temperatures, lighting, and cleanliness of the work environment can differ greatly between establishments. Farm equipment repair and maintenance tends to be very physical and require hard labor, walking, lifting, and bending. Farm equipment mechanics must follow safety precautions to guard against back strain, crush injuries, cuts and burns, chemical exposure, and machine accidents.

Relevant Skills and Abilities

Interpersonal/Social Skills
- Being able to work independently

Organization & Management Skills
- Following instructions
- Managing time
- Meeting goals and deadlines

Technical Skills
- Working with machines, tools or other objects

Unclassified Skills
- Performing work that produces tangible results

Work Environment Skills
- Traveling
- Working outdoors

Human Environment

A farm equipment mechanic's human interaction is limited to farmers, farm managers, and farm workers at farms, nurseries, ranches, slaughterhouses, and greenhouses. Those who work in shops for manufacturers or dealers may also interact with supervisors, equipment representatives, and trainees.

Technological Environment

Farm equipment mechanics use computerized diagnostic tools, hand tools, soldering equipment, saws, and welding tools to repair, maintain, diagnose, and rebuild farm equipment and machinery. Depending on the work environment, they may work on animal feeders, hay balers, mowers, plows, fertilizing equipment, pesticide sprayers, trucks, irrigation systems, tractors, chain saws, loading machines, conveyer belts, and milking machines. Farm equipment mechanics must also operate trucks to tow inoperable farm equipment and vehicles and to transport materials.

EDUCATION, TRAINING, AND ADVANCEMENT

High School/Secondary

High school students interested in pursuing a career as a farm equipment mechanic should prepare themselves by building good study habits. High school-level study of mechanics, mathematics, physics, chemistry, communications, metalworking, agricultural science, technical drafting, and technology can provide a strong foundation for work as a farm equipment mechanic. High school students interested in this career path will benefit from seeking internships or part-time work with local mechanics and farms.

Suggested High School Subjects
- Agricultural Mechanization
- Applied Math
- Applied Physics
- Auto Service Technology
- Blueprint Reading
- Diesel Maintenance Technology
- English
- Machining Technology
- Metals Technology
- Shop Math
- Shop Mechanics
- Welding

Famous First

The first diesel-powered tractor to be sold widely was the Caterpillar diesel tractor, manufactured in Peoria, Illinois, beginning in 1931. It was a track-type vehicle (as opposed to one with rubber tires), 12 tons in weight, and featured a draw strength of 68 horsepower.

College/Postsecondary

Aspiring farm equipment mechanics should earn an associate's degree or bachelor's degree in mechanics, agriculture, or farm management. Vocational schools also provide formal postsecondary training for farm equipment mechanics. Program participants study such subjects as diagnostic methods, diesel and gas mechanics, hydraulics, electronics, mathematics, engine repair, welding, and refrigeration. Coursework in business may also prove useful for those who intend to become self-employed or set up their own company. Postsecondary students can gain work experience and potential advantage in their future job searches by securing internships or part-time employment with local mechanics and farms.

Related College Majors
- Agricultural Mechanization, General
- Diesel Engine Mechanics & Repair

Adult Job Seekers

Prospective farm equipment mechanics should have, at a minimum, a high school diploma. Some jobs may require an associate's or bachelor's degree. Many farm equipment mechanics begin their careers as trainees, assistants, or other kinds of mechanics. Mechanics from related fields should find a transition to this career relatively easy. Although postsecondary training can provide greater opportunities for advancement in the field, employers provide ample on-the-job training for new farm equipment mechanics. Experienced farm equipment mechanics may be assigned tasks involving greater complexity, advance to supervisory positions, or establish their own businesses. Some farm equipment mechanics join unions, which offer worker protections, networking, and job opportunities.

Professional Certification and Licensure

Certification and licensure is not required for farm equipment mechanics.

Additional Requirements

Individuals who find satisfaction, success, and job security as farm workers will be knowledgeable about the profession's requirements, responsibilities, and opportunities. Farm equipment mechanics must comply with safety regulations and maintain clean driving records. In order to follow developments and trends in the field, they attend periodic refresher courses and trade shows or obtain additional training.

Fun Fact

The most commonly used piece of equipment on a farm is the tractor. First introduced in 1868, they were powered by steam. Today's tractors are outfitted with GPS and sensing systems that calibrate the machine's movements to reduce wasted fertilizer, seed, and fuel.

Source: ft.com/cms/s/0/a48ad98c-36c7-11e3-aaf1-00144feab7de.html#axzz3WxY4qLc7; http://inventors. about.com/od/tstartinventions/a/tractors.htm

EARNINGS AND ADVANCEMENT

Earnings of farm equipment mechanics depend on the type, size and geographic location of the employer, the equipment supplied and the particular duties performed by the employee. Mean annual earnings of farm equipment mechanics were $36,390 in 2013. The lowest ten percent earned less than $22,940, and the highest ten percent earned more than $51,510. Most farm equipment mechanics had the opportunity to earn overtime wages during planting and harvesting seasons. Some employers may require farm equipment mechanics to purchase and maintain their own hand tools. The cost can vary from several hundred to several thousand dollars.

Farm equipment mechanics may receive paid vacations, holidays, and sick days; life and health insurance; and retirement benefits. These are usually paid by the employer. Some employers also provide uniforms. Farm equipment repairers employed on large private farms may receive free or low-cost housing.

States with the Highest Employment Level in this Occupation

Metropolitan area	Employment [1]	Employment per thousand jobs	Hourly mean wage
Iowa	3,060	2.05	$17.73
California	2,490	0.17	$20.26
Illinois	2,400	0.42	$18.33
Texas	2,210	0.20	$17.05
Minnesota	2,180	0.81	$18.15

[1]Does not include self-employ ed. Source: Bureau of Labor Statistics

EMPLOYMENT AND OUTLOOK

Farm equipment mechanics held about 36,000 jobs nationally in 2012. Employment is expected to grow about as fast as the average for all occupations through the year 2022, which means employment is projected to increase 8 percent to 12 percent. The increasing complexity of equipment will force more farmers to rely on farm equipment mechanics for service and repairs, but the continued consolidation of farmland will allow equipment to be used more efficiently. Most job openings will arise from the need to replace experienced farm equipment mechanics who retire. Opportunities should be good for persons who have completed formal training in farm equipment repair, such as diesel mechanics.

Employment Trend, Projected 2012–22

Total, All Occupations: 11%

Farm Equipment Mechanics: 10%

Heavy Vehicle and Mobile Equipment Mechanics (All): 9%

Note: "All Occupations" includes all occupations in the U.S. Economy. Source: U.S. Bureau of Labor Statistics, Employment Projections Program

Related Occupations
- Automotive Technician
- Diesel Service Technician
- Heavy Equipment Service Technician
- Small Engine Mechanic

Conversation With . . .
DAVID DEERING

Master Technician
Champlain Valley Equipment, Middlebury, VT
Farm Equipment Mechanic and related jobs, 37 years

1. What was your individual career path in terms of education/training, entry-level job, or other significant opportunity?

I started in the agricultural business by working on our family dairy farm. I started working here at Champlain Valley Equipment (CVE) in my senior year of high school through the vocational agricultural co-op program. While doing maintenance and repairs on the farm, I also took welding and repair classes in high school and through the Vocational Ag program. Upon graduating from high school, I worked full time at Champlain Valley Equipment for two years, then returned to the farm to help out because of my father's health. Two years later, I attended Vermont Technical College and received an associate's degree in agribusiness management. After graduating in 1979, I returned full time to CVE. I have filled the roles of service technician, parts counter person, service manager, salesman and back to my current position as lead road technician since the mid- 1990s. I feel I am best suited to and most valuable in this position. The majority of my work is on self-propelled harvesters and high-horsepower tractors. I work lots of extra hours during the season to keep these machines operating and keep our customers satisfied, which is our goal.

2. What are the most important skills and/or qualities for someone in your profession?

Some of the most important skills for a farm equipment mechanic are being able to troubleshoot and diagnose electrical and hydraulic problems. Common sense and understanding the fundamentals of these systems, along with experience, are vital to making a repair quickly. Computers can help but can also sometimes lead you in the wrong direction.

3. What do you wish you had known going into this profession?

I wish I had known how much computers were going to be a part of everything today. Fifteen years ago, I would not have believed that I would have to rely on a computer to operate or repair a piece of farm equipment. Had I known, I would have taken a few computer classes.

4. Are there many job opportunities in your profession? In what specific areas?

There are many employment opportunities in the farm machinery business, especially on the repair and maintenance side. Computer and electronic diagnostic skills will be a vital part of any technician's training and will enable them to work on complicated machines such as combines, self-propelled choppers and high-horsepower tractors. Because GPS guidance systems are becoming very popular and require special training, it's a high-growth job area.

5. How do you see your profession changing in the next five years? What role will technology play in those changes, and what skills will be required?

Computer diagnostics will continue to grow in importance as emissions standards get stricter. I will probably be spending more time training customers in the operation of equipment and use of machines with "Tier 4 Final" emissions systems. Tier 4 is a federal clean emissions standard that diesel engines have to meet. Precision farming, or GPS, training will become more important as the popularity of these systems continues to grow, and repairing them will be inevitable.

6. What do you enjoy most about your job? What do you enjoy least about your job?

One of my favorite parts of the job is repairing a customer's machine quickly to get them back into the field again—for example, making a temporary repair so they can finish planting a field before the rain starts. Sometimes this requires working very late at night or early in the morning.

I also enjoy going to training classes on new machines and new technology. It allows me to be more productive when working on customers' machines and gives me the opportunity to network with technicians from other dealerships and discuss how they've addressed various problems.

I dislike not being able to solve a customer's issue or having to tell them that the problem is major and will require a lot of time and money to repair.

7. Can you suggest a valuable "try this" for students considering a career in your profession?

I would suggest that anyone contemplating a career in agricultural mechanics try working on a farm to see if the work environment is something they'd like to be exposed to on a daily basis. They could also contact a dealership to see if they could do a ride along with a service tech or shadow a technician in the shop.

SELECTED SCHOOLS

A number of technical and community colleges in farm states offer programs in farm equipment maintenance and repair. Commercial trade schools are also an option. Students are advised to consult with their school guidance counselor or research area post-secondary schools to find the right program.

MORE INFORMATION

Agricultural Industry Electronics Foundation
Association of Equipment Manufacturers
6737 W. Washington Street
Suite 2400
Milwaukee, WI 53214-5647
414.298.4158
www.aef-online.org

Associated Equipment Distributors
600 22nd Street, Suite 220
Oak Brook, IL 60523
630.574.0650
www.aedcareers.com

United Automobile, Aerospace and Agricultural Implement Workers of America (UAW)
8000 East Jefferson Avenue
Detroit, MI 48214
313.926.5000
www.uaw.org

Simone Isadora Flynn/Editor

General Maintenance Mechanic

Snapshot

Career Cluster: Construction; Maintenance & Repair
Interests: Machinery, mechanics, working with your hands, solving problems
Earnings (Yearly Average): $37,710
Employment & Outlook: Average Growth Expected

OVERVIEW

Sphere of Work

General maintenance mechanics are employed to perform routine maintenance tasks on a company or organization's plumbing and electrical systems, heating and air-conditioning units, and various other types of mechanical equipment. Maintenance mechanics are traditionally employed by large organizations housed in sprawling complexes, such as residential buildings, colleges and universities, hotels and resorts, hospitals, government buildings, and transportation centers. In addition to solving common problems in buildings and building systems, general

maintenance mechanics also use their experience to troubleshoot emergency issues that may arise due to everyday use or flood and storm damage. Factories and manufacturing complexes also employ general maintenance mechanics to monitor their machines and equipment so production is not delayed.

Work Environment

The work environment for general maintenance mechanics varies from day to day and project to project. Repair to heating and air-conditioning systems, roofs, and windows can require work outdoors in a variety of inclement conditions. Other common maintenance jobs, such as wall patching, replacement of lighting fixtures, plumbing, and door repair, are conducted indoors. Maintenance mechanics traditionally conduct their work during regular business hours in and around routine building traffic, placing a priority on safety, cleanliness, and organization regardless of the task at hand.

Profile

Working Conditions: Work both Indoors and Outdoors
Physical Strength: Heavy Work
Education Needs: On-The-Job Training, High School Diploma with Technical Education
Licensure/Certification: Recommended
Physical Abilities Not Required: N/A
Opportunities For Experience: Apprenticeship
Holland Interest Score*: REI
* See Appendix A

Occupation Interest

The job of a general maintenance mechanic attracts professionals of varying ages and backgrounds. Many are young workers employed at the assistant or apprenticeship level who use the job to develop knowledge and experience aimed at a future career in some field of mechanical maintenance. Veteran maintenance mechanics often have several years of previous experience in construction and contracting, public works, or the military. The field is also a popular transitional field for those looking for employment in specific maintenance fields or other related work.

A Day in the Life—Duties and Responsibilities

The varied nature of the everyday duties and responsibilities of maintenance mechanics is one of the hallmarks of the position. Maintenance mechanics are responsible for myriad technical repairs, adjustments, replacements, and services every day. Much of their work involves repairing structural and equipment damage resulting from everyday use by building occupants. These tasks include small structural repairs and fixing damaged walls, floors, heating and air-conditioning units, and plumbing.

Mechanics employed by factories or production facilities may spend their day analyzing machinery and other equipment to ensure that it is working properly. Those who work in transportation facilities may spend their day tending to the repair needs of a fleet of vehicles such as buses or other transit cars to make sure they are free of mechanical problems.

Maintenance mechanics may work in concert with janitorial service teams to provide repair and cleaning services in the event of emergencies such as spills, floods, plumbing backups, broken glass, and other unforeseen damage.

Duties and Responsibilities

- Building partitions
- Repairing plaster or drywall
- Inspecting and diagnosing problems
- Repairing or installing electrical, plumbing and temperature- control machinery
- Checking blueprints, repair manuals and parts catalogs
- Obtaining supplies and parts
- Using hand tools and special equipment
- Keeping records of their work
- Performing routine preventive maintenance

OCCUPATION SPECIALTIES

Factory/Mill Maintenance Repairers

Factory/Mill Maintenance Repairers inspect, fix and maintain machinery, plumbing, electricity and structures of commercial and industrial establishments.

Building Maintenance Repairers

Building Maintenance Repairers inspect, fix and maintain structures such as factories, office buildings, apartment houses and logging and mining constructions.

WORK ENVIRONMENT

Physical Environment

General maintenance mechanics are employed in numerous industries and professional environments, including corporate offices, hospitals, residences, transportation facilities, and university campuses.

Human Environment

Work as a general maintenance mechanic requires strong collaboration skills. Maintenance mechanics often work individually or in small groups in order to tend to repairs quickly and without major disruption. In addition to working closely with other members of facility maintenance staff, mechanics must also be able to communicate effectively with building occupants and other staff members.

Relevant Skills and Abilities

Interpersonal/Social Skills
- Being able to work independently

Organization & Management Skills
- Paying attention to and handling details
- Performing duties which change frequently

Research & Planning Skills
- Developing evaluation strategies

Technical Skills
- Performing technical work
- Working with machines, tools or other objects

Unclassified Skills
- Working long hours as needed

Work Environment Skills
- Working in a dangerous setting
- Working in awkward or uncomfortable positions
- Working under different weather conditions

Technological Environment

General maintenance mechanics must be skilled in general carpentry and the use of basic hand tools. Experience with basic plumbing and wiring concepts is often a prerequisite for the position.

EDUCATION, TRAINING, AND ADVANCEMENT

High School/Secondary

High school students can best prepare for a career in maintenance with courses in geometry, chemistry, physics, and industrial arts. Candidates from vocational high schools often have an advantage over other applicants. Drafting, architecture, and art classes can also serve as precursors for future work in and around building systems and technological schematics.

Suggested High School Subjects
- Applied Math
- Applied Physics
- Blueprint Reading
- Electricity & Electronics
- English
- Machining Technology
- Mechanical Drawing
- Science
- Shop Math
- Shop Mechanics
- Woodshop

Famous First

The first time an escalator was put into use was at the Old Iron Pier on Coney Island, New York, in 1896. Designed by Jesse Reno a few years earlier, the escalator featured a conveyor belt with iron cleats on the surface to provide traction to users. The Reno escalator was later installed at the Brooklyn Bridge and the Boston subway. So durable was it that some units in Boston were still functioning a hundred years later, when the Big Dig construction project forced their removal.

College/Postsecondary

Postsecondary education is not traditionally a requirement for those seeking a career as a general maintenance mechanic. Much of the education and knowledge necessary for the position is attained on the job.

Related College Majors
- Building/Property Maintenance & Management
- Heating, Air Conditioning & Refrigeration Mechanics & Repair

Adult Job Seekers

The field of general maintenance offers flexibility and minimal education requirements, making it an attractive position for individuals from a variety of professional, academic, and experiential backgrounds. Young workers can use their time in the role to acquire hands-on experience in general maintenance while continuing their education or planning a future role in another realm of mechanics, such as automobile, aviation, or heating, ventilation, and air conditioning (HVAC) repair. Maintenance mechanics traditionally work regular business hours, though some may have options for second and third shifts, particularly those employed in the commercial or industrial realm, where maintenance staff is often required to be on call on an as-needed basis.

Professional Certification and Licensure

General maintenance mechanics do not traditionally need specific licensure or certification for employment; however, certified HVAC professionals, electricians, and plumbing professionals are often given preference for open positions.

Additional Requirements

General maintenance mechanics must possess a sound frame of reference, as they must rely on this experience to analyze and address mechanical, systematic, and structural problems quickly without major disruption in their place of work. Patience, amicability, and the ability to work well in small groups are also qualities that can benefit those who work as maintenance mechanics.

EARNINGS AND ADVANCEMENT

Earnings of general maintenance mechanics vary widely by industry, geographic location of the employer and skill level. They are highest in transportation companies and utilities and lowest in service firms.

In 2013, general maintenance mechanics had mean annual earnings of $37,710. The lowest ten percent earned less than $21,070, and the highest ten percent earned more than $57,990.

General maintenance mechanics may receive paid vacations, holidays, and sick days; life and health insurance; and retirement benefits. These are usually paid by the employer.

Metropolitan Areas with the Highest Employment Level in this Occupation

Metropolitan area	Employment [1]	Employment per thousand jobs	Hourly mean wage
New York-White Plains-Wayne, NY-NJ	59,760	11.40	$20.80
Chicago-Joliet-Naperville, IL	28,000	7.57	$20.04
Los Angeles-Long Beach-Glendale, CA	27,350	6.88	$20.16
Houston-Sugar Land-Baytown, TX	27,090	9.82	$17.78
Atlanta-Sandy Springs-Marietta, GA	22,000	9.53	$18.34
Dallas-Plano-Irving, TX	19,590	9.11	$17.50
Philadelphia, PA	17,680	9.61	$19.63
Washington-Arlington-Alexandria, DC-VA-MD-WV	17,350	7.33	$21.37
Phoenix-Mesa-Glendale, AZ	15,840	8.89	$17.62
Pittsburgh, PA	13,120	11.60	$18.75

[1]Does not include self-employ ed. Source: Bureau of Labor Statistics

EMPLOYMENT AND OUTLOOK

General maintenance mechanics held over 1.3 million jobs nationally in 2012. Employment is expected to grow about as fast as the average for all occupations through the year 2022, which means employment is projected to increase 6 percent to 12 percent. Employment growth is related to the number of buildings--for example, office and apartment buildings, stores, schools, hospitals, hotels and factories - and the amount of equipment needing maintenance and repair. However, as machinery becomes more advanced and requires less maintenance, the need for general maintenance mechanics diminishes.

Employment Trend, Projected 2012–22

Installation, Maintenance, and Repair Occupations (All): 12%

Total, All Occupations: 11%

General Maintenance Mechanics: 9%

Note: "All Occupations" includes all occupations in the U.S. Economy. Source: U.S. Bureau of Labor Statistics, Employment Projections Program

Related Occupations
- Carpenter
- Electrician
- Industrial Machinery Mechanic
- Plumber & Pipe Fitter

Conversation With . . .
JOHN CHANDO

Lead Maintenance Mechanic
C.H. Nash Museum at Chucalissa, Memphis, TN
General Maintenance Mechanic, 9 years

1. What was your general career path in terms of education/training, entry-level job, or other significant opportunity?

I went to college right after high school but left after three semesters and started working as a chemical operator in a chemical plant. While working there, I did go back to school part time and eventually got an associate's degree. After working in the chemical plant, I took a job as a utilityman apprentice in the water department of a small town in New Jersey. I worked there for about four years and learned a variety of skills—all through hands-on training—like repairing broken water mains and fire hydrants, installing water meters, unplugging sewer lines, maintaining the town's pumping stations, doing minor maintenance on pumps and motors, etc.
This helped give me the experience that led to my next job as general maintenance mechanic for a small museum owned by the University of Memphis. Some of the duties of a general maintenance mechanic are inspecting the facilities and grounds to determine if any preventive maintenance is needed; maintenance tasks such as repairing roof leaks, fixing broken windows and doors, changing fuses, painting, routine plumbing, changing lightbulbs, exterminating insects, maintaining tools and equipment, mowing grass, and other basic landscaping, like edging and trimming. About three years ago, I became a Lead Maintenance Mechanic and took on additional duties, such as submitting work orders, ordering supplies, supervising maintenance staff, scheduling, reports, and inspections.

2. What are the most important skills and /or qualities for someone in your profession?

You need to have at least a little working knowledge of all the trades that it would take to oversee the maintenance of a facility: minor plumbing, carpentry, electricity, masonry, painting, landscaping, etc. You need at least moderate skills in all of these trades to do the job correctly. You don't need to be licensed in any trade to do this job, but should have a good working knowledge of all of them.

3. What do you wish you had known going into this profession?

Going into this profession I wish I had known that if I went to school for one of these trades I could have become licensed and would be making quite a bit more money because I'd have a broader knowledge of one specific trade, instead of just knowing a moderate amount about several.

4. Are there many job opportunities in your profession? In What specific areas?

There are many job opportunities in this profession. The job title may not always read "general maintenance mechanic." It might be "maintenance helper" or " handyman." Any college campus, factory, warehouse, mall, or other setting where things break and need to be fixed are typical places where you would see this profession.

5. How do you see your profession changing in the next five years? What role will technology play in those changes, and what skills will be required?

I don't see much change happening in this field over the next five years. We do need to keep up to date with things, particularly when we get new equipment, such as a HVAC system or a security system. I need to familiarize myself with it to know how it works and what needs to be done when it breaks.

6. What do you enjoy most about your job? What do you enjoy least about your job?

I enjoy the satisfaction you get when something is not working and you get it to work, or when you finish a project that you weren't sure you would be able to do without someone else's help. It gets frustrating when you're close to finishing a project or fixing something and you just don't have the knowledge that someone trained in that particular field has so you have to call someone in to finish it for you.

7. Can you suggest a valuable "try this" for student considering a career in your profession?

I suggest trying to maintain one's own house or apartment by yourself: everything from changing lightbulbs to preparing a room for painting and painting it, to repairing small water leaks or replacing rotted wood. If you're not sure if you can do it, check the Internet. There are lots of "how to" videos to use for a guide. You have to attempt things within reason though—you don't want to do anything that will put yourself or others in danger, like trying to change an electrical panel.

SELECTED SCHOOLS

A college degree is not necessary in most cases to work as a maintenance mechanic. For those interested in the field, however, a technical or community college is a good place to start. Many commercial trade schools are also available. Students are advised to consult with their school guidance counselor or research area post-secondary schools to find the right program.

MORE INFORMATION

American Society of Mechanical Engineers
2 Park Avenue
New York, NY 10016-5990
800.843.2763
www.asme.org

Associated Builders and Contractors
4250 N. Fairfax Drive, 9th Floor
Arlington, VA 22203
703.812.2000
www.abc.org

Building Trades Association
16th Street, NW
Washington, DC 20006
800.326.7800
www.buildingtrades.com

Mechanical Contractors Association of America
1385 Piccard Drive
Rockville, MD 20850
301.869.5800
www.mcaa.org

Society for Maintenance and Reliability Professionals
1100 Johnson Ferry Road, Suite 300
Atlanta, GA 30342
800.950.7354
www.smrp.org

John Pritchard/Editor

Heating & Cooling Technician

Snapshot

Career Cluster: Construction; Maintenance & Repair

Interests: Mechanics, working with your hands, communicating with others

Earnings (Yearly Average): $46,110

Employment & Outlook: Faster than Average Growth Expected

OVERVIEW

Sphere of Work

Heating and cooling technicians—also called heating, ventilation, air conditioning, and refrigeration (HVACR) technicians—install and maintain heating and cooling systems in homes and businesses. Some heating and cooling technicians are employed by large companies while others work as private contractors. The job of a heating and cooling technician is to repair and maintain the machines that control air temperature and air quality in homes and businesses and in buildings of various sizes. Heating and cooling technicians perform a variety of tasks, including the construction of ductwork and routine checks for

ventilation efficiency. They are also responsible for ensuring that a building or home is compliant with local air quality regulations.

Work Environment

The work environment of heating and cooling technicians varies from job to job. The work they perform is generally indoors, though some machines, such as large heat pumps or industrial air conditioning units, require them to work outside. Heating and cooling technicians must take proper precautions to minimize their risk of injuries related to both heating and cooling machines.

Profile

Working Conditions: Work both Indoors and Outdoors
Physical Strength: Medium Work
Education Needs: On-The-Job Training, High School Diploma with Technical, Education, Technical/Community College
Licensure/Certification: Required
Physical Abilities Not Required: N/A
Opportunities For Experience: Apprenticeship, Military Service
Holland Interest Score*: REC

* See Appendix A

Occupation Interest

Like engineers or engineering technicians, people who pursue a career as a heating and cooling technician enjoy science and mathematics. They also like taking things apart and putting them back together again. The job requires meticulous attention to detail and an extensive knowledge of heating and cooling mechanics.

A Day in the Life—Duties and Responsibilities

No two days are alike for a heating and cooling technician. Sometimes independent or residential contractors schedule projects in advance, while others receive a list of the day's jobs each morning. Heating and cooling technicians work eight to ten hours a day. Some heating and cooling technicians work overtime or weekends. Independent contractors have more control over how often and how long they work.

The responsibilities of heating and cooling technicians include reading and following blueprints and design specifications, installing electrical wiring, testing machine components, replacing old parts, and installing ductwork. In addition to doing repairs and installations, some heating and cooling technicians sell maintenance contracts to consumers. Because they often work independently, heating and cooling technicians must check their work on-site to ensure that technical and mechanical issues have been addressed.

Some heating and cooling technicians perform tasks as needed for heating and cooling systems, while others who work for a large company might be responsible for only one task such as the installation of a particular machine or system.

Duties and Responsibilities

- Diagnosing causes of breakdowns
- Installing and repairing units
- Lifting parts into position
- Disassembling and assembling parts
- Screwing, bolting, welding and brazing parts
- Cutting, threading and connecting pipes
- Connecting motors to control panels
- Connecting control panels to power sources
- Testing parts using instruments
- Adjusting valves
- Lubricating machinery

OCCUPATION SPECIALTIES

Refrigeration Technicians

Refrigeration Mechanics install, service and repair industrial and commercial refrigeration and cooling systems in supermarkets, freezer plants and other industrial establishments.

Furnace Installers and Repairers

Furnace Installers and Repairers install and repair oil, gas, electric, solid-fuel and multifuel heating systems.

WORK ENVIRONMENT

Physical Environment

Heating and cooling technicians sometimes work in tight or cramped spaces in homes, schools, offices, or factories. However, the daily activities of most technicians are varied enough that they spend equal amounts of time sitting and standing as they travel to jobs and communicate with colleagues and customers.

Relevant Skills and Abilities

Interpersonal/Social Skills
- Being able to work independently

Organization & Management Skills
- Following instructions
- Performing duties which change frequently

Research & Planning Skills
- Using logical reasoning

Technical Skills
- Performing technical work
- Working with machines, tools or other objects

Unclassified Skills
- Using set methods and standards in your work

Human Environment

On the job, heating and cooling technicians interact regularly with customers. Technicians and their customers discuss problems with air quality systems. If necessary, technicians will also explain the installation task. Some technicians do sales work, so a professional manner and a comfort in dealing with people is important. Heating and cooling technicians must be able to explain problems, repairs, and installations to the satisfaction of the customer.

Technological Environment

Heating and cooling technicians work with a number of technologies that range from simple hand tools (such as wrenches or screwdrivers) to acetylene torches and combustion analyzers that are built for testing machines. They also need to be familiar with computer hardware that is design to operate air quality systems as well as heating and cooling systems.

EDUCATION, TRAINING, AND ADVANCEMENT

High School/Secondary

An aspiring heating and cooling technician should enroll in physics, mathematics, science, and shop classes. A working knowledge of computers and electronics is also helpful. Most heating and cooling technicians are required by employers to earn a high school degree or pass a General Educational Development (GED) test.

Suggested High School Subjects
- Applied Math
- Applied Physics
- Blueprint Reading
- Chemistry
- Electricity & Electronics
- English
- Heating/Air Cond./Refrigeration
- Mechanical Drawing
- Metals Technology
- Physics
- Shop Math
- Trade/Industrial Education
- Welding

Famous First

The first successful refrigeration service for local customers began operating in 1889 in Denver, Colorado, under the name Colorado Automatic Refrigeration Company. A 50,000-square-foot cold storage warehouse and a 30-ton ice machine supplied area businesses with their refrigeration and ice-making needs. The system operated on liquid ammonia. Old fashioned system pictured.

College/Postsecondary

Most companies prefer to hire heating and cooling technicians with some postsecondary training. Aspiring heating and cooling technicians can apply for programs through a technical school. These programs can last anywhere for six to twenty-four months and will teach basic skills that are related to the field. Educational programs and vocational schools award graduates with certificates or associate's degrees in a specialized field related to heating and cooling.

After the completion of postsecondary training, heating and cooling technicians can apply for formal apprenticeships. Some technicians apply for a formal apprenticeship directly after high school. A number of organizations, including the Air Conditioning Contractors of America, the National Association of Home Builders, the Mechanical Contractors Association of America, the Plumbing-Heating-Cooling Contractors Association, and Associated Builders and Contractors offer apprenticeships under an experienced professional. Apprenticeship programs usually last three to five years.

Related College Majors
* Heating, Air Conditioning & Refrigeration Mechanics & Repair
* Heating, Air Conditioning & Refrigeration Technology

Adult Job Seekers

Adult job seekers who wish to begin a career as a heating and cooling technician should enroll in a postsecondary education program.

Individuals with transferrable skills, such as prior experience as a mechanic, should apply for an apprenticeship.

Professional Certification and Licensure

There are several tests and licenses available to heating and cooling technicians. Technician associations and trade groups offer licensing and certification for different stages of a technician's career. Many states require heating and cooling technicians to attain some form of licensure. Though they are not always required, certification and licensure makes a heating and cooling technician more employable. Technician certifications do not expire, though most are staggered to test both basic and more advanced knowledge and specializations. Heating and cooling technicians who work with refrigerants must be certified through the Environmental Protection Agency. Technicians must pass one of three written specialization exams servicing small appliances, high-pressure refrigerants, and low-pressure refrigerants. Other heating and cooling technicians are eligible to take exams after at least one year of installation experience and two years of experience in maintenance and repairs.

Additional Requirements

Heating and cooling technicians often have to lift heavy pieces of equipment or mechanical parts. They also often work in difficult physical positions and locations. For these reasons, heating and cooling technicians should maintain their physical fitness. They must also be adept at working with their hands and have good hand-eye coordination.

Fun Fact

The New York Stock Exchange building in New York was one of the first structures to use an air conditioning system, back in 1903.

Source: http://www.americanweathermakers.com/fun-facts.php

EARNINGS AND ADVANCEMENT

Earnings depend on the employee's skill and experience, type of equipment being repaired and the geographic location and extent of unionization of the employer. Skilled electricians, pipefitters or sheet metal workers who have specialized in air conditioning, refrigeration and/or heating work usually earn higher wages.

In 2013, heating and cooling technicians had mean annual earnings of $46,110. The lowest ten percent earned less than $27,210, and the highest ten percent earned more than $69,740. Apprentices usually begin at about fifty percent of the wage rate paid to experienced workers. As they gain experience and improve skills, they receive periodic increases.

Heating and cooling technicians may receive paid vacations, holidays, and sick days; life and health insurance; and retirement benefits. These are usually paid by the employer. Uniforms and safety equipment may also be provided.

Metropolitan Areas with the Highest
Employment Level in this Occupation

Metropolitan area	Employment [1]	Employment per thousand jobs	Hourly mean wage
New York-White Plains-Wayne, NY-NJ	7,330	1.40	$27.35
Chicago-Joliet-Naperville, IL	5,460	1.48	$28.40
Houston-Sugar Land-Baytown, TX	5,380	1.95	$20.91
Dallas-Plano-Irving, TX	4,690	2.18	$22.49
Atlanta-Sandy Springs-Marietta, GA	4,660	2.02	$20.68
Washington-Arlington-Alexandria, DC-VA-MD-WV	4,520	1.91	$25.67
Phoenix-Mesa-Glendale, AZ	4,130	2.32	$23.12
Philadelphia, PA	4,050	2.20	$23.33
Los Angeles-Long Beach-Glendale, CA	4,040	1.02	$26.29
Boston-Cambridge-Quincy, MA	3,440	1.97	$28.49

[1]Does not include self-employ ed. Source: Bureau of Labor Statistics

EMPLOYMENT AND OUTLOOK

There were approximately 268,000 heating and cooling technicians employed nationally in 2012. Employment is expected to grow much faster than the average for all occupations through the year 2022, which means employment is projected to increase 20 percent or more. As the population and number of buildings grow, so does the demand for new residential, commercial, and industrial climate-control systems. In addition, a renewed concern about energy conservation should continue to prompt the development and installation of new energy-saving heating and air-conditioning systems.

Employment Trend, Projected 2012–22

Heating and Cooling Technicians: 21%

Total, All Occupations: 11%

Installation, Maintenance, and Repair Occupations: 10%

Note: "All Occupations" includes all occupations in the U.S. Economy. Source: U.S. Bureau of Labor Statistics, Employment Projections Program

Related Occupations
- Energy Auditor
- Energy Engineer
- Home Appliance Repairer
- Plumber & Pipe Fitter
- Renewable Energy Technician
- Sheet Metal Worker
- Solar Energy System Installer
- Stationary Engineer

Related Military Occupations
- Heating & Cooling Mechanic

Conversation With . . .
LOUIS SKAGGS, Sr.

Owner, Zone Heating and Air Conditioning, 40 Years
New Orleans, LA
Heating and Cooling Business, 43 Years

1. What was your individual career path in terms of education/training, entry-level job, or other significant opportunity?

I was in the U.S. Marine Corps and also hold a BS in aerodynamics from Louisiana Tech. Originally, I wanted to go on and get a master's degree, and possibly a PhD. But I've always been an outside guy and mechanical. My father-in-law started this business with his brother in 1950. I bought it from him in 1975. He was retiring, his brother had passed away, they had built a good clientele, and I had worked for my father-in-law off and on going back to high school. I went on to build the business and improve it financially.

2. What are the most important skills and/or qualities for someone in your profession?

You've got to be mechanically- and electrically-inclined, a very logically-minded person who can ask yourself questions in order to work through a problem. You need to be able to read and understand schematics and go through them to deal with whatever is applicable for the problem at hand. For instance, you have to know where the current comes from, where it stops, and what's open and closed as far as diodes and resisters, safeties, pressure switches, and the like. You also have to be able to trace back; start at the problem and go back to see if everything else is functioning.

3. What do you wish you had known going into this profession?

As a business owner, you have three sources of stress you always have to be aware of: from your role as the service guy, from the liability standpoint, and from the customers.

4. Are there many job opportunities in your profession? In what specific areas?

There's plenty of opportunity. Some companies allow for commissions, some pay bonuses. HVAC companies have slow seasons – here in New Orleans, it's winter – and you need to know that if you're the new guy and if your company doesn't plan ahead, you're going to be out of a job in the wintertime.

5. How do you see your profession changing in the next five years, what role will technology play in those changes, and what skills will be required?

Today, I would really consider going for an electrical engineering degree first since the technology is so high-level and complex. These systems are run by electronics; they go back to a solid state board like a motherboard. We've got WiFi thermostats now that you can set from your phone from anywhere in the world. We still have the mechanics – things like motors and coils – and that hardware is going to remain the same. The software is where the industry is going. Continuous training is a requirement, including seminars taught by engineering people from the different manufacturers so you know how something operates.

6. What do you enjoy most about your job? What do you enjoy least about your job?

I really enjoy that I'm making people comfortable in their atmosphere. When I repair a system, especially one that really has a tough problem, I feel great. The people are happy, and it's gratifying. For me, the worst part is in the winter when I have to go under houses in mud and slush to do troubleshooting. It's muddy, wet, and even though I take proper precautions, I feel I run a chance of getting electrocuted. That's the only thing I don't really like.

7. Can you suggest a valuable "try this" for students considering a career in your profession?

Get on the web or pick up a few books on heating and air conditioning – or just air conditioning, which really is the most complex side of this trade – and see if you can figure out how these systems function. See if you can solve a problem. Also volunteer to tag along with a service technician because this is a hands-on trade.

SELECTED SCHOOLS

A college degree is not necessary in most cases to work as a heating and cooling technician. For those interested in the field, however, a technical or community college is a good place to start. Many commercial trade schools are also available. Students are advised to consult with their school guidance counselor or research area post-secondary schools to find the right program.

MORE INFORMATION

Air Conditioning Contractors of America
2800 Shirlington Road, Suite 300
Arlington, VA 22206
703.575.4477
www.acca.org

Air-Conditioning, Heating and Refrigeration Institute
2111 Wilson Boulevard, Suite 500
Arlington, VA 22201
703.524.8800
www.ari.org

American Society of Heating, Refrigerating and Air-Conditioning Engineers
Education Department
1791 Tullie Circle, NE
Atlanta, GA 30329
800.527.4723
www.ashrae.org

Associated Builders and Contractors
4250 N. Fairfax Drive, 9th Floor
Arlington, VA 22203
703.812.2000
www.abc.org

HVAC Excellence
1701 Pennsylvania Avenue, NW
Washington, DC 20006
800.394.5268
www.hvacexcellence.org

Mechanical Contractors Association of America
1385 Piccard Drive
Rockville, MD 20850
301.869.5800
www.mcaa.org

National Association of Home Builders
1201 15th Street, NW
Washington, DC 20005
800.368.5242
www.nahb.com

National Center for Construction Education and Research
13614 Progress Boulevard
Alachua, FL 32615
888.622.3720
www.nccer.org

Plumbing-Heating-Cooling Contractors-National Association
180 South Washington Street
P.O. Box 6808
Falls Church, VA 22040
800.533.7694
www.phccweb.org

Refrigerating Engineers & Technicians Association
P.O. Box 1819
Salinas, CA 93902
831.455.8783
www.reta.com

Refrigeration Service Engineers Society
1666 Rand Road
Des Plaines, IL 60016-3552
847.297.6464
www.rses.org

Sheetmetal and Air Conditioning Contractors National Association
4201 Lafayette Center Drive
Chantilly, VA 20151-1209
703.803.2980
www.smacna.org

Molly Hagan/Editor

Heavy Equipment Service Technician

Snapshot

Career Cluster: Engineering; Maintenance & Repair
Interests: Machinery, working with your hands, solving problems, working as a team
Earnings (Yearly Average): $47,830
Employment & Outlook: Average Growth Expected

OVERVIEW

Sphere of Work

Heavy equipment service technicians work in a variety of industries, maintaining and repairing a broad range of equipment. They identify problems with heavy machinery and repair them using hand tools and computerized equipment. They are able to disassemble and reassemble complex mechanical systems and electrical components. They also perform preventive maintenance, such as lubricating and inspecting pistons and bearings. Industries in which heavy equipment service technicians work include farming, construction, and transportation.

Work Environment

Heavy equipment service technicians work in an assortment of environments on a variety of machines and vehicles. They commonly work indoors at repair shops, but sometimes repairs need to be performed on jobsites or at other off-site locations. Although they are well ventilated and well lit, repair shops are noisy due to the presence of operational machinery. Heavy equipment service technicians may be required to perform repairs on dirty and greasy equipment while standing, kneeling, bending, or lying on their backs. The work environment presents many hazards, including high-voltage electricity, dangerous chemicals, and heavy machinery. Safety standards must be adhered to at all times.

Profile

Working Conditions: Work both Indoors and Outdoors

Physical Strength: Medium to Heavy Work

Education Needs: On-The-Job Training, High School Diploma with Technical Education, Technical/Community College

Licensure/Certification: Recommended

Physical Abilities Not Required: N/A

Opportunities For Experience: Apprenticeship, Military Service

Holland Interest Score*: REI

* See Appendix A

Occupation Interest

Heavy equipment service technicians work in a diverse range of industries. The profession tends to attract individuals who enjoy working with their hands and possess a strong understanding of how machinery works and operates. Heavy equipment service technicians are great problem solvers who are able to work under pressure, either alone or as members of a team.

A Day in the Life—Duties and Responsibilities

The heavy equipment used in the construction, farming, and railroad industries is essential to those industries' success, and heavy equipment service technicians keep this equipment running smoothly. Equipment serviced by technicians includes cranes, diesel engines, railcars, and more. Heavy equipment service technicians perform routine maintenance on these machines to ensure their performance, safety, and longevity.

Some machines require a heavy equipment service technician to use a diagnostic computer to identify which components are malfunctioning. Once the problem has been identified, the heavy equipment service technician will decide the best approach to solving it. Technicians use computers to help calibrate electronic systems. Depending on the service needed, a heavy equipment service technician may have to disassemble the equipment using hand and power tools. Besides repairing the equipment, technicians also clean and lubricate moving parts as needed and perform routine inspections. They check for leaks, worn or rusty parts, and a number of other issues. It is up to the heavy equipment service technician whether components should be repaired or replaced. Heavy equipment service technicians also identify electrical malfunctions, diagnose structural defects in mobile equipment such as railroad cars and tractors, and sometimes weld equipment as necessary.

Heavy equipment service technicians often specialize in one or more kinds of repair. While one technician in the shop may specialize in diesel-engine repair, another may specialize in electrical systems or hydraulics. The more specialties a heavy equipment service technician has, the more likely he or she is to find employment.

Duties and Responsibilities

- Performing routine but preventive maintenance
- Diagnosing the nature of the repairs required
- Partially dismantling the engine and examining parts
- Making field repairs in order to finish construction jobs
- Welding broken parts and structural members
- Replacing defective engines and subassemblies, such as transmission
- Testing repaired equipment to be sure it is working correctly
- Examining and repairing hydraulic apparatus that has lost power
- Diagnosing and correcting electrical problems

OCCUPATION SPECIALTIES

Mobile Heavy Equipment Mechanics

Mobile Heavy Equipment Mechanics adjust, maintain and repair gasoline, hydraulic and diesel-powered heavy equipment and accessories such as air compressors, cranes, donkey engines, generators and road graders.

Heavy Repairers

Heavy Repairers repair heavy automobile or truck units, such as motors, transmissions or differentials, before units are assembled into chassis.

Farm Equipment Mechanics

Farm Equipment Mechanics service and repair farm equipment, such as tractors and harvesters. They also work on smaller consumer-grade lawn and garden tractors. Most work for dealer repair shops, where farmers increasingly send their equipment for maintenance.

WORK ENVIRONMENT

Physical Environment

Heavy equipment service technicians commonly work inside repair shops, where equipment is taken for routine maintenance or major repairs. They frequently handle heavy equipment, which is often dirty and greasy. Heavy equipment can cause serious injury if mishandled, so technicians must follow safety standards. Heavy equipment service technicians are also sometimes called to jobsites to perform repairs.

Relevant Skills and Abilities

Communication Skills
- Reading well

Organization & Management Skills
- Paying attention to and handling details

Technical Skills
- Working with machines, tools or other objects

Work Environment Skills
- Working in a dirty environment
- Working in a noisy atmosphere

Human Environment

Being a heavy equipment service technician requires regular collaboration with other technicians and clients. Technicians may also interact with representatives from equipment and parts manufacturers.

Technological Environment

Heavy equipment service technicians use a wide range of tools, including small hand tools and sophisticated computerized equipment. Some common tools include welding equipment, pneumatic wrenches, jacks, and dynamometers to identify engine malfunctions. Voltmeters and ammeters are used while working on electrical systems.

EDUCATION, TRAINING, AND ADVANCEMENT

High School/Secondary

While there are no concrete educational requirements, employers are more likely to hire a heavy equipment service technician who has a high school diploma or the equivalent. Aspiring technicians should take high school courses in computers, mathematics, and mechanical drawing. Since heavy equipment service technicians often have to refer to service manuals, they need to be able to read and analyze mechanical drawings and instructions.

Many high schools also offer automotive shop classes, in which students learn the basics of automotive repair. Shop classes provide students with a background in engine repair and teach them how to use basic machine-shop tools.

Suggested High School Subjects
- Agricultural Mechanization
- Applied Math
- Applied Physics
- Auto Service Technology
- Blueprint Reading
- Chemistry
- Diesel Maintenance Technology
- English
- Machining Technology
- Mathematics
- Mechanical Drawing
- Physics
- Shop Math
- Shop Mechanics
- Trade/Industrial Education
- Welding

Famous First

The first crane was manufactured in 1883 by the Yale & Towne Company, Stamford, Connecticut, for the Pittsburgh Bessemer Steel Company. The crane was a two-ton, full-revolving steam crane mounted on a rail truck.

College/Postsecondary

There are several courses and programs offered at vocational and technical schools that will help strengthen the mechanical skills of anyone interested in becoming a heavy equipment service technician.
These courses and programs typically last one or two years. Some are designed specifically for heavy equipment service technicians, including programs in diesel technology, hydraulics, and electrical systems. Students in these courses will be instructed in equipment diagnostics, tools, hydraulics, and safety practices. Individuals who

complete postsecondary training will have a strong background in the field of heavy equipment service.

Related College Majors
- Heavy Equipment Maintenance & Repair

Adult Job Seekers

Aspiring heavy equipment service technicians who have no background in the industry are encouraged to enroll in a vocational or technical school offering relevant courses. Entry-level technicians with education credentials may require less on-the-job training. Networking is critical in the service technician industry, and vocational schools are a great place to meet experienced professionals. There are many facets to the service-technician profession, and applicants should take a multidisciplinary approach to their job search.

Professional Certification and Licensure

Many of the one- and two-year programs offered by technical and vocational schools provide certification upon completion. Many equipment manufacturers also offer certification programs in specialized areas of equipment repair and service. These programs typically last up to a week and provide heavy equipment service technicians with intensive instruction on the repair of the specific manufacturer's equipment. Employers often require their technicians to attend certification programs, and they are more likely to promote technicians who actively seek out further certification. The more certifications a heavy equipment service technician acquires, the greater his or her chances for career advancement.

The National Institute for Automotive Service Excellence (ASE) offers voluntary certification for heavy equipment service technicians. Technicians can take an ASE certification test online in any of over forty categories of machine operations, maintenance, and repair. Although this certification is not required, it demonstrates a heavy equipment service technician's skills and knowledge and increases his or her value to employers.

Additional Requirements

Heavy equipment service technicians need to have great mechanical aptitude and a commitment to further training. The industry uses a wide array of computer technology, so technicians must be comfortable working with computers. Heavy equipment service technicians should be in good physical shape to be able to meet the job's physical demands. They should also have great communication skills in order to collaborate and communicate with other technicians, supervisors, and clients.

EARNINGS AND ADVANCEMENT

Heavy equipment service technicians had mean annual earnings of $47,830 in 2013. The lowest ten percent earned less than $31,230, and the highest ten percent earned more than $67,210.

Heavy equipment service technicians may receive paid vacations, holidays, and sick days; life and health insurance; and retirement benefits. These are usually paid by the employer.

Metropolitan Areas with the Highest
Employment Level in this Occupation

Metropolitan area	Employment [1]	Employment per thousand jobs	Hourly mean wage
Houston-Sugar Land-Baytown, TX	6,150	2.23	$22.33
Los Angeles-Long Beach-Glendale, CA	2,320	0.58	$28.20
Phoenix-Mesa-Glendale, AZ	2,220	1.25	$22.14
Minneapolis-St. Paul-Bloomington, MN-WI	2,130	1.19	$25.03
Salt Lake City, UT	1,690	2.62	$25.15
Denver-Aurora-Broomfield, CO	1,350	1.05	$24.52
Dallas-Plano-Irving, TX	1,320	0.61	$21.23
Riverside-San Bernardino-Ontario, CA	1,230	1.02	$26.47
Pittsburgh, PA	1,110	0.98	$23.97
Birmingham-Hoover, AL	1,090	2.23	$19.97

[1]Does not include self-employ ed. Source: Bureau of Labor Statistics

EMPLOYMENT AND OUTLOOK

There were approximately 175,000 heavy equipment service technicians employed nationally in 2012. Employment is expected to grow about as fast as the average for all occupations through the year 2022, which means employment is projected to increase 6 percent to 12 percent. Increased demand will result from a growth in construction activity. In addition, many job openings will come from the need to replace workers who transfer to other occupations or leave the labor force.

Employment Trend, Projected 2012–22

Total, All Occupations: 11%

Farm Equipment Mechanics: 10%

Heavy Equipment Service Technicians: 9%

Note: "All Occupations" includes all occupations in the U.S. Economy. Source: U.S. Bureau of Labor Statistics, Employment Projections Program

Related Occupations
- Aircraft Mechanic
- Automotive Technician
- Bulldozer Operator
- Diesel Service Technician
- Farm Equipment Mechanic
- Industrial Machinery Mechanic

Related Military Occupations
- Automotive & Heavy Equipment Mechanic
- Construction Equipment Operator

Conversation With . . .
JEFF STEVENS

Heavy Equipment Mechanic
A.F. Amorello & Sons, Worcester, MA
Heavy Equipment Mechanic, 18 years

1. What was your individual career path in terms of education/training, entry-level job, or other significant opportunity?

When I was in high school, I worked in the garage at a road construction company where my father was a foreman. I always like working on cars. After I graduated from high school, I went to an 18-month program for heavy equipment/diesel repair at Universal Technical Institute (UTI) out in Illinois. At that point in time, it was the closest program, but they've since opened a school here in Massachusetts. After I finished, I got hired at the same company working on backhoes, loaders, pavers, trucks … all kinds of equipment.

2. What are the most important skills and/or qualities for someone in your profession?

I would have to say the ability to diagnose problems is the most important skill for a heavy equipment mechanic. Anybody, or almost anybody, can change out parts, but trying to figure out what the problem is—that's the heart of the job. You have to be logical and analytical, knowing what the next logical step is to take. That also requires patience. Obviously, you need to have mechanical aptitude. And you also need to have strength because most of the stuff that you deal with is going to be much bigger than in a car. It's hard to explain, but you have to really want to do this job.

3. What do you wish you had known going into this profession?

Tools cost a lot of money. With heavy equipment, everything's more money, because they're bigger—bigger sockets, bigger wrenches. You're going to have to spend a lot of money on tools. Some companies give you an allowance, but it's still a lot of money. And you want to have the right tools. The right tool can get the job done in half the time. Other than that, everything's pretty much as I expected.

4. Are there many job opportunities in your profession? In what specific areas?

Yes, there are. Just about every company with heavy equipment needs mechanics. Manufacturers like Caterpillar are always looking for mechanics. Then there are construction companies like the one I work for, and trucking companies.

5. How do you see your profession changing in the next five years? What role will technology play in those changes, and what skills will be required?

It's getting a lot more computerized. Every single piece of equipment has a computer in it, or multiple computers. A paver we have here has, I think, 13 computer nodules in it. The manufacturers all offer training programs. And a lot of times you're calling the manufacturer for help. Caterpillar has a hotline that you can call with questions. The work is basically the same, though. Before, injection pumps were mechanical; now they've changed to electronic because it's more efficient. But if you have to replace the injector, you're still replacing an injector—it may look different or be installed differently, but it's still an injector.

6. What do you enjoy most about your job? What do you enjoy least about your job?

Mostly, I enjoy fixing things, taking something that's broken and making it work. And I like the satisfaction of figuring out what the problem is. What I probably like least is the stress of a machine breaking down that's really needed or when a machine breaks down in the middle of a job. I often go out to job sites and work on equipment there when it breaks down. If something major breaks and everyone needs it and you're in the middle of the road, that can be very stressful.

7. Can you suggest a valuable "try this" for students considering a career in your profession?

Number one, be sure you like to get dirty! See if you like working on cars. Working on heavy equipment is pretty much the same as working on cars, but on a bigger scale. You could even try taking apart your bicycle and putting it back together.

SELECTED SCHOOLS

A college degree is not necessary to work as a heavy equipment mechanic. For those interested in the field, however, a technical or community college is a good place to start. Many commercial trade schools are also available. Students are advised to consult with their school guidance counselor or research area post-secondary schools to find the right program.

MORE INFORMATION

Association of Leaders in Equipment Distribution
615 W. 22nd Street, Suite 220
Oak Brook, IL 60523
630.574.0650
www.aednet.org

National Automotive Technicians Education Foundation
101 Blue Seal Drive SE, Suite 101
Leesburg, VA 20175
703.669.6650
www.natef.org

National Institute for Automotive Service Excellence
101 Blue Seal Drive SE, Suite 101
Leesburg, VA 20175
703.669.6600
www.ase.com

National Truck Equipment Association
37400 Hills Tech Drive
Farmington Hills, MI 48331-3414
800.441.6832
www.ntea.com

Patrick Cooper/Editor

Home Appliance Repairer

Snapshot

Career Cluster: Maintenance & Repair; Technology

Interests: Mechanics, working with your hands, communicating with others, solving problems

Earnings (Yearly Average): $37,220

Employment & Outlook: Slower than Average Growth Expected

OVERVIEW

Sphere of Work

Home appliance repairers investigate problems with and repair a variety of malfunctioning machines used in the home, including dishwashers, ovens, washers, and dryers. Traditionally, home appliance repairers are knowledgeable about the entire spectrum of home appliance technology and possess extensive training in plumbing and electrical systems. They are hands-on problem solvers who are skilled in deductive reasoning. Much of the knowledge required of the position is learned through on-the-job experience.

Work Environment

Home appliance repairers work in both repair shops and on location in homes and selected small businesses. Many are independent contractors who work as repairers and small-business owners, sometimes managing a small staff. Others are employed by home appliance distributors and retail outlets. Home appliance repairers spend much of their time traveling from job to job, traditionally in vans or light trucks outfitted with tools, spare parts, and other necessary equipment.

Profile

Working Conditions: Work Indoors
Physical Strength: Medium Work
Education Needs: On-The-Job Training, High School Diploma with Technical Education, Technical/Community College
Licensure/Certification: Required
Physical Abilities Not Required: No Heavy Labor
Opportunities For Experience: Apprenticeship, Part-Time Work
Holland Interest Score*: RES

* See Appendix A

Occupation Interest

Home appliance repair attracts technologically savvy individuals who enjoy mechanical problem solving. The individualized nature of the work of a home appliance repairer often attracts people who enjoy working alone or with small groups. Since customer service and technological explanation are a large part of the job; home appliance repairers often are both amicable and patient and possess effective interpersonal communication skills.

A Day in the Life—Duties and Responsibilities

Home appliance repairers have a variety of tasks other than repairing machinery. Repairers who are proprietors of their own home appliance repair business must also make time to tend to administrative and budgetary duties, as well as to tasks related to marketing and promotion of the business.

In addition to traveling to jobs, appliance professionals who are employed by repair shops or retail businesses must document both their travel and parts used and complete paperwork related to billing and hours worked. All home repairers must complete occasional training courses to stay abreast of emerging trends and developments in home appliance technology.

Appliance professionals traditionally work regionally in homes and small businesses within close proximity to their headquarters. Jobs are customarily aligned in the most efficient manner possible, taking into consideration the particular machinery, type of problem, and estimated length of repair. Home appliance repair trucks are normally outfitted with most of the parts, tools, and diagnostic instruments repair workers need to tackle the majority of repairs. Large-scale repairs may require return visits or transportation of some parts, or an entire machine, back to a repair center.

Duties and Responsibilities

- Locating source of problems
- Examining and removing worn-out parts
- Dealing with customers who may be upset
- Testing parts
- Installing piping to a gas main
- Repairing and adjusting parts
- Installing new parts
- Estimating cost of repairs
- Keeping records of parts used and hours worked
- Advising customers on use and care of appliances

WORK ENVIRONMENT

Physical Environment

Home appliance repairers work predominately in residential, small business, and commercial settings. Home appliance repairers can also work in a variety of settings where appliance machinery is utilized, from corporate offices to hospitals, and restaurants.

Relevant Skills and Abilities

Interpersonal/Social Skills
- Cooperating with others
- Working as a member of a team

Organization & Management Skills
- Making decisions
- Paying attention to and handling details

Research & Planning Skills
- Developing evaluation strategies

Technical Skills
- Performing technical work
- Working with machines, tools or other objects

Human Environment

Home appliance repair requires strong interpersonal communication skills. Home appliance professionals interact extensively with clients and vendors on a daily basis.

Technological Environment

Home appliance repairers utilize a wide variety of technologies that range from telephone and radio use to working with diagnostic software and highly calibrated tools and machinery.

EDUCATION, TRAINING, AND ADVANCEMENT

High School/Secondary

High school students can best prepare for a career in home appliance repair with coursework in algebra, geometry, chemistry, physics, and computers. Industrial art and design classes can also serve as precursors for future work in technology and engineering and with machinery.

Participation in science fairs and science clubs gives students the opportunity to conceive of, invent, and disassemble various technological and mechanical processes and functions prior to graduation. Many vocational high schools in the United States offer specific small-machinery courses to high school students.

Suggested High School Subjects
- Appliance Repair Technology
- Applied Math
- Applied Physics
- Blueprint Reading
- Electricity & Electronics
- English
- Heating/Air Cond./Refrigeration
- Shop Math
- Shop Mechanics
- Trade/Industrial Education
- Welding

Famous First

The first electric fan was invented in 1882 by Schuyler Skaats Wheeler, a 22-year-old electrical engineer who worked for a few years at the Edison Electric Company before leaving and eventually forming his own firm, the Crocker-Wheeler Company of Ampere, New Jersey.

College/Postsecondary

Postsecondary education is not traditionally a requirement for a career in home appliance repair. Much of the basics of the position can be acquired through the successful completion of vocational or associate's-level training programs. A variety of community college and adult education centers also offer instructional training in home appliance and small machinery repair.

Appliance repair professionals interested in opening their own small repair businesses benefit from postsecondary coursework in engineering, business administration, and management.

Related College Majors
- Electrical & Electronics Equipment Installation & Repair

Adult Job Seekers

Home appliance repair professionals traditionally work regular business hours, although some may work on weekends or an on-call, emergency basis that can require sporadic hours and holiday shifts. The minimal amount of training and high frequency of on-the-job experience potential in the role makes the occupation a popular transitional field for both young professionals and those trying out new career paths.

Professional Certification and Licensure

Specific certification and licensing regarding home appliance repair is dictated by state and district regulations.

Additional Requirements

Punctuality, responsibility, and problem-solving skills are important skills for home appliance repair professionals to possess. Technological advances in home appliances have made many systems more intricate, thus increasing the range of potential problems and the amount of knowledge and patience required to troubleshoot them.

Fun Fact

Due to the harsh North Dakota winters, J. Ross Moore didn't want his mom hanging wet clothes outside to dry. In 1935 he built an oil-heated drum—the first clothes dryer—in a shed next to the house. He later created gas and electric dryers, and sold his designs when he needed the cash.

Source: greatachievements.org/?id=3768

EARNINGS AND ADVANCEMENT

Earnings depend on the type of equipment serviced, the union affiliation and geographic location of the employer and the employee's skill and experience. Home appliance repairers had median annual earnings of $37,220 in 2013. The lowest ten percent earned less than $19,810, and the highest ten percent earned more than $58,160.

Home appliance repairers may receive paid vacations, holidays, and sick days; life and health insurance; and retirement benefits. These are usually paid by the employer.

Metropolitan Areas with the Highest Employment Level in this Occupation

Metropolitan area	Employment [1]	Employment per thousand jobs	Hourly mean wage
New York-White Plains-Wayne, NY-NJ	1,680	0.32	$19.59
Edison-New Brunswick, NJ	750	0.76	$29.82
Chicago-Joliet-Naperville, IL	740	0.20	$17.61
Phoenix-Mesa-Glendale, AZ	690	0.39	$21.07
Riverside-San Bernardino-Ontario, CA	670	0.56	$23.38
Miami-Miami Beach-Kendall, FL	610	0.59	$17.45
Tampa-St. Petersburg-Clearwater, FL	530	0.46	$18.48
Philadelphia, PA	510	0.28	$16.74
Baltimore-Towson, MD	490	0.38	$20.55
Minneapolis-St. Paul-Bloomington, MN-WI	450	0.25	$20.46

[1]Does not include self-employ ed. Source: Bureau of Labor Statistics

EMPLOYMENT AND OUTLOOK

There were approximately 45,000 home appliance repairers employed nationally in 2012. About one-third were self-employed. Employment is expected to grow slower than the average for all occupations through the year 2022, which means employment is projected to increase 2 percent to 8 percent. The number of home appliances in use is expected to increase with growth in the numbers of households and businesses. Appliances are also becoming more technologically advanced and will increasingly require a skilled repairer to diagnose and fix problems.

Related Occupations
- Heating & Cooling Technician
- Home entertainment equipment technician
- Office Machine Repairer
- Small Engine Mechanic
- Television & Radio Repairer
- Vending Machine Repairer

Conversation With . . . TANNA MARINO

Franchise Consultant
Mr. Appliance, Cypress, Texas
Appliance Repair professional, 7 years

1. What was your individual career path in terms of education/ training, entry-level job, or other significant opportunity?

I had little more than a high school diploma when I became a service technician for Mr. Appliance. I was a stay-at-home mom before that. Our four kids were getting older and I decided that I needed to help out financially. One day our refrigerator broke and we called Mr. Appliance. My husband and the repairman and myself were talking in the driveway after he fixed our fridge. He was actively trying to recruit my husband, but my husband's a firefighter and happy with his career. After he left, I asked my husband how he would feel if I went for the job. I didn't know anything about appliances, but I like to tinker. My mom taught my brother and me to lay tile when we were growing up because she had a tile business, so I had already been thrust into a male-dominated field. I was working for Mr. Appliance when I was chosen to be put on "Undercover Boss" with Dina Dwyer-Owns, the owner of The Dwyer Group, which owns Mr. Appliance. Not long after that, I was given the opportunity to be a Franchise Consultant, which I've done for the last three years.

2. What are the most important skills and/or qualities for someone in your profession?

The most important skill to have is the ability to listen to the customer and care about what they have to say. I have a mentor who reminds me of the quote by Theodore Roosevelt: "People don't care how much you know until they know how much you care."

Anyone who has determination and the ability to follow-through can do just fine in appliance repair. As part of my training, I rode with the top technician for two or three months. I had a list of tech support line phone numbers I could call if I needed help. It took about a year before I was on pretty solid ground.

3. What do you wish you had known going into this profession?

I guess the only real obstacle I had was being a female technician. You have to know how to let things roll off your back. I got comments like, "You're the technician?"

I never really took offense to the remarks. To me, it just meant I had something to prove.

4. Are there many job opportunities in your profession? In what specific areas?

There are always job opportunities for qualified applicants. There are jobs in residential and commercial settings. Anywhere that there's an appliance, there's a need for technicians—restaurants, hotels, hairdressers all have washers and dryers, assisted living facilities.

I was blessed to be a part of an initiative created by The Dwyer Group called Women in the Trades, which provides scholarships for women looking to further their education in the trades industry.

5. How do you see your profession changing in the next five years? What role will technology play in those changes, and what skills will be required?

Technology plays such a big role in most industries these days. Electronics are kind of the future of everything. It's just like with cars being less mechanical and more computer-based. Looking back over my career, I have seen a lot of changes. It's hard to predict what the future holds for us.

6. What do you enjoy most about your job? What do you enjoy least about your job?

When I was working as an appliance service technician, I truly enjoyed customer interactions and the analytical side of the service industry. I would say one of the least attractive parts of my job would have been the uniform! We wore blue dickies and blue and white striped shirts that were designed for men. I got to dress like a guy every day, I felt. Thanks to an initiative that came out of the "Undercover Boss" episode and Women in the Trades, we now have women's cut uniforms. I worked on that and it was fun. The women's-cut uniforms we were finding looked better, but the quality was not there. You're on your knees a lot and you're working under machines. The fabric has to withstand that.

7. Can you suggest a valuable "try this" for students considering a career in your profession?

I would suggest reaching out to any of The Dwyer Group franchises like Mr. Appliance and speaking to a local owner. There may be entry-level positions available for training purposes.

SELECTED SCHOOLS

A college degree is not necessary to work as a home appliance repairer. For those interested in the field, however, a technical or community college is a good place to start. Many commercial trade schools are also available. Students are advised to consult with their school guidance counselor or research area post-secondary schools to find the right program.

MORE INFORMATION

International Society of Certified Electronics Technicians
3608 Pershing Avenue
Fort Worth, TX 76107-4527
800.946.0201
www.iscet.org

National Electrical Contractors Association
3 Bethesda Metro Center, Suite 1100
Bethesda, MD 20814
301.657.3110
www.necanet.org/

National Electronics Service Dealers Association
3608 Pershing Avenue
Fort Worth, TX 76107-4527
817.921.9061
www.nesda.com

Professional Service Association
71 Columbia Street
Cohoes, NY 12047
888.777.8851
www.psaworld.com

United Servicers Association
3105 N. Ashland Avenue, Suite 199
Chicago, IL 60657
800.683.2558
www.unitedservicers.com

John Pritchard/Editor

Home Entertainment Equipment Technician

Snapshot

Career Cluster: Electronics; Maintenance & Repair; Technology

Interests: Mechanics, electronics, solving problems, helping others

Earnings (Yearly Average): $37,310

Employment & Outlook: Slower than Average Growth Expected

OVERVIEW

Sphere of Work

Home entertainment equipment technicians disassemble, clean, troubleshoot, and repair malfunctioning home entertainment systems. These technicians often specialize in one or more areas of home entertainment media, such as televisions and monitors or audio and surround-sound systems. Home entertainment equipment technicians often work independently of cable and Internet technicians. They may, however, double as home entertainment equipment installation professionals for both independent shops and national electronics retailers. Home

entertainment technicians are often on call to complete repairs in residences, businesses, and repair shops.

Work Environment

Many home entertainment equipment technicians spend a lot of time traveling, tending to repairs from work vans and visiting several clients each day. More complex repairs may require service by technicians at repair shops, which are outfitted with equipment that is not portable. Home entertainment equipment technicians work primarily indoors, though some outdoor projects may occasionally be required.

Profile

Working Conditions: Work Indoors
Physical Strength: Light to Medium Work
Education Needs: On-The-Job Training, High School Diploma with Technical Education
Licensure/Certification: Recommended
Physical Abilities Not Required: No Heavy Labor
Opportunities For Experience: Military Service
Holland Interest Score*: REI

* See Appendix A

Occupation Interest

Home entertainment equipment technicians come from a variety of backgrounds, interests, and occupations. They are almost exclusively technologically savvy people who enjoy working with electronics and computers. Many have extensive backgrounds as technology hobbyists. The field of home entertainment equipment repair traditionally attracts problem solvers who derive a sense of purpose and satisfaction from helping less knowledgeable people navigate complex and emerging home-entertainment technology.

A Day in the Life—Duties and Responsibilities

Customers will usually bring small, portable electronic equipment into retail locations for repair. Technicians who work in these settings are called bench technicians. They have a complete selection of tools, diagnostic machines, and parts to work with. When equipment is too large to transport to a retail site, customers will request a home or office visit by a field technician. Field technicians carry a limited number of tools and parts and work in the customer's home or business to clean parts and make repairs. If the repair is too involved to handle on-site, the technician will bring in defective or malfunctioning parts to the retail location for diagnosis and repair or replacement.

At retail locations, bench technicians may begin their day by reviewing the complexity of and time requirements for each specific repair. They may also communicate with management, staff, and outside vendors in order to obtain parts for specific fixes. Home entertainment equipment technicians who are employed by television and electronics stores may have duties related to the maintenance and upkeep of the retail environment. They also answer customer questions that are related to service, repair, or equipment maintenance.

Field technicians begin each day at a central service center and are given a list of repair locations. They are responsible for preparing for each repair job by packing the necessary equipment and tools and ensuring they arrive at customer locations at the scheduled time. Both field and bench technicians spend time cleaning and lubricating parts. Technicians also test equipment to help diagnose problems and replace broken or failed parts.

Duties and Responsibilities

- Checking for sources of trouble
- Talking to customers
- Reading service manuals and diagrams
- Checking circuits with test equipment
- Replacing faulty parts
- Adjusting loose components and parts
- Ordering equipment and supplies
- Installing radios in automobiles

OCCUPATION SPECIALTIES

Television and Radio Technicians

Television and Radio Technicians inspect and repair televisions and radios.

Production Technicians

Production Technicians repair rejected electronic equipment according to specifications with hand tools.

Audio-Video Technicians

Audio-Video Technicians install and repair audio-video equipment with hand tools and testing equipment.

WORK ENVIRONMENT

Physical Environment

Home entertainment equipment technicians work primarily in repair-shop settings. Many technicians are also required to spend time in customer's homes and in business settings in order to complete necessary repair or replacement of defective equipment. Work is almost exclusively conducted indoors.

Human Environment

Professionals in the equipment repair field frequently interact with both customers and vendors. Although repair work is primarily conducted in a solitary environment, equipment technicians will often meet with customers to explain the repairs in nontechnical terms.

Relevant Skills and Abilities

Interpersonal/Social Skills
- Being sensitive to others
- Cooperating with others

Research & Planning Skills
- Analyzing information

Research & Planning Skills
- Gathering information
- Solving problems

Technical Skills
- Working with machines, tools or other objects

Technological Environment

Home entertainment equipment technicians use a wide range of technologies, including complex hardware and software systems and highly calibrated diagnostic tools and machinery. These tools include instruments to measure voltage and current and to detect short circuits and blown fuses. Technicians also use hand tools to replace defective parts.

EDUCATION, TRAINING, AND ADVANCEMENT

High School/Secondary

High school students can best prepare for a career as a home entertainment equipment technician with courses in algebra, calculus, physics, robotics, and computer science. English and writing courses aid in the development of the communication and problem-solving skills that are vital for success in the field.

Many high school students can gain exposure to electronics and media devices by participating in science fairs and science clubs. Summer jobs and internships at relevant organizations can also provide a sound foundation of knowledge.

Suggested High School Subjects
- Applied Math
- Blueprint Reading
- Electricity & Electronics
- English
- Machining Technology

- Radio & TV Repair
- Shop Math
- Shop Mechanics
- Welding

Famous First

The first pay television system, called Phonovision, was established in 1951 in Chicago. Station KS2KSBS, owned by the Zenith Radio Corporation, transmitted a scrambled radio signal that could only be received by customers who had paid for a "key signal" sent via telephone circuit. During the first four weeks, 2,561 sales were made.

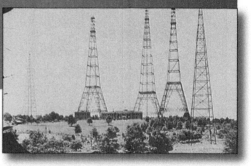

College/Postsecondary

There are numerous postsecondary vocational, technical, and associate's degree programs in electronics repair. Postsecondary education is not always a requirement for those entering the field, given the large amount of on-the-job training. However, the competency and knowledge demonstrated by an advanced education in electronics can be of tremendous benefit to job applicants.

Basic postsecondary education related to electronics repair includes classes in circuitry, processors, computer chips, computer software, applications, and programming. Courses also instruct future electronics repair professionals on the technical intricacies of television transmission, broadcasting, and other facets of telecommunications systems. Students of electronics repair learn how to read and interpret circuitry diagrams, machine specifications, service manuals, and other documentation related to the engineering, production, and maintenance of home entertainment equipment.

Related College Majors
- Electrical & Electronics Equipment Installation & Repair
- Major Appliance Installation & Repair

Adult Job Seekers

Home entertainment equipment technicians work traditional weekday business hours. Occasional weekend work may also be required. The role is a popular transitional field for electronics and entertainment technology hobbyists looking to make their passion for video, audio, and recording technology a viable career. A return to employment for an unrelated field may require significant transition time, involving either extensive on-the-job training or formal instruction.

Professional Certification and Licensure

Electronics professionals are encouraged to seek and acquire certification or licensing according to national, state, and district regulations. Several organizations provide certification for electronics repair professionals.

Additional Requirements

Home entertainment equipment technicians should have a strong commitment to customer service and the ability to explain complex technical concepts to less informed clientele.

Fun Fact

When President Harry S Truman gave the first televised White House address in 1947, asking Americans to eat less and give more to those starving in war-ravaged Europe, 44,000 homes in the country had television sets. By 1954, more than half of U.S. homes had a TV and today, the average American home has three.

Source: http://learning.blogs.nytimes.com/2011/10/05/oct-5-1947-president-truman-uses-first-ever-tv-address-to-ask-americans-to-conserve-food; politico.com/news/stories/1010/43100.html

EARNINGS AND ADVANCEMENT

Earnings depend on the geographic location of the employer and the employee's skill level. Median annual earnings of home entertainment equipment technicians were $37,310 in 2013. The lowest ten percent earned less than $21,500, and the highest ten percent earned more than $56,440.

Home entertainment equipment technicians may receive paid vacations, holidays, and sick days; life and health insurance; and retirement benefits. The employer usually pays at least part of these benefits.

Metropolitan Areas with the Highest Employment Level in this Occupation

Metropolitan area	Employment [1]	Employment per thousand jobs	Hourly mean wage
Chicago-Joliet-Naperville, IL	1,050	0.28	$20.15
Miami-Miami Beach-Kendall, FL	770	0.76	$17.33
Edison-New Brunswick, NJ	680	0.69	$24.40
Baltimore-Towson, MD	620	0.48	$20.37
Dallas-Plano-Irving, TX	570	0.27	$15.10
Louisville-Jefferson County, KY-IN	540	0.89	$16.24
Indianapolis-Carmel, IN	530	0.58	$16.57
Los Angeles-Long Beach-Glendale, CA	460	0.12	$18.52
St. Louis, MO-IL	430	0.33	$16.66
Riverside-San Bernardino-Ontario, CA	420	0.35	$20.92

[1]Does not include self-employ ed. Source: Bureau of Labor Statistics

EMPLOYMENT AND OUTLOOK

Home entertainment equipment technicians held about 35,000 jobs in 2012. About one-fourth were self-employed. Most worked in electronics and appliance stores. Employment is expected to grow slower than the average for all occupations through the year 2022, which means employment is projected to increase 1 percent to 7 percent. This is due to the continued growing sales of home entertainment equipment, even while such equipment is less expensive and more reliable than in the past. When malfunctions do occur, it often is cheaper for consumers to replace equipment rather than to pay for repairs. Some job growth will occur due to the continued growth of installation services and maintenance of sophisticated digital equipment.

Employment Trend, Projected 2012–22

Total, All Occupations: 11%

Home Entertainment Equipment Technicians: 4%

Electronic Equipment Repairers: 1%

Note: "All Occupations" includes all occupations in the U.S. Economy. Source: U.S. Bureau of Labor Statistics, Employment Projections Program

Related Occupations
- Computer Service Technician
- Electronic Engineering Technician
- Electronic Equipment Repairer
- Home Appliance Repairer
- Office Machine Repairer
- Television & Radio Repairer

Related Military Occupations
- Audiovisual & Broadcast Technician
- Electrical Products Repairer
- Electronic Instrument Repairer
- Photographic Equipment Repairer

Conversation With . . .
STEVE BROWN

Vice President, Sales Design
Great Choice AV, Edmond OK
Home Entertainment Installation/Repair, 31 years

1. **What was your individual career path in terms of education/training, entry-level job, or other significant opportunity?**

   I got into this business because I liked music. Back then, stereo was the big thing, and I learned to not only enjoy it, but to sell it to others. Before I got into this business, I was an assistant manager at a grocery store. My partner and I started Great Choice AV in 2009. We install and repair home theater systems, and also are involved in home automation: whole house audio, lighting control, cameras, climate control, remote control of your pool or spa temperature, door looks, security systems and irrigation systems. You can control an entire system from an iPad or iPhone, just as you would from a touch panel.

2. **What are the most important skills and/or qualities for someone in your profession?**

   Knowledge of the industry and the ability to listen to customers' needs are the two most important skills. If you listen to the customer (and read his/her facial expressions), it isn't that hard to figure out where they're at with their technical knowledge. Sometimes, I just slow down to make sure they fully understand what I'm talking about.

   As a business owner, you realize that obtaining and maintaining relationships with clients and with other business professionals is important. Most of the equipment manufacturers offer training, and I attend as much of it as possible to keep up with new technology.

3. **What do you wish you had known going into this profession?**

   I wish I had known that I wouldn't be making as much today as I did 25 years ago! Seriously, though, margins are shallow, so a sale doesn't yield as much profit as before. But if I didn't love the field I'm in, I would've looked for something else long ago.

4. Are there many job opportunities in your profession? In what specific areas?

There are job opportunities in this field. A person has to really want to do this work, not just want a job and a paycheck. If someone doesn't have a true interest in the home entertainment business, he or she will fail quickly. Most of the jobs are with smaller companies like ours. We'll hire anybody we feel has a genuine interest in the industry, but the manufacturers typically won't hire people who don't already have experience in the business.

5. How do you see your profession changing in the next five years? What role will technology play in those changes, and what skills will be required?

Technology changes rapidly in this business, and we'll likely have to be trained in new areas that we can't even image. The biggest challenges and problems we face on a daily basis have to do with anything wireless. Wireless still isn't there. I'm always telling our customers, "If wireless was that good, there wouldn't be any such thing as wire!"

6. What do you enjoy most about your job? What do you enjoy least about your job?

I enjoy the relationships I build with my customers. It's fun to see a person happy when we've provided them with true entertainment. The thing that I dislike the most is the customer (who really isn't a customer) who just wants the "best price" on something he/she knows little or nothing about. That person is destined to get what they pay for … and deserve.

7. Can you suggest a valuable "try this" for students considering a career in your profession?

I started off my interest in this field when my parents purchased a subscription to *Stereo Review* magazine when I was about 16 years old. Reading articles in that magazine really sparked my interest in this business. Many people start off by working at a business such as Best Buy. That's not a bad place to start. Then, when you want to get more involved, look for a job with a business like ours.

SELECTED SCHOOLS

A college degree is not necessary in most cases to work as a home entertainment equipment technician. For those interested in the field, however, a technical or community college is a good place to start. Many commercial trade schools are also available. Students are advised to consult with their school guidance counselor or research area post-secondary schools to find the right program.

MORE INFORMATION

Federal Communications Commission
445 12th Street, NW
Washington, DC 20554
888.225.5322
www.fcc.gov

National Electrical Contractors Association
3 Bethesda Metro Center, Suite 1100
Bethesda, MD 20814
301.657.3110
www.necanet.org

International Society of Certified Electronics Technicians
3608 Pershing Avenue
Fort Worth, TX 76107-4527
800.946.0201
www.iscet.org

National Electronics Service Dealers Association
3608 Pershing Avenue
Fort Worth, TX 76107-4527
817.921.9061
www.nesda.com

John Pritchard/Editor

Industrial Machinery Mechanic

Snapshot

Career Cluster: Engineering; Maintenance & Repair; Manufacturing

Interests: Machinery, mechanics, working with your hands, solving problems, using tools and computers

Earnings (Yearly Average): $49,560

Employment & Outlook: Faster than Average Growth Expected

OVERVIEW

Sphere of Work

Industrial machinery mechanics maintain industrial machines including factory equipment, conveying systems, and production and packing machinery. Most of their job is preventive—an industrial machinery mechanic tries to diagnose problems with a machine before it breaks down—but they are also trained to make repairs when a machine does stop working. When machines break, production is slowed or stopped, so mechanics must make repairs quickly and efficiently.

Industrial machinery mechanics are also known as industrial machine repairers or maintenance machinists. They are responsible

for keeping a number of complex machines in a factory or plant in working order. Industrial machinery mechanics are also responsible for keeping factories or plants stocked with the proper machine parts necessary to make repairs.

Work Environment

Industrial machinery mechanics work in factories, power plants, and on construction sites. They are sometimes required to work overtime, or on nights and weekends, if a machine breaks down outside of regular workday hours. The job of an industrial machinery mechanic can be dangerous. They are required to follow specific safety precautions and wear protective gear while working.

Profile

Working Conditions: Work Indoors
Physical Strength: Medium Work
Education Needs: On-The-Job Training, High School Diploma with Technical Education, Technical/Community College
Licensure/Certification: Recommended
Physical Abilities Not Required: N/A
Opportunities For Experience: Apprenticeship, Part-Time Work
Holland Interest Score*: REI

* See Appendix A

Occupation Interest

Industrial machinery mechanics are interested in how machines work. They analyze and solve complex problems on a daily basis and enjoy working with their hands. Industrial machinery mechanics apply instructions from manuals and diagrams to machines and machine parts, and they are adept at using a number of tools. They will often use computers or other electronic devices to analyze equipment.

A Day in the Life—Duties and Responsibilities

Industrial machinery mechanics work regular work hours, though they are sometimes required to work overtime. Throughout a normal day, they perform a number of tasks related to the maintenance and upkeep of machines in factories and production plants. These machines include conveyor belts, robotic arms, and hydraulic lifts.

When there is a problem with a machine, industrial machinery mechanics must diagnose the issue and figure out the best way to solve it. They talk with machine operators and inspect the machinery. They check initially for loose connectors or worn parts. If a part needs replacing, industrial machinery mechanics will replace it. They are also responsible for having the right parts on hand for such a situation. If there are no loose or worn parts, industrial machinery mechanics must perform tests to determine the problem. Sometimes these tests involve computer programs or electronic testing equipment. Industrial machinery mechanics analyzes the test results to decide his or her next course of action.

Sometimes, industrial machinery mechanics must take entire machines apart and put them back together. This is often done by following a manual or diagram. Industrial machinery mechanics routinely use hand tools. They also use larger tools like lathes, grinders, and drill presses. Some industrial machinery mechanics perform welding tasks. After they have replaced an old part or performed a repair, they will test the machine to make sure it works.

Duties and Responsibilities

- Observing and inspecting equipment regularly to locate causes of trouble
- Oiling, greasing and cleaning machine parts
- Dismantling machines and equipment
- Repairing or replacing defective parts
- Installing special parts
- Sketching a required part to be manufactured by the plant's machine shop
- Operating basic tool machines to make needed parts
- Adjusting controls on machinery and equipment
- Reassembling machinery and equipment
- Starting and testing equipment
- Keeping maintenance records of the equipment serviced

WORK ENVIRONMENT

Physical Environment

The most common environments of industrial machinery mechanics are factories, plants, and construction sites. These sites can often be noisy and dirty. It is important for industrial machinery mechanics to be able to tune out the distractions of their environment in order to focus on making repairs.

Relevant Skills and Abilities

Organization & Management Skills
- Following instructions
- Making decisions
- Paying attention to and handling details
- Performing duties which change frequently

Technical Skills
- Performing technical work
- Working with machines, tools or other objects

Human Environment

There are a number of people working around industrial machinery mechanics, performing any number of tasks at any given time. They must work well with others, including colleagues and clients. They must also be adept at dealing with machine operators. Often, industrial machinery mechanics will have to ask an operator questions to diagnose a problem with a machine. In a factory environment, every person performs a specialized task in service of a larger production scheme. Industrial machinery mechanics monitor equipment to keep the whole operation running smoothly and are an important part of this equation.

Technological Environment

Industrial machinery mechanics regularly use computers, computerized machines, and testing devices in their work. The majority of industrial machines have computerized components, and many are operated by way of computer software.

EDUCATION, TRAINING, AND ADVANCEMENT

High School/Secondary

An aspiring industrial machinery mechanic should enroll in courses focusing on mathematics, physics, computer science, and English. Shop courses, which instruct students on basic engineering and machinery operation, are also important for aspiring industrial machinery mechanics. Most employers require industrial machinery mechanics to have a high school diploma or pass a General Education Development (GED) test.

Suggested High School Subjects
- Applied Math
- Applied Physics
- Blueprint Reading
- Computer Science
- Drafting
- Electricity & Electronics
- English
- Industrial Arts
- Machining Technology
- Mathematics
- Mechanical Drawing
- Physics
- Shop Mechanics

Famous First

The first heavy-duty cable factory was built in 1841 in Saxonburg, Pennsylvania, by John A. Roebling, who also created the machinery. Roebling's "wire rope" consisted of wire that was wound into strands and then turned onto great reels. Several of these strands were then themselves wound together to form a thick rope or cable. The cable was used in the construction of suspension bridges, example shown here, including the Brooklyn Bridge.

College/Postsecondary

Most industrial machinery mechanics need at least one year of postsecondary education or specialized training in their field. Courses in such a program include blueprint reading, computer programming, mechanical drawing, mathematics, or electronics. Many employers require industrial machinery mechanics to have advanced degrees. Most industrial machinery mechanics are required to be familiar with and trained in repairing all types of industrial machinery.

Some industrial machinery mechanics complete a two-year associate's degree in industrial maintenance at a technical school. Others begin working in a different factory job and take classes provided by their employer in order to become industrial machinery mechanics. In either case, hands-on training is a very important part of any training program. Industrial machinery mechanics must be comfortable with the machines they spend their time monitoring.

Related College Majors
- Heavy Equipment Maintenance & Repair

Adult Job Seekers

A person who has had a job in a factory or has been a mechanic in a different field is a good candidate for becoming an industrial machinery mechanic. The career also draws on a number of other transferable skills, including knowledge of computers or experience working with heavy machinery. Individuals with no background in a related field should enroll in a college or a technical or vocational school that offers a program in industrial machinery mechanics. Technical schools are also a great place for job seekers to network. Communication technologies and standards are always changing, so mechanics should be willing to continue learning throughout their career.

Professional Certification and Licensure

Though it is not required, industrial machinery mechanics can acquire certification through the Society of Maintenance and Reliability Professionals (SMRP). A program called Certified Industrial Maintenance Mechanic, or CIMM, is offered by SMRP. Certification exams test a candidate's knowledge of their field. Those who gain certification must maintain it by participating in fifty hours of skill development and training (offered through SMRP) over the course of a three-year period, or they simply retake the exam.

Additional Requirements

Because troubleshooting is a large part of an industrial machinery mechanic's job, a person in this career must be a creative thinker. He or she must be willing to test different solutions and identify problems based on little information. Industrial machinery mechanics must also keep their cool in stressful situations. A broken machine shuts down production, so mechanics must work quickly, yet efficiently, to keep the factory up and running on schedule.

EARNINGS AND ADVANCEMENT

Earnings of industrial machinery mechanics depend on the type, geographic location and union affiliation of the employer and the employee's skill. Mean annual earnings of industrial machinery mechanics were $49,560 in 2013. The lowest ten percent earned less than $31,090, and the highest ten percent earned more than $71,930.

Industrial machinery mechanics may receive paid vacations, holidays, and sick days; life and health insurance; and retirement benefits. These are usually paid by the employer.

Metropolitan Areas with the Highest Employment Level in this Occupation

Metropolitan area	Employment [1]	Employment per thousand jobs	Hourly mean wage
Houston-Sugar Land-Baytown, TX	11,230	4.07	$24.70
Chicago-Joliet-Naperville, IL	5,490	1.48	$26.83
Los Angeles-Long Beach-Glendale, CA	5,320	1.34	$28.84
Atlanta-Sandy Springs-Marietta, GA	4,020	1.74	$22.25
Cincinnati-Middletown, OH-KY-IN	3,990	4.01	$25.44
Philadelphia, PA	3,740	2.03	$23.51
St. Louis, MO-IL	3,380	2.62	$24.37
Dallas-Plano-Irving, TX	3,330	1.55	$23.02
Gary, IN	3,160	11.82	$26.31
New York-White Plains-Wayne, NY-NJ	3,090	0.59	$25.83

[1]Does not include self-employ ed. Source: Bureau of Labor Statistics

EMPLOYMENT AND OUTLOOK

There were approximately 320,000 industrial machinery mechanics employed nationally in 2012. Employment is expected to grow faster than the average for all occupations through the year 2022, which means employment is projected to increase up to 20 percent. As more companies introduce new automated equipment, these workers will be needed to ensure that these machines are kept in good condition. However, many new machines are capable of self-diagnosis, increasing their reliability and reducing the need for these workers. Many job openings will result from the need to replace workers who transfer to other occupations or retire.

Employment Trend, Projected 2012–22

Industrial Machinery Mechanics: 19%

Total, All Occupations: 11%

Maintenance Workers, Machinery: 11%

Note: "All Occupations" includes all occupations in the U.S. Economy. Source: U.S. Bureau of Labor Statistics, Employment Projections Program

Related Occupations
- Diesel Service Technician
- General Maintenance Mechanic
- Heavy Equipment Service Technician
- Machinist

Conversation With . . .
TRICIA KEEGAN

Facility Manager
Tiverton Power Plant, Tiverton, R.I.
Industrial Machinery Mechanic & Manager, 21 years

1. What was your individual career path in terms of education/training, entry-level job, or other significant opportunity?

I went to high school at Boston Latin School, then went to Boston University to be a math teacher. A friend of mine wanted to visit the Massachusetts Maritime Academy and asked me to drive her down for Women's Day. A woman who spoke there had graduated from Mass Maritime and was a math teacher. I always wanted to travel and always loved books about ships and decided to apply without even telling my parents. I gave up a full academic scholarship to B.U. I had no idea what I was getting into in terms of engineering. I just knew I could still become a math teacher, go to this school and travel all over the world. We did a term at sea each year. I graduated with a bachelor's degree in marine engineering, with a concentration in facilities engineering. A power plant has the same engine as a ship, just on a larger scale. It's the same equipment and the same philosophy. Upon graduation, I was hired by General Electric (GE) Power Systems. I worked as a field service engineer, working on gas turbines, mostly. Then I became a control specialist, working on electronics that run the plant and doing mechanical work. GE manufactures the power-generating equipment that power plants own. I worked on equipment in Oklahoma, Iowa, Newfoundland, the Netherlands, the Dominican Republic, Panama. After I got married and had kids, I went part-time for a while. In 2009, I became the plant manager in Tiverton.

2. What are the most important skills and/or qualities for someone in your profession?

You have to have mechanical aptitude, and that comes with experience. Early on in your career, you're really learning from the people around you. You have to be able to identify preventive and predictive maintenance, rather than unplanned maintenance, by recognizing trends when things go wrong. You have to keep good, detailed logs—how you fixed something, who you worked with. I still refer back to a log I had in 1996.

As a facilities manager, the four things I'm always focused on are: safety of employees and contractors; compliance with environmental and other regulations; productivity; and people. I'm learning more and more how important it is to communicate well and to get input and ideas from many people—the operations department, the maintenance department, the electronics department.

3. What do you wish you had known going into this profession?

One thing I wish I had done more is seek advice, just about day-to-day things. Also, I would be myself more. Being a woman in a male-dominated field, I always tried to tone it down and keep it serious. If people were all going out to dinner after work, the normal me would have gone, but I felt that I had to draw a line. I didn't want to give the wrong impression.

4. Are there many job opportunities in your profession? In what specific areas?

In power generation, the sky's the limit. I could work at a refinery, at a manufacturing facility, a hospital, a natural gas facility, an airport.

5. How do you see your profession changing in the next five years? What role will technology play in those changes, and what skills will be required?

We're looking at renewables, wind power and solar, and we're waiting for that break-through for better storage and transmission, probably through nanotechnology—but it probably won't happen in the next five years. Right now they're studying how your clothes can charge your cell phone, using friction, where the fibers carry electronics to the phone. So what's our future look like? Probably micro-systems where your house will run on a battery pack and doesn't have to be attached to the grid.

6. What do you enjoy most about your job? What do you enjoy least about your job?

There's a new challenge every day. And there's no shortage of work to be done; we're very busy people. What I enjoy least is time away from my three children. Finding that work/life balance is challenging. Also, you worry a lot, you take it home with you, worrying about the safety of your coworkers. You're under a lot of pressure.

7. Can you suggest a valuable "try this" for students considering a career in your profession?

Reach out to someone in the field, maybe through alumni associations at schools. You can visit a power plant, do a tour, or tour ships. I think most people would be willing to give you a couple of hours. If you know a nurse, ask her about arranging for you to visit the hospital's facilities department: they have a back-up generator, they have water sterilization. Or if your father works in the Financial District, all the big buildings have facilities departments. You may think, "Oh, they're just custodians," but they're doing all kinds of important stuff.

SELECTED SCHOOLS

A college degree is not necessary to work as an industrial machinery mechanic. For those interested in the field, however, a technical or community college is a good place to start. Many commercial trade schools are also available. Students are advised to consult with their school guidance counselor or research area post-secondary schools to find the right program.

MORE INFORMATION

International Association of Machinists & Aerospace Workers
Apprenticeship Department
9000 Machinists Place
Upper Marlboro, MD 20772-2687
301.967.4500
www.iamaw.org

National Association of Manufacturers
733 10th Street NW, Suite 700
Washington, DC 20001
202.637.3000
www.nam.org

Society for Maintenance and Reliability Professionals
1100 Johnson Ferry Road, Suite 300
Atlanta, Georgia 30342
800.950.7354
www.smrp.org

Molly Hagan/Editor

Laser Technician

Snapshot

Career Cluster: Engineering; Manufacturing; Science; Technology

Interests: Science, technology, solving problems, communicating with others

Earnings (Yearly Average): $58,401

Employment & Outlook: Average Growth Expected

OVERVIEW

Sphere of Work

Laser technicians, also known as photonics technicians, repair and operate lasers and related equipment. Due to the numerous applications of laser technology, technicians work in a wide range of fields, including the medical, manufacturing, defense, construction, and telecommunications industries. Laser technicians align lenses and mirrors, check power supplies, and prepare tubes, rods, semiconductor chips, and other parts of the laser equipment, typically under the supervision of senior engineers or scientists. They may work on one site exclusively, performing routine maintenance as well as operations, or travel between client facilities to perform maintenance as needed.

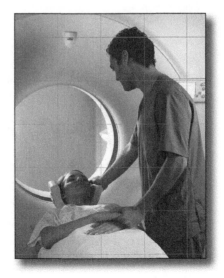

Work Environment

Laser technicians may work in a wide range of locations, including manufacturing facilities, scientific laboratories, hospitals, construction sites, and research and development plants. Work environments are kept extremely clean and well ventilated in order to prevent any dust or other particles from infiltrating and corrupting the laser equipment's optics and mechanics. Temperature and humidity are also carefully regulated. Laser technicians typically work a forty-hour week, although they may work extra hours when equipment malfunctions. As there is some risk of injury when working with laser equipment, it is essential that safety protocols be followed at all times.

Profile

Working Conditions: Work Indoors
Physical Strength: Light Work
Education Needs:
  Technical/Community College,
  Bachelor's Degree
Licensure/Certification:
  Recommended
Physical Abilities Not Required: No
  Heavy Labor
Opportunities For Experience:
  Internship, Apprenticeship
Holland Interest Score*: IRE

* See Appendix A

Occupation Interest

Individuals interested in a career as a laser technician typically enjoy science and are skilled in working with complex technology. Laser technicians must be quick to identify and solve problems and have excellent communication skills, as they may need to explain technical issues to individuals from different professional backgrounds. Lasers are used in a wide range of industries, so technicians have the opportunity to explore a variety of fields, from medicine to telecommunications.

A Day in the Life—Duties and Responsibilities

Laser technicians help build, repair, and modify laser equipment to suit the needs of the laboratory, department, or business in which they work. Technicians repair or replace essential parts of the equipment, which may include semiconductors or optical fibers, and maintain control consoles, recorders, cables, and power sources. They must also clean and position mirrors and lenses so that laser streams are precise and uncorrupted. Laser technicians frequently test equipment to ensure that it operates safely and fulfills its specific function. In addition to making repairs, some laser technicians also operate the equipment themselves, performing tasks such as engraving materials or removing tattoos.

Additional duties vary based on the industry in which the laser technicians work. For example, technicians who work in scientific laboratories may be involved in extensive data collection in addition to maintaining and operating the equipment, while those working in the telecommunications and manufacturing sectors may spend more time using equipment to weld seams or splice fibers. Some laser technicians are based at one work site, while others visit several clients to troubleshoot and operate laser equipment on an on-call basis.

Laser technicians are typically required to keep detailed records of the use of laser equipment, including test schedules, maintenance reports, and assessments of the wavelength, intensity, and duration of the laser beams produced. Technicians are also required to adhere to all safety protocols, including the wearing of protective clothing or eyewear when necessary.

Duties and Responsibilities

- Repairing laser systems
- Performing alignment procedures on optical systems
- Operating laser systems
- Utilizing basic laser and electrical safety practices
- Performing tests and measurements using electronic devices
- Reading and preparing shop drawings and schematics
- Analyzing test data and report results
- Keeping careful records of work performed

WORK ENVIRONMENT

Physical Environment

Laser technicians work in factories, laboratories, medical centers, construction sites, and other facilities that use laser technology. Work environments must be very clean, with environmental conditions such as humidity heavily regulated. Some technicians travel to client facilities in order to operate, repair, and maintain laser equipment.

Relevant Skills and Abilities

Communication Skills
- Speaking effectively
- Writing concisely

Interpersonal/Social Skills
- Having good judgment

Research & Planning Skills
- Solving problems

Technical Skills
- Performing scientific, mathematical and technical work
- Working with machines, tools or other objects
- Using set methods and standards in your work

Human Environment

Laser technicians work with a wide range of individuals that varies based on the industry in which they work. Technicians may interact with engineers and scientists as well as medical personnel, construction workers, foremen, line workers, laboratory technicians, and building maintenance personnel.

Technological Environment

When constructing, installing, and maintaining laser equipment, laser technicians use oscilloscopes, interferometers, semiconductors, gas cells, diodes, and various power saws. They also rely on computers, using computer-aided design (CAD), photo imaging, scientific, and office suite software.

EDUCATION, TRAINING, AND ADVANCEMENT

High School/Secondary

High school students interested in pursuing a career as a laser technician should study mathematics and science, particularly geometry, trigonometry, chemistry, and physics. Industrial arts courses that cover electronics and machinery are useful, as are courses that teach students to read and draw blueprints. As laser technicians rely heavily on computer technology, high school students should also take classes in information technology and computer science.

Suggested High School Subjects

- Algebra
- Applied Math
- Applied Physics
- Blueprint Reading
- Chemistry
- Computer Science
- Drafting
- Electricity & Electronics
- English
- Geometry
- Physical Science
- Trade/Industrial Education
- Trigonometry

Famous First

The first working laser, based on the prototype developed by Charles H. Townes in 1957, was demonstrated in 1960 by a team at the Hughes Aircraft Company in Malibu, California, pictured. The team, headed by Theodore H. Maiman, used a ruby cylinder with polished ends, one of which had a small hole for the beam to exit.

College/Postsecondary

Laser technicians generally need at least an associate's degree from a two-year college or technical school. These programs include studies in photonics and optics. Some technicians choose to earn a bachelor's degree in a similar field. Postsecondary students should educate themselves about the educational requirements of their prospective employers, areas of specialization, and states in which they work, as requirements may vary.

Related College Majors
- Laser & Optical Technology

Adult Job Seekers

Qualified laser technicians may apply directly to laboratories, manufacturers, hospitals, and other employers with open positions. Many technicians find job postings and networking opportunities through membership in professional organizations, such as the Laser Institute of America and the Optical Society.

Professional Certification and Licensure

Some states require professional certification or licensure for laser technicians working in laser scar removal or other medical specialties. Many organizations and businesses also offer voluntary certification in certain laser systems. As with any voluntary certification process, it is beneficial to consult credible professional associations within the field and follow professional debate as to the relevancy and value of any certification program.

Additional Requirements

Laser technicians must be skilled with complex machinery and systems, as well as computers.

Fun Fact

From barcode scanners to eye surgery, lasers are everywhere. LASER is an acronym for Light Application by Stimulated Emission of Radiation.
Source: http://hyperphysics.phy-astr.gsu.edu/hbase/optmod/lasapp.html

EARNINGS AND ADVANCEMENT

Earnings depend on the type and geographic location of the employer and the employee's education, ability and experience. Laser technicians earned average first year salaries of $48,499 in 2012. Laser technicians with five years of experience earned salaries averaging $68,302.

Laser technicians may receive paid vacations, holidays, and sick days; life and health insurance; and retirement benefits. These are usually paid by the employer.

EMPLOYMENT AND OUTLOOK

Nationally, there were approximately 62,000 life, physical and social science technicians, of which laser technicians are a part, employed in 2012. Employment is expected to grow about as fast as the average for all occupations through the year 2022, which means employment is projected to increase 6 percent to 12 percent. With continued emphasis on laser technology, job opportunities should be good.

Related Occupations
- Electrical and Electronics Engineer
- Nuclear Medicine Technologist

Conversation With . . .
JESSICA HUDSON

Engineering Technician
Wasatch Photonics, Durham, N.C.
Laser and Photonics Technician, 3 years

1. What was your individual career path in terms of education/training, entry-level job, or other significant opportunity?

When I decided to go to school for laser and photonics, I didn't have any background or experience with the field. I had just graduated from high school and I was working as a cashier in a grocery store when I first heard of lasers and photonics. I had gone to Central Carolina Community College to turn in some paperwork and tour the campus when an office worker told me about her daughter, who had gone through the program. After hearing a few details, I was talked into signing up for classes. I had very little information, but everything sounded so interesting.

In my job at Wasatch, I make spectrometers that use lasers. Customers use them in machinery or in research projects. It's hard to say exactly what the customer uses the spectrometer for, because sometimes the client doesn't even want to tell us what they're using it for because they want to keep it a secret. But there are numerous applications for spectrometers and new ones are coming out every day. They can be used in a lab to study and analyze different samples. Some spectrometers are being used to study things in space. They can also be used to detect weapons of mass destruction.

2. What are the most important skills and/or qualities for someone in your profession?

I use a lot of problem solving and math skills every day in the workplace. I work with electronics, optical assemblies, and lasers, so hands-on skill and manual dexterity are needed. Being patient was something I had to work on. When I'm learning something, I like to understand it immediately. But I've learned that there are many things to understand in this profession, so it's OK to not understand and to ask questions.

3. What do you wish you had known going into this profession?

Even though there are a lot of big words and everything sounds so complicated, you can learn if you stop and listen. When I first started classes, I felt overwhelmed because I didn't have any prior experience or knowledge. Honestly, I thought I had made a huge mistake in choosing Lasers and Photonics Technology as my major. But as I went to classes, I started understanding everything and realized how amazing this profession really is.

4. Are there many job opportunities in your profession? In what specific areas?

I personally decided not to move far from home for a job. There are, however, job opportunities everywhere. There are so many types of jobs with a degree in lasers and photonics. They could be anywhere from manufacturing to research and development.

5. How do you see your profession changing in the next five years? What role will technology play in those changes, and what skills will be required?

I see technology in this profession expanding in the next five years. If you look back five years, you can see how far we have come, which means good things for the future. There is more and more demand for laser and photonics technicians out in the workplace. When I started my current job, it was a small company that had been up and running for only two years. But in the three years that I've been here, there have been many new applications for laser and photonics.

Technology is changing every day and people are always striving to make it better and better. Someone is always coming out with the next new and better device.

In the future, there will be more to learn as technology moves forward and some older things become obsolete, but I think the same basic skills will always be used.

6. What do you enjoy most about your job? What do you enjoy least about your job?

I like seeing everything evolve and things made easier thanks to new technology in this field. I get to work with my hands every day, and love that I really understand everything that is going on even though it's complicated. I also like when people ask me what I do at my job, then look at me kind of crazy when I tell them!

Honestly, I can't complain about anything at my job. The worst thing I can think of is when parts are delivered late and I have to wait to work on something.

7. Can you suggest a valuable "try this" for students considering a career in your profession?

It's hard to suggest a "try this" since lasers and photonics can be a bit dangerous. Just looking up lasers and photonics technology on the Internet will amaze you and show you all the different types of applications. You can buy kits online to do different types of projects that include electronics and lasers and photonics.

SELECTED SCHOOLS

Many technical and community colleges offer programs in or related to laser technology maintenance and repair. Commercial trade schools are also an option. Students are advised to consult with their school guidance counselor or research area post-secondary schools to find the right program.

MORE INFORMATION

Institute of Electrical and Electronics Engineers Photonics Society
445 Hoes Lane
Piscataway, NJ 08855
www.photonicssociety.org

Laser Institute of America
13501 Ingenuity Drive, Suite 128
Orlando, FL 32826
800.345.2737
www.laserinstitute.org

National Center for Optics and Photonics Education
324B Kelly Drive
Waco, TX 76710
254.741.8338
www.op-tec.org

Optical Society
2010 Massachusetts Avenue NW
Washington, DC 20036
202.223.8130
www.osa.org

Michael Auerbach/Editor

Locomotive Engineer

Snapshot

Career Cluster: Engineering; Transportation

Interests: Travel, machinery, analyzing details, organizing information

Earnings (Yearly Average): $55,660

Employment & Outlook: Slower than Average Growth Expected

OVERVIEW

Sphere of Work

Locomotive engineers operate large freight and passenger trains, subway trains, and light rail (intra-city) train cars. Most engineers run diesel-powered engines to their destinations along an inter-rail system, although many trains are also powered by electricity. Locomotive engineers monitor their trains' operations, interpret the signal lights alongside the tracks, keep track of the weight they are carrying on board, and communicate with dispatchers (train traffic controllers). Engineers must conduct pre-trip checks for mechanical problems and file reports upon disembarking. They ensure that the train leaves and arrives on schedule, prepare reports on any issues that occur in transit, and read and react to switching orders from train yard dispatchers.

Work Environment

Locomotive engineers work on passenger trains, freight trains, subways, and light rail vehicles. Trains are extremely heavy and are difficult to slow or bring to a stop when they are moving at normal speed. The work can be dangerous, with the constant risk of cars, live animals, and careless or emotionally disturbed people stopping unexpectedly on the tracks. Locomotive engineers (particularly freight locomotive engineers) work erratic hours and are subject to the health risks of other shift workers. When not on board moving trains, engineers work in train yards or engine terminals performing inspections on stationary engines and cars, or may be travelling to their next assignment or resting in company lodgings for federally-mandated rest periods.

Profile

Working Conditions: Work both Indoors and Outdoors
Physical Strength: Light to Medium Work
Education Needs: High School Diploma or G.E.D., On-the-Job Training
Licensure/Certification: Required
Physical Abilities Not Required: No Heavy Labor
Opportunities For Experience: Apprenticeship, Military Service, Part-Time Work
Holland Interest Score*: IRS

* See Appendix A

Occupation Interest

Locomotive engineers play an integral role in the country's transportation and commerce systems. Urban and commuter lines get people to work each day in cities like Boston, New York, Philadelphia, Chicago, and San Francisco. In the Northeast, passenger rail travel extends from Boston to Washington DC and is frequently used. Freight railroads in the United States move between 42 and 47 percent of the nation's freight.

Locomotive engineers often travel great distances, including cross-country, viewing the country in a way that few people do. The field attracts individuals who have an aptitude for complex machinery, as diesel- and electric-powered trains tow massive cargoes of freight and people over long trips. Additionally, freight train engineers can earn significant paychecks if they draw a long trip that will require several days' commitment or incur overtime pay. Opportunities for locomotive engineers continue to grow at a modest rate, as freight transport is seen as a more cost effective and green way of carrying cargo and as the United States seeks to develop passenger rail systems across the country.

A Day in the Life—Duties and Responsibilities

Prior to departure, locomotive engineers must check their trains for any mechanical issues, making small repairs, lubricating machinery, and ensuring that the train meets state and federal safety standards. Engineers must also inspect their cargo, assessing weight and looking for leaks. They also check routes, railroad rules, weather updates, and switching orders from yard dispatchers and trainmasters. Once the train departs, locomotive engineers operate the throttle, air brakes, horns, electric, and other equipment, coordinate with railroad dispatchers via radio, and monitor fuel, battery, and brake air pressure gauges. In transit, railroad engineers carefully watch the track for any obstructions, trespassers, and other problems. In the event that the train must make an unscheduled stop or an accident occurs, locomotive engineers must log in detail what occurred and any actions taken. Although the Federal Railroad Administration, (FRA) regulates the amount of sleep engineers must get in a twenty-four hour period, they still must cope with fatigue, stress, and adverse weather conditions.

Locomotive engineers who work on passenger car systems (particularly subways and commuter rail systems) run relatively shorter routes and have more consistent schedules. Freight locomotive engineers, however, may travel for days in daylight and at night. In light of the modern safety equipment that is built into trains, most trains only operate with a conductor and a locomotive engineer.

Duties and Responsibilities

- Inspecting the train before and after the run for defective equipment
- Interpreting train orders, signals and railroad rules and regulations
- Controlling starts, stops and the speed of train
- Communicating information or instructions concerning stops, delays or oncoming trains
- Reporting defects to the engine foreman
- Preparing reports explaining accidents, unscheduled stops or delays
- Lubricating moving parts

OCCUPATION SPECIALTIES

Yard Engineers

Yard Engineers operate switching locomotives within the yard of a railroad, industrial plant, quarry, construction project or similar location to switch railroad cars for loading, unloading and makeup or breakup of trains.

Hostlers

Hostlers receive locomotives from engineers at the end of their runs, drive the locomotives to various stations in the roundhouse for cleaning, refueling and repairs and deliver serviced locomotives to engine crews.

WORK ENVIRONMENT

Physical Environment

Locomotive engineers primarily work in diesel- and electric-powered freight and passenger trains, commuter trains, subways, monorails and streetcars. Passenger cars are built to provide passengers with a degree of comfort, while freight cars have less insulation and lack or limit cushioned seating and heat or air conditioning. There is always a danger of impact with obstacles on the tracks and/or derailment.

Human Environment

Locomotive engineers interact with on-board conductors, dispatchers, trainmasters, switching operators, rail traffic controllers, brake operators, and passengers. They also coordinate with public safety officers, government inspectors and officials, and corporate executives (both from within their respective companies and from client organizations).

Relevant Skills and Abilities

Organization & Management Skills
- Paying attention to and handling details
- Performing duties which change frequently
- Performing routine work

Research & Planning Skills
- Analyzing information
- Developing evaluation strategies

Technical Skills
- Working with machines, tools or other objects

Technological Environment

Locomotive engineers must work with many types of mechanical technology, including diesel and electric passenger and freight train engines, automatic and manual rail switches, air braking systems, gauges and meters, hand tools and flashlights, global positioning systems, and two-way radios. Most modern trains have computer-based systems with which engineers must familiarize themselves as well. Engineers are periodically tested on federal rules governing the movement of trains; these rules are revised, reprinted, and distributed annually by government agencies to railroad employees.

EDUCATION, TRAINING, AND ADVANCEMENT

High School/Secondary

High school students are encouraged to take mathematics courses, such as algebra and geometry. Training in electronics, engines, and other subjects covered in industrial arts classes is useful. Furthermore, developing communication skills is essential to those seeking to enter this industry. A high school diploma is required for all locomotive engineers.

Suggested High School Subjects
- Algebra
- Applied Math
- Auto Service Technology
- Blueprint Reading
- Electricity & Electronics
- English

Famous First

The first train operated exclusively by women was placed in service in 1979 by the Long Island Rail Road. The train ran between Port Washington, on Long Island, and Pennsylvania Station, in New York City. The conductor, Deirdre Hickey, was the first woman to qualify in yard, freight, and passenger service. The ticket collector and brakeperson were also women.

College/Postsecondary

Most locomotive engineers have a high school degree, receiving the remainder of their professional training on the job with a railroad company. However, a small percentage of locomotive engineers have postsecondary degrees, such as a bachelor's degree or some undergraduate-level coursework. A criminal background check and periodic drug testing are usually mandatory conditions of employment due to the fact that train engineers' jobs involve public safety.

Adult Job Seekers

Many locomotive engineers begin their careers as railroad yard workers, brake operators, or conductors. The minimum age for locomotive engineers is twenty-two years, and railroad experience is a requirement. Some job seekers may tour a railroad company and/ or shadow other engineers. Some locomotive engineering training programs place individuals who have completed the required courses in brake operator positions as they wait for engineer positions to open. Many qualified individuals also apply directly to railroad companies and transit authorities.

Professional Certification and Licensure

Locomotive engineers must pass training and instruction from an FRA-sanctioned program. Upon completion of such a program, engineers must also pass a comprehensive exam and a background check through their employer in order to receive an engineer's license (which must be renewed periodically).

Additional Requirements

Locomotive engineers should have above average mathematical and analytical skills, enabling them to solve complex problems and understand mechanical systems. They must be attentive enough to notice mechanical problems, leaks, and other safety hazards. Locomotive engineers should also demonstrate a working knowledge of trains and the railroad system. Furthermore, because many of today's trains are operated using sophisticated computer technology, computer skills are a valuable asset for locomotive engineers. Because working on large engines entails climbing and lifting, physical fitness is desirable, particularly since the shift worker lifestyle of erratic sleep, little exercise, and poor diet fails to promote it.

Although not a requirement, those interested in a career as a locomotive engineer should know that more than 76 percent of railroad employees belong to unions, to which they pay dues. The unions ensure reasonable wages and health care, and are authorized to negotiate with employers when conflicts arise.

Fun Fact

Early locomotives were referred to as iron horses, but early trains were actually horse-drawn. In 1827 the Baltimore & Ohio Railroad was granted a charter for transporting freight and passengers, but due to uneven terrain, B&O couldn't come up with a strong-enough steam engine, so they uses horses to pull the train.

Source: history.com/news/history-lists/8-things-you-may-not-know-about-trains

EARNINGS AND ADVANCEMENT

Earnings depend on the size of the locomotive, type of service, number of miles traveled and number of hours worked. Mean annual earnings of locomotive engineers were $55,660 in 2013. The lowest ten percent earned less than $37,460, and the highest ten percent earned more than $81,720.

Locomotive engineers may receive paid vacations, holidays, and sick days; life and health insurance; and retirement benefits. These are usually paid by the employer.

States with the Highest Employment Level in this Occupation

Metropolitan area	Employment [1]	Employment per thousand jobs	Hourly mean wage
Texas	3,910	0.36	$21.51
Illinois	2,290	0.40	$28.50
Missouri	1,900	0.72	$25.28
Ohio	1,590	0.31	$28.71
Virginia	1,560	0.43	$25.24

[1]Does not include self-employ ed. Source: Bureau of Labor Statistics

EMPLOYMENT AND OUTLOOK

There were approximately 39,000 locomotive engineers employed nationally in 2012. Employment is expected to grow slower than the average for all occupations through the year 2022, which means employment is projected to increase 0 percent to 5 percent. There is a continued need for train operators on open rail. The need to replace workers who transfer to other occupations or retire will also be a main source of job openings.

Employment Trend, Projected 2012–22

Total, All Occupations: 14%

Rail Transportation Workers: 3%

Train Engineers and Operators: 1%

Note: "All Occupations" includes all occupations in the U.S. Economy. Source: U.S. Bureau of Labor Statistics, Employment Projections Program

Related Occupations
- Rail Transportation Worker

Conversation With . . .
ADARE GHIST

Locomotive Engineer
Amtrak, New Haven, CT
Locomotive Engineer, 1 year

1. What was your individual career path in terms of education/training, entry-level job, or other significant opportunity?

I went to college at Wright State University in Dayton, Ohio, and got a degree in English. Finding a job where I would use that degree was difficult. I worked at various jobs for five years before I applied to Amtrak at the suggestion of a friend. I started on the railroad as an assistant conductor and then as conductor for a total of 1½ years before being promoted to locomotive engineer. The engineer is responsible for the operation of the train, while the conductor deals with passengers and collects revenue. Also, conductors with an assignment in the rail yard may rearrange the cars of a train before it goes to the station, or leave a car for repair and take another one. They actually hook up the connections between the engine and the cars and between each car so that the cars have brakes, electricity, and air pressure for the bathrooms.

I started in Boston, but recently moved to New Haven, CT., because there are more jobs here at the moment.

2. What are the most important skills and/or qualities for someone in your profession?

It's important to be able to multi-task and focus on several things happening at once. The job requires a certain amount of mechanical aptitude, especially with regards to diesel engines and electrical circuits. There's a lot of memorization of written material in the rule books and manuals.

3. What do you wish you had known going into this profession?

Extensive training programs provided me everything I needed to know in order to perform my job. Each railroad company has its own training program. Amtrak sends students to a training center for 13 weeks of classroom training, with some hands-on segments. This includes operating rules and regulation, company policies, technical information about the locomotives, and troubleshooting. Upon returning to their local region, students do on-the-job training with a current engineer—first learning the territory and learning to operate from an instructor, then operating the train under supervision for approximately one to two years.

4. Are there many job opportunities in your profession? In what specific areas?

Training as a locomotive engineer would make you a valuable asset for any railroad company. There are railroads around the globe and there are many different types of operations: local commuter trains, cross-country trains, or mile-long freight trains. I am not aware of any schools or programs outside of those offered by the railroad companies. At Amtrak, you're on probation as an employee until successful completion of the training.

5. How do you see your profession changing in the next five years? What role will technology play in those changes, and what skills will be required?

Locomotives are becoming more and more electronic rather than mechanical. New safety devices are also electronic. Computer skills are becoming necessary for troubleshooting. The infrastructure also has changed from manual to remotely controlled, in regards to signals and track switches. As that technology advances, our procedures and rules also will continue to change.

6. What do you enjoy most about your job? What do you enjoy least about your job?

Even though the job is very serious, I have a lot of fun moving trains. I come to work each day looking forward to helping people get from one place to another and I leave knowing that I accomplished something.

The least enjoyable part is scheduling. Working on call means a two-hour notice for a job at any time of the day or night. Normally, new employees (conductors and engineers alike) do not have enough seniority to choose a job with a regular schedule, so we are often on-call all the time, with one day off per week. As you move up the seniority list, you get more opportunities to work the schedule you would like to work.

7. Can you suggest a valuable "try this" for students considering a career in your profession?

The next time you're on the school bus, pay close attention to the driver. Could you focus on all the external dangers of the road and on other drivers while at the same time ensuring the safety of the children riding in the back? Could you do this for several hours without a break? You could also try this the next time you're on a city bus. Keep in mind that the railroad does not allow for mistakes like running red lights or speeding. These mistakes can have dire consequences when you're operating a train.

SELECTED SCHOOLS

A college degree is not necessary to work as a locomotive engineer. For those interested in the field, however, a technical or community college may be considered. A commercial trade school may also be an option. Students are advised to consult with their school guidance counselor or research area post-secondary schools to find the right program.

MORE INFORMATION

American Short Line and Regional Railroad Association
50 F Street NW, Suite 7020
Washington, DC 20001
202.628.4500
www.aslrra.org

Association of American Railroads
425 Third Street, SW, Suite 1000
Washington, DC 20024
202.639.2100
www.aar.org

Brotherhood of Locomotive Engineers
1370 Ontario Street, Mezzanine
Cleveland, OH 44113
216.241.2630
www.ble-t.org

Burlington Northern Santa Fe Railway
2650 Lou Menk Drive
Fort Worth, TX 76131-2830
800.795.2673
www.bnsf.com

CSX
Corporate Headquarters
500 Water Street, 15th Floor
Jacksonville, FL 32202
904.359.3200
www.csx.com

Mordoc Railroad Academy
P.O. Box 432
Madison, CA 95653
916.965.5515
www.mordocrailroadacademy.com

National Railroad Passenger Corporation (Amtrak)
60 Massachusetts Avenue NE
Washington, DC 20002
202.906.2739
www.amtrak.com

Transport Workers Union of America AFL-CIO
501 3rd Street NW, 9th Floor
Washington, DC 20001
202.719.3900
www.twu.org

U.S. Department of Transportation
Federal Railroad Administration
1200 New Jersey Avenue SE
Washington, DC 20590
www.fra.dot.gov/index.shtml

Michael Auerbach/Editor

Maintenance Supervisor

Snapshot

Career Cluster: Construction; Engineering; Maintenance & Repair

Interests: Mechanical repair, engineering, construction, managing others

Earnings (Yearly Average): $62,201

Employment & Outlook: Faster than Average Growth Expected

OVERVIEW

Sphere of Work

Maintenance supervisors, often called maintenance directors, manage staffs of mechanics, janitors, and other utility personnel. Maintenance supervisors are employed by both large and small institutions and may hold positions within small town or municipal governments. The role of a maintenance supervisor is to oversee the daily activities of their staff, prioritize work, and organize budgetary needs for supplies and routine facility maintenance. They also make the final decision on major structural, mechanical, or operational projects.

Maintenance supervisors are skilled in both operational and staff management. They also possess an extensive knowledge of basic engineering, building infrastructure, light machinery, and state and regional maintenance policies and procedures.

Work Environment

Supervisors work in a variety of different environments, depending on the organization for which they are employed. In addition to overseeing all structural, systematic, and logistical repairs for buildings and substructures, maintenance supervisors are also often responsible for exterior maintenance, including landscaping and snow and trash removal. Outdoor responsibilities are less common under the authority of maintenance directors employed by organizations in urban environments.

Profile

Working Conditions: Work both Indoors and Outdoors
Physical Strength: Light Work
Education Needs: High School Diploma with Technical Education, Technical/Community College
Licensure/Certification: Usually Not Required
Physical Abilities Not Required: N/A
Opportunities For Experience: Part-Time Work
Holland Interest Score*: ERS

* See Appendix A

Occupation Interest

Maintenance supervisors are often derived from professionals with an interest in the trades, mechanical systems, and engineering. In addition to their diverse set of mechanical and industrial skills, supervisors possess acute leadership abilities and experience with the administrative functions related to mechanical repair and engineering. Managerial interest is usually the result of willingness to advance professionally after several years of experience working as an integral part of a maintenance, engineering, or construction team.

A Day in the Life—Duties and Responsibilities

Maintenance supervisors have numerous responsibilities, including the hiring and firing of maintenance staff. Supervisors traditionally interview all potential candidates, vetting their experience, capabilities, and examining references. Supervisors are also responsible for the coordination of schedules, determining avenues for advancement, and resolving workplace disputes on behalf of current employees.

In addition to overseeing routine cleaning and maintenance jobs, supervisors are also responsible for prioritizing both major projects and maintenance related issues that arise due to structural damage from weather and other causes, such as overuse or mistreatment. Effective maintenance supervisors are able to coordinate staff members in the most efficient way possible to see that each task is tended to in a timely manner.

In addition to prioritizing projects, maintenance supervisors oversee all financial and budgetary needs of their maintenance staff, from supplies and uniforms to the purchase of related tools, machinery, and other supplies.

Much of this planning is conducted in partnership with other members of a facility or organization's executive staff who traditionally have final say in budgetary allocation. The maintenance supervisor represents the concerns and needs of the entire maintenance staff within the corporate or organizational hierarchy.

Duties and Responsibilities

- Scheduling workers and contractors to perform work
- Filling in on an emergency basis for other maintenance personnel
- Managing complaints and problems among subordinates
- Overseeing the work of assistants
- Being responsible for maintaining expensive machinery and real estate

OCCUPATION SPECIALTIES

Utilities Supervisors

Utilities Supervisors are responsible for the maintenance and repair of equipment in electrical, mechanical and water utility plants serving communities and industries.

Custodial Supervisors

Custodial Supervisors are responsible for cleaning and maintaining the premises of business and community buildings. They often times work with a staff, and must anticipate and meet the needs for a clean and smoothly functioning building.

Building Maintenance Supervisors

Building Maintenance Supervisors tend to the physical and aesthetic needs of one or more buildings. They oversee the staff that maintains the physical structure, operation, and cleanliness of a building.

WORK ENVIRONMENT

Physical Environment

The work environment for maintenance supervisors can vary from day to day and project to project. While much of their work is conducted in an office setting, their responsibilities also require field work.

Plant Environment

Maintenance supervisors are employed by commercial building complexes, schools and universities, transportation hubs, hotels and resorts, theme parks and stadiums, as well as by hospitals, municipalities, and private organizations.

Relevant Skills and Abilities

Communication Skills
- Speaking effectively
- Writing concisely

Interpersonal/Social Skills
- Being able to remain calm
- Working as a member of a team

Organization & Management Skills
- Coordinating tasks
- Demonstrating leadership
- Handling challenging situations
- Making decisions
- Managing people/groups
- Managing time
- Organizing information or materials

Research & Planning Skills
- Solving problems
- Using logical reasoning

Human Environment

Professional maintenance supervisors interact with a variety of vendors, coworkers, and other staff members on a daily basis. In addition to a willingness to motivate their own staff, they must also support and communicate regularly with other staff departments.

Technological Environment

The role of maintenance supervisor requires extensive technical skills. In addition to knowledge of traditional administrative software and tools, such as e-mail, telephone, and financial software, directors must be well versed in a variety of tools, systems, and infrastructure such as carpentry, plumbing, electrical wiring and HVAC.

EDUCATION, TRAINING, AND ADVANCEMENT

High School/Secondary

High school students can best prepare for a career as a maintenance supervisor by enrolling in courses pertaining to industrial arts, algebra, calculus, geometry, trigonometry, chemistry, physics, and computer science. Students with vocational training in mechanics or carpentry also have an advantage in the marketplace. Experience in sports and other extracurricular activities also help lay important educational groundwork for future managers.

Summer work in one or many trades, such as plumbing, carpentry, or electrical wiring, can also be useful for those interested in a career in maintenance engineering.

Suggested High School Subjects
- Appliance Repair Technology
- Applied Math
- Blueprint Reading
- Building & Grounds Maintenance
- Building Trades & Carpentry
- English
- Heating/Air Cond./Refrigeration
- Machining Technology
- Masonry
- Metals Technology
- Shop Mechanics
- Small Engine Repair
- Welding

Famous First

The first airline to go beyond Federal Aviation Administration requirements and achieve ISO 9000 registration—the standard for superior quality control—was United Airlines, whose engine maintenance division attained this distinction in 1997. By adhering to the ISO quality control standards, the airline saw significant reductions in engine overhaul cycles (every 120 days on average instead of every 60 days) and parts maintenance/repair cycles (52 days instead of 26).

College/Postsecondary

Postsecondary educational requirements for maintenance director vacancies are common, although extensive experience in both trade work and small-staff management can often be as viable. Most maintenance supervisors have at minimum certificate or associate's level training in one or more vocations, ranging from HVAC systems, small machinery repair, construction, or engineering. Post-secondary coursework for technical professionals customarily includes building and construction courses, instruction on building and inspection codes, zoning laws, facility operation, plumbing, fire protection, and architectural planning.

A bachelor's degree in administration, engineering, civic planning or any relevant technical field is the best way for young professionals lacking extensive field experience to become viable candidates for open positions in the industry.

Related College Majors
• Building/Property Maintenance & Management
• Operations Management & Supervision

Adult Job Seekers

Individuals with no background in a related field should enroll in a college or a technical or vocational school that offers a program in industrial management. Technical schools are also a great place for job seekers to network. Communication technologies and standards are always changing, so maintenance supervisors should be willing to continue learning throughout their career. Maintenance directors are often required to work lengthy and sporadic hours, including weekends and holidays. This may make the position untenable for professionals attempting to balance their work with family or continuing education. Immersion into the job is a must for maintenance directors to effectively exert leadership skills across both staff and the management of many different projects simultaneously.

Professional Certification and Licensure

Mechanical and building professionals are encouraged to acquire certification or licensing according to national, state, and district regulations.

Additional Requirements

Strong leadership skills are an important requirement of the position. Staying organized and managing several projects simultaneously are hallmarks of successful maintenance directors. In addition to good communication skills, maintenance directors must also have the desire to stay with the pace of developments in their field through frequent participation in industry conferences.

Fun Fact

More people report to maintenance supervisors than any other management level.

Source: Ricky Smith, reliability solutions advisor at maintenance consulting firm People and Processes Inc.

EARNINGS AND ADVANCEMENT

Maintenance supervisors advance up through the ranks based on experience and capability. Median annual earnings of maintenance supervisors were $62,201 in 2012.

Maintenance supervisors may receive paid vacations, holidays, and sick days; life and health insurance; and retirement benefits. These are usually paid by the employer. Some employers may also provide company transportation.

EMPLOYMENT AND OUTLOOK

Maintenance supervisors held about 555,000 jobs nationally in 2012. Employment is expected to grow faster than the average for all occupations through the year 2022, which means employment is projected to increase 12 percent to 18 percent. Most were employed in manufacturing. Other industries employing maintenance supervisors were wholesale and retail trade, public utilities, repair shops, transportation and government..

Related Occupations
- Building Manager
- Electrician
- Supervisor

Conversation With . . .
SAM DEAL

Facilities Maintenance Supervisor, 12 years
University of North Carolina at
Chapel Hill School of Nursing

1. What was your individual career path in terms of education/training, entry-level job, or other significant opportunity?

I actually kind of stumbled into this. I went to school for computer science but didn't have the money to finance my education so I left early. I needed to work. I needed to make money to support myself. I held a host of trade-type jobs both while in high school and college and afterwards. Most of it was in the construction field. I used a lot of skills, including carpentry, plumbing, light electrical work, even upholstery. It wasn't really a traditional career path in terms of setting me up for this type of job but each experience has proved invaluable to me in my current position. My initial computer training also helped me immensely.

After I left school, my first job was in security. That also helped me immensely in this job because one of the facets of it is building security. In 1999, I took a job at UNC as a general laborer for the grounds department. Several months later, I switched to a job maintaining office equipment on campus. That brought me into contact with 11 buildings and schools on campus, including the School of Nursing, where I got to know several folks, including my predecessor. He'd told me he was planning to leave and I told him I was interested in the job. And I ended up getting it.

2. What are the most important skills and/or qualities for someone in your profession?

One of the most important skills is to be a diplomat. When I say that, I mean being able to deal with all sorts of people. At times, I deal with deans and directors or stakeholders who are helping to fund a large project. But I also deal with the people who have boots on the ground and who are actually doing the work. You have to go between the different groups and deal with their different dynamics and connect with them all and make sure everyone has one focused goal.

3. What do you wish you had known going into this profession?

Probably the amount of general knowledge that's necessary for the many different trades that I deal with. I cover everything from housekeeping needs to heating and air-conditioning to building security. I also deal with ergonomic issues that people have with their work space as well as big renovation and addition projects. Fortunately, I have been able to fill in gaps in my knowledge as I go along.

4. Are there many job opportunities in your profession? In what specific areas?

I think it goes to the particular demands of the job. At the university level, there are probably not a lot of job opportunities once you reach my level. In the private sector, I think there are a lot of job opportunities in everything from apartments to businesses to private schools.

5. How do you see your profession changing in the next five years, what role will technology play in those changes, and what skills will be required?

In my job, technology is having an effect in terms of what is being demanded and desired of the facility by its users. There are changes in the sorts of common-area furniture and desks that we order because people need places to plug in their phones and laptops.

6. What do you enjoy most about your job? What do you enjoy least about your job?

I do enjoy my job although at times I feel overwhelmed. It's just because I find myself switching gears a lot. One hour I could be meeting with the dean or a director and the next I could be crawling over an air handler. It's a very broad range of general knowledge that you kind of need to have. I'm a jack of all trades and I like to think I'm a master of at least a couple. I love what I do and particularly who I do it for. I can't think of a better group of caring individuals than those in the nursing profession.

7. Can you suggest a valuable "try this" for students considering a career in your profession?

I think it would be useful simply to walk around your house and note the different utilities that your home uses, whether it's heating, air-conditioning or plumbing, then look at the structure of the home itself and what all went into that, whether it's masonry, carpentry or prefab. Those are all important things to know about a building that you're responsible for maintaining even if it's as a homeowner, not a professional.

SELECTED SCHOOLS

A college degree is not necessary in most cases to work as a maintenance supervisor. For those interested in the field, however, a technical or community college is a good place to start. Many commercial trade schools are also available. Students are advised to consult with their school guidance counselor or research area post-secondary schools to find the right program.

MORE INFORMATION

Association for Maintenance Professionals
P.O. Box 60075
Fort Myers, FL 33906
239.333.2500
www.maintenance.org

Association for Operations Management
8430 West Bryn Mawr Avenue
Suite 1000
Chicago, IL 60631
800.444.2742
www.apics.org

John Pritchard/Editor

Office Machine Repairer

Snapshot

Career Cluster: Electronics; Maintenance & Repair; Technology
Interests: Machine repair, working with your hands
Earnings (Yearly Average): $38,310
Employment & Outlook: Slower than Average Growth Expected

OVERVIEW

Sphere of Work

Office machine repairers install, troubleshoot, and fix business equipment such as printers, fax machines, copiers, and scanners. Office machine professionals are employed by office supply retailers and by small businesses specializing in office systems repair. Some office machine repairers are employed by large corporations or singular enterprises and are responsible for servicing all machines within one company.

Work Environment

Office machine specialists work in business settings such as offices, warehouses, manufacturing facilities, and any other environment that utilizes office systems technology. Major repairs may take place at workshops or headquarters of office machine repair firms. Much of the work of office machine repairers takes place in active work environments, requiring specialists to be respectful of those in surrounding workspaces.

Profile

Working Conditions: Work Indoors
Physical Strength: Light Work
Education Needs: On-The-Job Training, High School Diploma with Technical Education
Licensure/Certification: Recommended
Physical Abilities Not Required: No Heavy Labor
Opportunities For Experience: Part-Time Work
Holland Interest Score*: RES

* See Appendix A

Occupation Interest

The field of office machine repair attracts individuals who are interested in computers, electronics, and mechanical processes. These professionals also enjoy troubleshooting problems and analyzing mechanical issues. They are good listeners who excel at examining evidence. Office machine specialists enjoy helping others. They possess the patience explain the complexities of advanced technologies to less knowledgeable people.

A Day in the Life—Duties and Responsibilities

Office machine repair specialists often investigate and repair several machines on a daily basis. Specialists employed by retail outlets or repair companies often begin their day at headquarters reviewing the day's scheduled jobs. They also organize the equipment and tools required by each job.

Some repair specialists concentrate on one specific type of business machine, while others are well versed in a variety of different technologies. Most office machine repairers work alone. Installation of large machines such as copiers and printers may require specialists to work in pairs.

Troubleshooting business machines usually requires extensive disassembly, which workers must be careful to conduct in a nondisruptive and organized manner. Testing of machinery may require use of specific diagnostic tools.

Once a specialist discovers the specific problem, the repair process begins, either by performing maintenance on faulty machine parts or by replacing them entirely. After parts are repaired or replaced, it is the role of the machine repair specialist to run a series of tests to make sure everything is in working order. Many specialists also conclude repairs by informing administrative and office staff members on how to prevent future disruptions.

Duties and Responsibilities

- Inspecting and testing office machines
- Disassembling and examining parts for repair or replacement
- Giving instructions on the operation and care of the machines
- Assembling new machines
- Making out proper repair bills, shop records and time cards

WORK ENVIRONMENT

Physical Environment

Office machine repairers work primarily in office settings. They also work in and around business of all kinds, often near other professionals and in active office environments during business hours.

Human Environment

Most office machine repairers work alone. However, strong interpersonal and communication skills are a perquisite of the position because of the extensive interaction with other professionals at job locations.

Relevant Skills and Abilities

Interpersonal/Social Skills
- Being able to work independently

Organization & Management Skills
- Following instructions

Research & Planning Skills
- Using logical reasoning

Technical Skills
- Working with machines, tools or other objects

Technological Environment

Office machine repairers utilize a variety of technological equipment ranging from diagnostic software to hand tools and power tools. They must also be well versed in the technological infrastructure and internal software of the machines they service.

EDUCATION, TRAINING, AND ADVANCEMENT

High School/Secondary

High school students can best prepare for a career in office machine repair by completing coursework in algebra, calculus, introductory robotics, and computer science. Drafting, design, and industrial art classes can also serve as precursors for work in machine schematics. English, composition, and rhetorical communication courses also provide an important foundation for the interpersonal communication and problem-solving skills that are vital for success in the field.

Suggested High School Subjects
- Applied Math
- Business & Computer Technology
- Driver Training
- Electricity & Electronics
- English
- Industrial Arts
- Machining Technology
- Mathematics

Famous First

The first copy made by xerography was in 1938 in Astoria, Queens, New York City, by Chester F. Carlson. Carlson used wax paper pressed against an electrostatically charged, sulfur-coated zinc plate dusted with fine dark powder to make a copy of the original. This process was dry rather than wet, as in mimeography. Carlson filed a patent for the process in 1942, but he never succeeded in producing a commercial device for office use. Other firms accomplished this in the late 1940s and early 1950s.

College/Postsecondary

A postsecondary degree is not traditionally a requirement for job vacancies in office machine repair. However, most positions do recommend applicants have certification or some kind of formal education in electronics. Many employers give preference to applicants with electronics training attained from vocational or technical schools or from military experience. Applicants with more extensive training in electronics and machine repair have increased promotional opportunities that can lead to positions working with more complex systems as well as supervisorial and management roles.

Related College Majors
- Business Machine Repair
- Computer Installation & Repair
- Electrical & Electronics Equipment Installation & Repair

Adult Job Seekers

Office machine repairers work conventional business hours with the exception of on-call technicians who may be required to repair machines on an emergency basis. The limited amount of formal training and professional experience required of applicants makes the field of office machine repair a viable entry-level profession for professionals interested in a career in electronics or computer systems. Since office machines are utilized in businesses around the world, the skills and experience attained through work as an office machine repairer are viable in many places.

Professional Certification and Licensure

Several organizations and certifying bodies throughout the United States offer licensure and certificates demonstrating aptitude in office machine repair. Certification is normally achieved through the successful completion of written or online examinations. Possession of certification from such organizations as the Electronics Technicians Association International can give applicants increased prospects for employment.

Additional Requirements

Patience and organization are the hallmarks of successful office machine repairers. In addition to possessing the composure to analyze and address complex technological problems, office machine specialists must also be willing to examine several potential solutions in order to get the systems functioning properly.

EARNINGS AND ADVANCEMENT

Earnings of office machine repairers depend on the geographic location of the employer, the complexity of the equipment serviced and the experience of the individual. Office machine repairers had median annual earnings of $38,310 in 2013. The lowest ten percent earned less than $21,890, and the highest ten percent earned more than $57,880.

Office machine repairers may receive paid vacations, holidays, and sick days; life and health insurance; and retirement benefits. These are usually paid by the employer. Some employers also reimburse travel expenses.

Metropolitan Areas with the Highest
Employment Level in this Occupation

Metropolitan area	Employment [1]	Employment per thousand jobs	Hourly mean wage
Dallas-Plano-Irving, TX	4,280	1.99	$16.82
New York-White Plains-Wayne, NY-NJ	3,570	0.68	$19.97
Atlanta-Sandy Springs-Marietta, GA	2,850	1.24	$18.01
Houston-Sugar Land-Baytown, TX	2,670	0.97	$17.93
Chicago-Joliet-Naperville, IL	2,660	0.72	$19.13
Los Angeles-Long Beach-Glendale, CA	2,530	0.64	$21.26
Philadelphia, PA	2,260	1.23	$19.77
Minneapolis-St. Paul-Bloomington, MN-WI	2,100	1.17	$18.66
Fort Worth-Arlington, TX	1,910	2.10	$13.65
Santa Ana-Anaheim-Irvine, CA	1,720	1.19	$22.36

[1]Does not include self-employ ed. Source: Bureau of Labor Statistics

EMPLOYMENT AND OUTLOOK

Nationally, there were about 133,000 computer, ATM, and office machine repairers employed in 2012. Employment of office machine repairers is expected to grow slower than the average for all occupations through the year 2022, which means employment is projected to increase 1 percent to 7 percent. Computers and other office equipment will continue to require preventative maintenance and also need to have parts repaired or replaced.

Employment Trend, Projected 2012–22

Total, All Occupations: 11%

Installation, Maintenance, and Repair Occupations: 10%

Office Machine Repairers: 4%

Note: "All Occupations" includes all occupations in the U.S. Economy. Source: U.S. Bureau of Labor Statistics, Employment Projections Program

Related Occupations
- Computer Service Technician
- Electromechanical Equipment Assembler
- Electronic Equipment Repairer
- Home Appliance Repairer
- Home entertainment equipment technician
- Telecommunications Equipment Repairer
- Television & Radio Repairer

Conversation With . . .
JERRY SMITH

Owner
TCT Office Products, Inc., Holland, MI, 22 years

1. What was your individual career path in terms of education/training, entry-level job, or other significant opportunity?

I was a welder for about 15 years, then was unemployed, then painting houses. I was looking for a change in my career. The church I attended was getting ready to have a 24-hour prayer chain and the organizers were getting a list of prayers together. The organizer approached me and I told him I needed a full-time job. And he said, "I'm going to be looking for somebody who would like to learn to repair typewriters." So that's how I started, in 1984, with IBM typewriters. My brother and I bought out a company that also maintained FAX machines, copiers and printers. I travel in my area to repair machines; occasionally they come to me because my business includes an in-house shop. We also have a copy and printing business here. I'm acquainted with a lot of equipment, although I don't repair computers out in the field.

2. What are the most important skills and/or qualities for someone in your profession?

Being mechanical, patient, willing to learn, and willing to stick to it. You also need to be willing to fail and not be afraid of it, and to learn all that you can from failing.

3. What do you wish you had known going into this profession?

It's difficult; there's no school for learning to be inquisitive. You need to learn how things look when they come apart, and what they are supposed to look like when they're not broken. Most everything I've done in my life has been on-the-job training. You can go to school, but you still have to acquire skills for yourself. You have to know what you're doing, think the process through, and accomplish your mission.

4. Are there many job opportunities in your profession? In what specific areas?

Not a lot, at least in my area. I do service a lot of nearby communities and companies. I fix a range of different types of copiers, and I don't know of anybody who does exactly what I do.

5. How do you see your profession changing in the next five years, what role will technology play in those changes, and what skills will be required?

It's hard to say. In many ways, I'm the last of a type because because I don't know a lot of independent office machine repairmen and, at this point, I am semi-retired. You could train through one of the large corporations and perhaps find work that way.

You will need to be proficient at learning. Say you want to get hired by one of the big corporations like Cannon or Xerox to repair their copiers and you're a technician. They may send you to school if there's a need. The industry is changing very fast. Office machines are becoming more complicated and electronic, and require different skills than those required when office machines were largely mechanical.

6. What do you enjoy most about your job? What do you enjoy least about your job?

I enjoy doing service for the community and traveling around. I like working on the different machines; it's challenging. What I enjoy the least is when people take too long to pay their bills and then call and say we charge too much.

7. Can you suggest a valuable "try this" for students considering a career in your profession?

Look at the industry and find someone in the business who is maybe five years out from retirement. Work for them to see how you like it. Who knows, maybe you'll find you can become an owner.

SELECTED SCHOOLS

A college degree is not necessary in most cases to work as an office machine repairer. For those interested in the field, however, a technical or community college is a good place to start. Many commercial trade schools are also available. Students are advised to consult with their school guidance counselor or research area post-secondary schools to find the right program.

MORE INFORMATION

Business Solutions Association
3601 East Joppa Road
Baltimore, MD 21234
410.931.8100
www.opwa.org

Independent Office Products and Furniture Dealers Association (IOPFDA)
301 N. Fairfax Street, Suite 200
Alexandria, VA 22314
800.542.6672
www.iopfda.org

John Pritchard/Editor

Renewable Energy Technician

Snapshot

Career Cluster: Architecture & Construction; Environment & Conservation; Natural Resources Development

Interests: Hydroelectric, solar, and geothermal energy; environmental science; maintenance and repair

Earnings (Yearly Average): $47,741

Employment & Outlook: Faster Than Average Growth Expected

OVERVIEW

Sphere of Work

Renewable energy technicians design, install, manage, and care for the mechanical systems used in the generation of wind, solar, geothermal, biological, and hydroelectric energy. They inspect and maintain solar panels, wind turbines, power generators and other equipment, most often at electric power plants. If these technologies fail, energy technicians may recommend shutting down affected equipment until repairs can be completed. Many renewable

energy technicians work at multiple sites, providing assessment, maintenance, and repair services as requested by the site managers or owners. Some renewable energy technicians design, install, and maintain renewable energy technologies at private residences, educational institutions, or businesses.

Work Environment

Renewable energy technicians work at energy-generating facilities, for example, hydroelectric dams, wind farms, solar farms, geothermal energy plants, and bioenergy installations. Many of these facilities, particularly wind and solar farms and hydroelectric dams, may be located in remote locations, so renewable energy technicians must live close by or be willing to spend a significant amount of time traveling. While on site, much of the work is done outdoors—in varying weather conditions. There are physical risks associated with some job duties, as certain technicians frequently climb to the top of very tall wind turbines or other tall structures to perform their work. Technicians may also be at risk of exposure to extreme heat or electrocution when working close to renewable energy collectors or generators.

Profile

Working Conditions: Work both Indoors and Outdoors
Physical Strength: Medium Work
Education Needs: Junior/ Technical/Community College, Bachelor's Degree
Licensure/Certification: Recommended
Physical Abilities Not Required: N/A
Opportunities For Experience: Apprenticeship, Part-Time Work
Holland Interest Score*: RCI

* See Appendix A

Occupation Interest

Renewable energy technicians provide expertise and services to an exciting new industry that has grown significantly in a relatively short time. The work they do helps to lessen the environmental impact of electric power by reducing society's use of fossil fuels. A young field, renewable energy requires a range of skills, with some technicians dealing directly with electrical systems, others skilled in system installation, and still others participating in system design. Successful renewable energy technicians are well aware of the dynamic nature of the industry and keep abreast, as well as contribute to, the advances in the field. Renewable energy technicians spend much of their time working outdoors, and should be able to climb, kneel, carry tools and equipment, and walk long distances. Working in a relatively new technical field may appeal to individuals interested in being at the forefront of technological development.

A Day in the Life—Duties and Responsibilities

TRenewable energy technicians' daily responsibilities vary according to their particular area of expertise. For example, wind energy technicians work at wind farms, frequently climbing hundreds of feet into the air to work inside a nacelle (the housing at the center of a wind turbine) where they clean and lubricate bearings, shafts, and gears. Geothermal energy technicians also work outdoors, monitoring energy and heat outputs, replacing and installing new piping systems, and testing the efficiency of residential and commercial geothermal heat pumps. Hydroelectric power technicians spend time inside hydroelectric power plants to monitor generators, flow tunnels, and computers that track the efficiency of turbines.

When beginning a project, renewable energy technicians may assess a site to determine the proper systems and methods for the installation of equipment used to collect solar energy, wind power, bioenergy, hydroelectricity, or geothermal energy. After installing the equipment, they prepare it for connection to the electric power grid by priming, flushing, purging, or performing other practices. According to schedule and at the request of the energy company or the facility director, renewable energy technicians also travel periodically to the dam, farm, or other facility to inspect equipment, assess productivity, diagnose any malfunctions, and make repairs. Based on information about the output and efficiency of the facility, technicians will make recommendations for upgrades or modifications.

Duties and Responsibilities

- Designing, installing, operating and maintaining systems that use renewable energy
- Recommending energy efficiency and alternative energy solutions
- Researching the latest information concerning renewable energy advances
- Consulting with and supervising other technicians and installers
- Working with individual clients and government agencies

OCCUPATION SPECIALTIES

Wind Turbine Service Technicians

Wind Turbine Service Technicians inspect, adjust and maintain wind turbines that harness wind energy.

Solar Energy System Installers & Technicians

Solar Energy System Installers & Technicians build, install and maintain systems on roofs and other structures that harness solar energy. They also install and repair systems that collect, store and circulate solar-heated water.

Hydropower Energy Technicians

Hydropower Energy Technicians maintain hydropower plants that convert water to energy.

Geothermal Energy Technicians

Geothermal Energy Technicians maintain geothermal power plants that convert energy from the earth's core.

Bioenergy Technicians

Bioenergy Technicians maintain bioenergy power plants that convert energy from biomass, such as wood, crops, plants, waste materials and alcohol fuels.

Fuel Cell Technicians

Fuel Cell Technicians research and perform the assembly and testing of fuel cells and also install and maintain existing fuel cells.

WORK ENVIRONMENT

Relevant Skills and Abilities

Communication Skills
- Speaking effectively
- Writing concisely

Interpersonal/Social Skills
- Being able to work independently
- Working as a member of a team

Organization & Management Skills
- Paying attention to and handling details
- Coordinating tasks
- Making decisions
- Performing duties which change frequently

Research & Planning Skills
- Analyzing information
- Developing evaluation strategies
- Using logical reasoning

Technical Skills
- Understanding which technology is appropriate for a task
- Applying the technology to a task
- Maintaining and repairing technology
- Working with your hands
- Working with machines, tools or other objects

Physical Environment

Renewable energy technicians work at renewable energy facilities, such as wind and solar farms, hydroelectric dams, and bioenergy and geothermal energy processing plants. Many of these facilities are located in remote, open areas. Because the facilities process electricity, there may be a risk of electrocution when working on technical equipment. There is also a risk of other physical injuries at different types of electric power plants and wind farms.

Human Environment

Depending on the sub-field in which they work, renewable energy technicians work with a number different people, including environmental engineers, environmental scientists, business executives, construction personnel, utility workers, and energy auditors.

Technological Environment

Nursery workers use machinery and eIn addition to the hand-held tools used to install renewable energy equipment and systems, technicians use and work in close proximity to a wide range of energy-related technologies. Among these devices are portable data input terminals, digital refractometers, temperature gauges, water pressure gauges, nacelles, and photovoltaic cells. Technicians also use computer software, including input/output tracking software, databases, and analytical software.

EDUCATION, TRAINING, AND ADVANCEMENT

High School/Secondary

High school students should study algebra, geometry, and other mathematics courses. Natural sciences such as chemistry, physics, and environmental studies are equally important. Computer science, drafting, and industrial arts courses (such as welding, building trades, carpentry, and electronics) are also useful preparation for this field.

Suggested High School Subjects
- Algebra
- Applied Math
- Blueprint Reading
- Building Trades & Carpentry
- Chemistry
- College Preparatory
- Computer Science
- Drafting
- Electricity & Electronics
- English
- Geometry
- Heating/Air Cond./Refrigeration
- Machining Technology
- Mathematics
- Mechanical Drawing
- Metals Technology
- Physics
- Science
- Shop Math
- Shop Mechanics
- Welding

Famous First

The first hydroelectric power plant to use a storage battery was the Hartford Electric Light Company, Hartford, Conn., in 1896. The storage battery made it possible to supply the company's peak-load requirements from water power that would otherwise have gone to waste during the periods of relatively small demand. Hartford plant pictured.

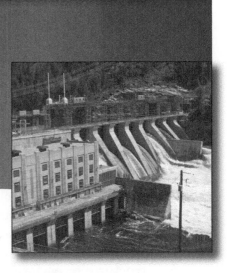

College/Postsecondary

Although employers value practical experience in this occupation, many employers prefer candidates to have an associate's or bachelor's degree. Renewable energy technicians can increase their competitiveness as job candidates by obtaining technical certificates and degrees in related fields, such as hydroelectricity maintenance and wind turbine maintenance. Such programs are increasingly becoming available at two-year community and technical colleges.

Related College Majors
- Electromechanical Technology
- Heating, Air Conditioning & Refrigeration Technology
- Solar Technology

Adult Job Seekers

Some renewable energy technician jobs may be found through technical and community college placement offices. Candidates may also apply directly to companies who advertise in print or online. Individuals with limited experience may join renewable energy firms as interns, or obtain part-time or summer jobs as a means of entry into the field.

Professional Certification and Licensure

There is no required certification for renewable energy technicians. Voluntary certification programs in specialized fields, such as wind turbine maintenance and geothermal energy maintenance, are increasingly available through professional trade associations. Such certification can bolster a candidate's credentials, especially in light of the fact that the renewable energy field is becoming more competitive. As with any voluntary endeavor, candidates should consult credible professional associations within the field and follow professional debate as to the relevancy and value of any certification program.

Additional Requirements

Renewable energy technicians should be detail-oriented and possess the ability to analyze complex systems and problems, as well as excellent mechanical skills. They must be willing to travel, sometimes for long periods of time. Many renewable energy technician positions spend a great deal of time working outdoors and often need to climb tall structures or perform heavy lifting activities. To work effectively with a team of colleagues from different fields, they should have strong communication and people skills.

EARNINGS AND ADVANCEMENT

Median annual earnings of renewable energy technicians were $47,741 in 2013.

Renewable energy technicians may receive paid vacations, holidays, and sick days; life and health insurance and retirement benefits. These are usually paid by the employer.

EMPLOYMENT AND OUTLOOK

Employment of renewable energy technicians is expected to grow much faster than the average for all occupations through the year 2022, which means employment is projected to increase 20 percent or more. Energy and its relationship to sustaining the environment is a rapidly growing field that will continue to create demand for new jobs for many years to come.

Related Occupations

- Energy Auditor
- Energy Conservation & Use Technician
- Energy Engineer
- Heating and Cooling Technician
- Solar Energy System Installer
- Wind Energy Engineer

SELECTED SCHOOLS

Many technical and community colleges offer programs in energy systems installation and repair, often with a concentration in renewable energy. Interested students are advised to consult with their school guidance counselor or to research area postsecondary schools and training programs. For those interested in pursuing a bachelor's degree, a state land-grant college or technical institute is probably the best place to start.

MORE INFORMATION

American Council on Renewable Energy
1600 K Street NW, Suite 700
Washington, DC 20006
202.393.0001
www.acore.org

American Solar Energy Society
4760 Walnut Street, Suite 106
Boulder, CO 80301
303.443.3130
www.ases.org

American Wind Energy Association
1501 M Street, NW, Suite 1000
Washington, DC 20005
202.383.2500
www.awea.org

Biomass Power Association
100 Middle Street
P.O. Box 9729
Portland, ME 04104-9729
703.889.8504
www.usabiomass.org

Energy Efficiency & Renewable Energy Network
Department of Energy
1000 Independence Avenue, SW
Washington, DC 20585
800.342.5363
www.eere.energy.gov

Geothermal Resources Council
P.O. Box 1350
Davis, CA 95617
530.758.2360
www.geothermal.org

National Hydropower Association
25 Massachusetts Avenue, NW
Suite 450
Washington, DC 20001
202.682.1700
www.hydro.org

Renewable Fuels Association
425 Third Street, SW, Suite 1150
Washington, DC 20024
202.289.3835
www.ethanolrfa.org

Solar Energy Industries Association (SEIA)
575 7th Street, NW, Suite 400
Washington, DC 20004
202.682.0556
www.seia.org

Windustry
2105 First Avenue South
Minneapolis, MN 55404
800.946.3640
www.windustry.org

Michael Auerbach/Editor

Robotics Technician

Snapshot

Career Cluster: Engineering; Manufacturing; Maintenance & Repair; Technology

Interests: Robotics technology, engineering, computer science, electrical systems, machinery

Earnings (Yearly Average): $54,160

Employment & Outlook: Slower than Average Growth Expected

OVERVIEW

Sphere of Work

Robotics technicians, also known as electromechanical technicians, build and repair robots and mechanical devices in a manufacturing setting. Drawing on their knowledge of electrical and computer systems, robotics technicians develop efficient robots and keep them in good working order. Some technicians assist at all levels of a robot's conception, production, and installation. Others are experts when it comes to the machines they are assigned to maintain.

Technicians install new systems and replace old ones. Some robotics

technicians work closely with engineers in development and design. Others spend their time inspecting sites and making repairs. Robotics technicians read and interpret manuals and instructions, but they also think critically to find solutions to unusual or difficult problems with machines.

Work Environment

Most robotics technicians work in factories or similar manufacturing settings. Using a number of technologies, ranging from sophisticated computer programs to hand tools, technicians test machines and look for problems. A technician's work can be dangerous, so it is important for technicians to take proper safety precautions and follow correct procedures.

Profile

Working Conditions: Work Indoors
Physical Strength: Light Work
Education Needs:
Technical/Community College
Licensure/Certification:
Recommended
Physical Abilities Not Required: No
Heavy Labor
Opportunities For Experience:
Internship
Holland Interest Score*: REC

* See Appendix A

Occupation Interest

A robotics technician should be interested in engineering. He or she should enjoy taking machines apart and putting them back together again. Technicians are meticulous, and they always double-check their work. A robotics technician plays an important role within the larger framework of a factory operation.

A Day in the Life—Duties and Responsibilities

Every day is different for robotics technicians. Their responsibilities include building and installing new robotic devices, replacing old or outdated parts and machines, testing robot performance, troubleshooting problems within a system, maintaining inventories of necessary parts and tools, and programming computers.

There are generally two types of robotics technicians: those who work with engineers to design and assemble robots and those who maintain and repair those robots. The first type thinks creatively to find a way for machines to simulate the work of humans. Robot manipulators, or robots that simulate the work of arms or hands, are common in industrial settings, particularly when the work is repetitive or performed in a dangerous environment. Technicians work with engineers to develop machines like manipulators that perform a very specialized task within the larger framework of the factory or plant.

The second kind of robotics technician monitors the use of these machines. After the robot has been tested and installed, a technician routinely inspects it for missing or malfunctioning parts. This work is largely preventative, as a broken or worn-down machine can stall production across the plant. When a machine does break down, robotics technicians have the knowledge and skill to repair them.

Technicians typically work a regular forty-hour week, though sometimes companies schedule repairs of robotic equipment during weekends or holidays. In this event, a technician might have to work overtime.

Duties and Responsibilities

- Assisting engineers in designing and applying robot systems
- Inspecting electronic components prior to robot assembly
- Inspecting and testing robots for defects after assembly
- Installing robots or robot systems at users' sites
- Providing start-up assistance to users, including fine tuning performance and accuracy of robots
- Training other technicians and skilled workers to operate, program, repair and service robots
- Keeping records of test procedures and results

WORK ENVIRONMENT

Physical Environment

Robotics technicians work in factories, plants, and other industrial settings.

Plant Environment

The plants and factories in which robotics technicians work are often dirty and loud. Technicians are often required to wear protective gear when performing their job. Working with large machines can be dangerous, so people must follow strict safety precautions.

Relevant Skills and Abilities

Communication Skills
- Speaking effectively
- Writing concisely

Organization & Management Skills
- Paying attention to and handling details

Research & Planning Skills
- Analyzing information
- Developing evaluation strategies
- Using logical reasoning

Technical Skills
- Applying the technology to a task
- Performing scientific, mathematical and technical work
- Working with machines, tools or other objects
- Working with your hands

Human Environment

Most robotics technicians work in teams that include other technicians, technologists, engineers, and machine operators. A robotics technician rarely works alone. Even minor repairs require assistance from or interaction with others.

Technological Environment

A robotics technician must be familiar with a range of technologies. In terms of computers and computer programming, most technicians use computer-aided design (CAD) software and industrial control software programs.

EDUCATION, TRAINING, AND ADVANCEMENT

High School/Secondary

Aspiring robotics technicians should enroll in courses focusing on mathematics, physics, computer science, and English. Shop classes and extracurricular activities related to robotics or simple machinery are also valuable. A robotics technician is familiar with various kinds of machines and understands why and how those machines work. They are comfortable using the scientific method and solving equations. They are also adept at reading manuals and diagrams and are able to explain complex instructions with ease. A job as a robotics technician requires a high school diploma or equivalent.

Suggested High School Subjects
- Algebra
- Applied Math
- Applied Physics
- Blueprint Reading
- Computer Science
- Electricity & Electronics
- English
- Geometry
- Machining Technology
- Mathematics

Famous First

The first Robot Olympics was the ROBOlympics (later renamed RoboGames) held in San Francisco in March 2004. Under the sponsorship of the Robotics Society of America, participants entered their robots in 31 events, including sumo, soccer, combat, and wrestling. The games have been held annually since then.

College/Postsecondary

Most robotics technician jobs require only two years of postsecondary training, culminating in an associate's degree or certificate. Community colleges and technical schools offer degree programs in electromechanics, robotics technology, industrial maintenance, and computer-integrated manufacturing. Many of these programs are accredited by the Accreditation Board for Engineering and Technology (ABET) and include courses in trigonometry, algebra, science, and engineering specializations.

Similar fields of study, including electrical engineering technology and mechanical engineering technology, are available in four-year bachelor's degree programs, but most robotics technicians do not pursue this career path. Students who earn a bachelor's degree are much more likely to pursue a career as an engineering technologist.

Related College Majors
* Robotics Technology

Adult Job Seekers

Robotics technicians draw upon a number of transferrable skills, including those of an electrician, mechanic, and computer programmer. Adults who already work as industrial machine operators or simply work in a factory setting might pursue work as a robotics technician. However, they will most likely need to return to school to acquire the proper training; it is unusual for a robotics technician to learn his or her trade completely on the job, though many complete internships.

Professional Certification and Licensure

Robotics technicians are not required to seek certification or licensure in their field, but it is recommended. Some companies offers a number of certifications tailored to different careers in and principles of robotics. For example, one can take certification tests in categories such as application lifecycle management, business planning and alignment, complex and embedded systems, design and development, and enterprise modernization. Local robotics societies also offer workshops and seminars for professional development.

Additional Requirements

Robotics technicians must be efficient and precise. They should work well with others, appreciate the needs of organizations, and be able to execute their job in the fulfillment of those needs. They enjoy working with their hands but are also adept at working with computers. Technicians must be able to think both analytically and creatively. The creation and maintenance of robotic systems requires technicians to draw upon all of their talents and knowledge. Due to the noisy conditions common in factories and plants, it is important that robotics technicians be able to focus on their work despite distractions.

Fun Fact

One of the earliest uses of the word "robot" was in the 1920s play, *Rossum's Universal Robots*, by Czech writer Karel Capek. It comes from the Slavonic word "robota," which means servitude, drudgery, or forced labor. In the play, robots, which are produced to do the work humans prefer not to, eventually rise up in revolt.

Source: sciencefriday.com/segment/04/22/2011/science-diction-the-origin-of-the-word-robot.html

EARNINGS AND ADVANCEMENT

Earnings of robotics technicians depend on the type and size of the employer and the individual's education, experience and job responsibilities. Mean annual earnings of robotics technicians were $54,160 in 2013. The lowest ten percent earned less than $33,490, and the highest ten percent earned more than $80,070.

Robotics technicians may receive paid vacations, holidays, and sick days; life and health insurance; and retirement benefits. These are usually paid by the employer. Some employers have profit-sharing and/or tuition reimbursement plans and also reimburse job-related travel expenses.

Metropolitan Areas with the Highest
Employment Level in this Occupation

Metropolitan area	Employment [1]	Employment per thousand jobs	Hourly mean wage
San Jose-Sunnyvale-Santa Clara, CA	690	0.75	$25.11
Boston-Cambridge-Quincy, MA	670	0.38	$28.94
Phoenix-Mesa-Glendale, AZ	590	0.33	$24.77
Santa Ana-Anaheim-Irvine, CA	440	0.31	$22.10
Los Angeles-Long Beach-Glendale, CA	360	0.09	$26.67
San Diego-Carlsbad-San Marcos, CA	330	0.25	$28.42
Baltimore-Towson, MD	290	0.23	$32.47
Atlanta-Sandy Springs-Marietta, GA	290	0.13	$27.60
Chicago-Joliet-Naperville, IL	270	0.07	$32.01
Oklahoma City, OK	270	0.45	$18.53

[1]Does not include self-employ ed. Source: Bureau of Labor Statistics

EMPLOYMENT AND OUTLOOK

Nationally, there were approximately 17,500 electro-mechanical technicians, of which robotics technicians are a part, employed in 2012. Employment is expected to grow slower than the average for all occupations through the year 2022, which means employment is projected to increase 1 percent to 7 percent. Many job openings will result from the need to replace robotics technicians who transfer to other occupations or retire.

Employment Trend, Projected 2012–22

Total, All Occupations: 11%

Robotics Technicians: 4%

Engineering Technicians (All): 1%

Note: "All Occupations" includes all occupations in the U.S. Economy. Source: U.S. Bureau of Labor Statistics, Employment Projections Program

Related Occupations
- Computer Service Technician
- Computer-Control Machine Tool Operator
- Computer-Control Tool Programmer
- Electrical & Electronics Engineer
- Electrician
- Electromechanical Equipment Assembler
- Engineering Technician

Conversation With . . .
PAUL CARUSO

Robotics Technician
iRobot Corporation, Bedford, MA
Electronics & Robotics Professional, 33 years

1. What was your individual career path in terms of education/training, entry-level job, or other significant opportunity?

After graduating from James Madison High School in New York, I went on to earn a two-year degree from The College of Staten Island in electrical engineering and a one-year certificate in electronic technology at the PSI Institute. In the past, I worked as a technician for Tandy Corporation. I was a field technician for Circuit City for almost seven years, before going to work for iRobot in 2006. Today, I'm a Senior Quality Engineering Technician with iRobot Corporation.

2. What are the most important skills and/or qualities for someone in your profession?

This position requires a lot of troubleshooting. Working in robotics, it's important to take a methodical approach to solving a problem—starting at one point and working step-by step until you solve the issue. That requires patience.

3. What do you wish you had known going into this profession?

If I had known what I know now, I would have continued with my studies to get my bachelor's degree, plus take other classes along the way to broaden my knowledge in areas outside of electronics and electrical engineering.

4. Are there many job opportunities in your profession? In what specif-ic areas?

Yes, there are many opportunities in robotics, including video conferencing/remote presence; medical electronics and telemedicine (which is the remote delivery of clinical information and health care services via the Internet or satellite, etc.); home and elderly independent-living robotics; and many more.

Robotics technicians often find themselves working for a robotics company, such as iRobot, in a diagnostic lab environment. Since robots are such complicated machines, special parts and tools are required to service them that are not always accessible away from the lab. As robots become more pervasive in society, there will be a need for technicians to travel into the field for troubleshooting, updates, and repairs—particularly for larger robots installed in hospitals, manufacturing plants, and elderly care facilities that are not easily transportable.

5. **How do you see your profession changing in the next five years? What role will technology play in those changes, and what skills will be required?**

Constant breakthroughs in technology mean we will see advances in robotics that were impossible to consider only a few years ago. You will soon be able to buy cars that drive themselves. There will be robots working together to clean the house and ambidextrous robots helping the elderly with daily tasks. This will create a need for more technical people to design and maintain these robots. We will need people with mechanical, software and electrical engineering degrees who can work together to solve complicated problems.

6. **What do you enjoy most about your job? What do you enjoy least about your job?**

I truly enjoy working with my hands. And there's great satisfaction that comes with solving a difficult problem in a way that will help improve the quality of the product. What I don't enjoy? Of course, there's always paperwork involved with any job, which isn't quite as exciting.

7. **Can you suggest a valuable "try this" for students considering a ca-reer in your profession?**

I suggest that students attend electronic trade shows, where they can walk the show floor and get a glimpse at the latest technology hitting markets. Not only is it a great way to see cutting-edge technology, but it's also a great way to make connections with companies that may be hiring or seeking internship candidates. Internships are critical to breaking into a career in robotics.

SELECTED SCHOOLS

Many technical and community colleges offer programs in or related to robotics technology. Commercial trade schools are also an option. Students are advised to consult with their school guidance counselor or research area post-secondary schools to find the right program.

MORE INFORMATION

American Society for Engineering Education
1818 N Street NW, Suite 600
Washington, DC 20036-2479
202.331.3500
www.asee.org

Association for Unmanned Vehicle Systems International
2700 S. Quincy Street, Suite 400
Arlington, VA 22206
703.845.9671
www.auvsi.org

Institute of Electrical and Electronics Engineers
3 Park Avenue, 17th Floor
New York, NY 10016-5997
212.419.7900
www.ieee.org

National Robotics Training Center
1951 Pisgah Road
P.O. Box 100549
Florence, SC 29501-0549
800.228.5745
www.nrtcenter.com

Technology Student Association
1914 Association Drive
Reston, VA 20191-1540
703.860.9000
www.tsaweb.org

Molly Hagan/Editor

Small Engine Mechanic

Snapshot

Career Cluster: Engineering; Maintenance & Repair
Interests: Engine mechanics, small motor technology, electronics, engineering, customer interaction
Earnings (Yearly Average): $32,180
Employment & Outlook: Slower than Average Growth Expected

OVERVIEW

Sphere of Work

Small engine mechanics repair small gasoline-powered or electronic engines. Traditionally self-employed or staff members at hardware stores or other small-engine retail outlets, such mechanics most commonly repair engines in lawnmowers, snowblowers, line trimmers, and golf carts. Small engine mechanics may also specialize in outboard marine engines, small-scale carnival rides, and other motorized carts. Many small engine mechanics are seasonal employees who repair small motors part time in addition to holding other jobs.

Work Environment

Small engine mechanics work in repair shops. Also, many self-employed small engine mechanics set up shops in their own garages or basements. Much of the work of small engine mechanics is done solitarily. Most, if not all, small engine mechanics interact with their customers directly, placing an importance on their ability to communicate, explain work processes and procedures, and explicate billing.

Profile

Working Conditions: Work both Indoors and Outdoors
Physical Strength: Medium to Heavy Work
Education Needs: On-The-Job Training, High School Diploma with Technical Education
Licensure/Certification: Usually Not Required
Physical Abilities Not Required: N/A
Opportunities For Experience: Military Service, Part-Time Work
Holland Interest Score*: REC

* See Appendix A

Occupation Interest

Small engine repair attracts both young professionals and hobbyists, who undertake the role as part of their training and interest in advancing toward more complex roles in engineering and mechanics, and older workers and retirees, who take on small engine repair as a means of part-time employment. Small engine repair is traditionally seasonal or part-time work, and few professionals have the clientele to maintain business on a year-round basis.

A Day in the Life—Duties and Responsibilities

Small engine mechanics analyze, investigate, and repair problems with small engines. The first step is usually a consultation with the client or engine owner to discuss the problem. Other clients bring small engine tools and equipment to be repaired annually as part of routine maintenance.

Small engine mechanics rely primarily on previous experience when troubleshooting common engine problems. Most problems require engine disassembly, a process that requires analytical discipline, organization, and patience. Small engine mechanics are technologically savvy thinkers who are skilled at troubleshooting basic mechanical schemes.

After repairs are complete, it is the role of small engine mechanics to test the engine to make sure it will be returned to the client in proper working order. If the problem remains or the engine is still not functioning properly, the mechanic must troubleshoot the engine further.

Small engine mechanics return repaired engines to clients upon completion of their work, preferably with an explanation regarding the engine's malfunction as well as strategies and potential maintenance processes that can prevent further malfunction in the future.

Duties and Responsibilities

- Troubleshooting engines
- Performing routine maintenance on engines
- Dismantling engines and examining parts for wear or breakage
- Repairing or replacing worn or defective parts
- Cleaning and adjusting carburetors, voltage regulators
- Adjusting timing and drive components
- Lubricating engines
- Installing spark plugs, filters and accessories

OCCUPATION SPECIALTIES

Outboard Motor Mechanics

Outboard Motor Mechanics check out and adjust or repair electrical and mechanical systems of outboard motors. They may change or replace parts such as gears and propellers, or install and repair steering and throttle controls.

Motorcycle Repairers

Motorcycle Repairers overhaul and repair motorcycles, motor scooters and other similar motor vehicles. They may also repair or replace other parts of the motorcycle such as the frame, brakes, spring fork, headlight, horn, handlebar controls, gas and oil tanks, mufflers and wheels.

Gas Engine Repairers

Gas Engine Repairers maintain and repair gas-driven, internal combustion engines that power electric generators, compressors and similar equipment.

WORK ENVIRONMENT

Physical Environment

Small engine mechanics work primarily in garage and repair shop settings.

Small engine mechanics may be employed by construction firms, landscaping companies, resort hotels and amusement parks, country clubs, and colleges and universities. The majority of small engine mechanics are self-employed.

Relevant Skills and Abilities

Organization & Management Skills
- Paying attention to and handling details

Technical Skills
- Performing technical work
- Working with machines, tools or other objects

Human Environment

Being a small engine mechanic requires strong customer interaction skills. Many self-employed small engine mechanics wear multiple hats within their small business, acting as client liaison, mechanic, and head of finance for their small operation.

Technological Environment

Small engine mechanics utilize a variety of industrial and mechanical tools, ranging from dials, gauges, hand tools such as wrenches and chisels, and electronic engine testing and diagnostic devices.

EDUCATION, TRAINING, AND ADVANCEMENT

High School/Secondary

High school students can best prepare for a career in small engine mechanics with courses in algebra, geometry, chemistry, physics, and introductory computer science. Students with a vocational high school background in construction, carpentry, or auto repair often have an advantage in grasping the technical know-how inherent in the position.

Suggested High School Subjects
- Applied Math
- Applied Physics
- Auto Service Technology
- Blueprint Reading
- Business Math
- Electricity & Electronics
- English
- Mathematics

- Science
- Shop Mechanics
- Small Engine Repair
- Trade/Industrial Education
- Welding

Famous First

The first gasoline-powered lawn mower in the United States was manufactured in 1914 by Ideal Power Mower Company of Lansing, Michigan. The mower was based on a patent by Ransom E. Olds, founder of the Oldsmobile auto company. Ideal Power Mower also developed the first ride-on lawn mower (tractor type) in 1922.

College/Postsecondary

Postsecondary coursework is not required for a career in small engine mechanics.

Related College Majors
- Aircraft Mechanics Airframe
- Small Engine Mechanics & Repair

Adult Job Seekers

Small engine mechanics traditionally work regular business hours, though those who repair small engines as a secondary job may be required to work evenings and weekends. Small engine repair professionals who work in places with weather-related attractions, such as ski resorts, golf courses, and amusement parks, may work only seasonally while having another job during the off-season months.

Professional Certification and Licensure

No specific certification or licensure is required to become a small engine mechanic, although informal certification by a nationwide body such as the American Society of Mechanical Engineers may be beneficial in applying for open positions or attracting clientele.

Additional Requirements

One of the most difficult aspects of being a small engine mechanic is staying abreast of developments in small motor technology. Workers can take advantage of course work at local vocational learning centers and training seminars in order to stay informed in developments in the field.

EARNINGS AND ADVANCEMENT

Earnings depend on the employer and the individual's skill and experience. Experienced small engine mechanics usually earn two to three times as much as a trainee. Small engine mechanics may be paid either hourly wages or a commission.

Mean annual earnings of small engine mechanics were $32,180 in 2013. The lowest ten percent earned less than $19,900, and the highest ten percent earned more than $47,090.

Small engine mechanics may receive paid vacations, holidays, and sick days; life and health insurance; and retirement benefits. These are usually paid by the employer. Small engine mechanics working for dealers may receive discounts on equipment, parts and accessories. Employers may also provide uniforms. Small engine mechanics may be required to purchase their own hand tools.

States with the Highest Employment
Level in this Occupation

Metropolitan area	Employment [1]	Employment per thousand jobs	Hourly mean wage
Florida	2,830	0.38	$14.07
Texas	1,860	0.17	$16.32
Pennsylvania	1,550	0.28	$14.77
California	1,520	0.10	$17.30
Ohio	1,160	0.23	$14.25

[1]Does not include self-employ ed. Source: Bureau of Labor Statistics

EMPLOYMENT AND OUTLOOK

There were about 68,000 small engine mechanics employed nationally in 2012. Employment of small engine mechanics is expected to grow slower than the average for all occupations through the year 2022, which means employment is projected to increase 3 percent to 9 percent.

Growth in the number of registered motorcycles and the increasing sophistication and complexity of motorboat engines and lawn and garden power equipment will contribute to job demand. In addition, routine maintenance will always be a large source of work for small engine mechanics. Job openings will also occur because many experienced small engine mechanics leave the field each year to transfer to other jobs or retire. Job prospects should be very good for persons who complete mechanic training programs in a high school, vocational school or community college.

Employment Trend, Projected 2012–22

Total, All Occupations: 11%

Motorcycle Mechanics: 6%

Small Engine Mechanics: 6%

Motorboat Mechanics : 5%

Outdoor Power Equipment Mechanics: 5%

Note: "All Occupations" includes all occupations in the U.S. Economy. Source: U.S. Bureau of Labor Statistics, Employment Projections Program

Related Occupations
- Automotive Technician
- Diesel Service Technician
- Farm Equipment Mechanic
- Home Appliance Repairer

Related Occupations
- Powerhouse Mechanic

Conversation With . . .
VINCE SQUITIERI

Owner/Operator
Vince Christian Small Engine Repair, Maryland
Small engine repair, 9 years

1. What was your individual career path in terms of education/training, entry-level job, or other significant opportunity?

After high school, I started my career as an auto mechanic, then became a mechanic for the Maryland State Police for about a year and a half. I went on to become a Maryland State Trooper for about 14 years. I retired in 2006 because I was hit by a drunk driver while I was on duty and sustained injuries that meant I no longer met the physical requirements to be a trooper. Since I'm a single father, I needed a job where I could be a stay-at-home parent. I had borrowed a snow blower from a neighbor that needed repair, and started calling around to shops. These places were charging $60 to $90 and were totally booked. A light went on: I can do this. I'm a mechanic, I have the tools, I have a trailer, and, I realized, I can do it from home. I turned a large shed at my home into a workshop and life's been great ever since. I service a five-county geographical area around Annapolis and Kent Island.

2. What are the most important skills and/or qualities for someone in your profession?

You need to be somebody who enjoys working with your hands. To work on small engines, you have to understand how an internal combustion engine operates. You need to understand carburetion, transmissions, hydraulics, electricity, and electronics because that's what you're going to be fixing. You have to develop good diagnostic skills, and that requires you to have a good understanding of these areas. I primarily work on lawn mowers—four-cycle engines—but also work on two-cycle engines, such as those in weed trimmers, chain saws, or leaf blowers.

From the standpoint of a small business owner, you have to interact with customers intelligently. You need to present yourself well. When you're in business, unless you're selling space heaters on a day where it's 15 degrees below zero, you're not just selling your service, you're selling yourself. I make sure I'm clean shaven, my shirt is tucked in. You shake the person's hand, speak in a polite and professional manner. I think that's very important.

When people come to you with their $1,000, $2,000, or $3,000 lawnmower, they want to talk to somebody who sounds like they know what they're talking about.

It's important to be polite, and when I go to pick up their machines I wear a shirt or jacket with my name and company name on it.

You also need business skills such as accounting, marketing, and advertising. You need math skills. I would definitely suggest going to a community college and taking a couple of classes on how to run a small business. You need to understand the Internet and websites, because that's where I get 95 percent of my customers. And you need to be organized.

3. What do you wish you had known going into this profession?

Going into this business, I had all the mechanical skills I needed. I wish I'd known more about the business side of things.

4. Are there many job opportunities in your profession? In what specific areas?

In my geographical area, it's kind of seasonal because most work comes in summer when people are cutting grass. In winter, you hope for snow so you get snow blowers and generators. But you can get enough work in summer so that you can practically take the winter off.

5. How do you see your profession changing in the next five years, what role will technology play in those changes, and what skills will be required?

The engines are going to change so there are more electronics controlling exhaust, like with a car. You're going to have to keep up with the electronics.

6. What do you enjoy most about your job? What do you enjoy least about your job?

I most enjoy working for myself and having the freedom to take off when I want to and work when I want to. I like meeting people and making friends, and I do that every day. I also enjoy working with my hands. What I don't like is that it's hard to find good, responsible, dependable help. I've recently hired an employee who will work out, but I have hired a lot of people who just didn't have a work ethic.

7. Can you suggest a valuable "try this" for students considering a career in your profession?

Find a place that repairs small engines and go see exactly what they do. Or, do what I did before I started this business: spend a lot of time watching YouTube videos. Type in "small engine repair" or "lawn mower repair." You can find out what it would take, physically and mentally, to do this occupation. Finally, if somebody is throwing away a lawnmower, drag it home, take it apart and try to put it back together. Then you'll know. Maybe you don't like grease and gas.

SELECTED SCHOOLS

A college degree is not necessary to work as a small engine mechanic. For those interested in the field, however, a technical or community college is a good place to start. Many commercial trade schools are also available. Students are advised to consult with their school guidance counselor or research area post-secondary schools to find the right program.

MORE INFORMATION

American Society of Mechanical Engineers
2 Park Avenue
New York, NY 10016-5990
800.843.2763
www.asme.org

Association of Marine Technicians
513 River Estates Parkway
Canton, GA 30115
770.720.4324
www.natef.org

Equipment and Engine Training Council
3880 Press Wallace Drive
York, SC 29745
803.222.6149
www.eetc.org

John Pritchard/Editor

Stationary Engineer

Snapshot

Career Cluster: Engineering; Maintenance & Repair
Interests: Mechanics, working with your hands, working with tools, troubleshooting, communicating with others
Earnings (Yearly Average): $56,190
Employment & Outlook: Slower than Average Growth Expected

OVERVIEW

Sphere of Work

Stationary engineers operate and maintain systems and equipment in commercial and business facilities. They specialize in working with engines, boilers, turbines, and other mechanical apparatuses at shopping malls, factories, offices, and hospitals. Stationary engineers worked with fixed, rather than mobile, equipment. They operate and maintain heating, air conditioning, and ventilation systems (HVAC), as well as electrical systems. Maintenance performed by engineers can include making repairs and replacing parts.

Work Environment

Stationary engineers work in large commercial buildings and industrial environments where mechanical equipment is permanently housed. These areas include basements, rooftops, and floor spaces that are designated for stationary equipment. Depending on the size of the building, engineers may work alone or with a team of other engineers. These kinds of environments can present several hazards, including dust, loud noise, and heat. Proper safety standards must be followed to avoid workplace injuries.

Profile

Working Conditions: Work Indoors
Physical Strength: Medium Work
Education Needs: On-The-Job Training, High School Diploma with Technical Education
Licensure/Certification: Required
Physical Abilities Not Required: N/A
Opportunities For Experience: Apprenticeship, Military Service
Holland Interest Score*: REI

* See Appendix A

Occupation Interest

Being a stationary engineer involves working with a wide range of equipment and tools. The job tends to interest people with excellent mechanical skills who enjoy working with their hands. In order to troubleshoot problems, a stationary engineer must be very analytical and have excellent critical-thinking skills. Stationary engineers are good communicators with the ability to work efficiently by themselves or as a member of a team.

A Day in the Life—Duties and Responsibilities

Stationary engineers start up, maintain, and shut down the mechanical equipment that operates building utilities. They work with the heating, air conditioning, and electrical systems that most people never think about. The majority of their workday is spent monitoring equipment to ensure that it is running properly. In addition to regular maintenance, they perform repairs on equipment that is malfunctioning or damaged. Stationary engineers who work in large buildings work with a team to ensure equipment operates smoothly.

While monitoring equipment, a stationary engineer will examine gauges, meters, fuel levels, and indicators to ensure that the equipment is operating correctly and safely. This can include adjusting the system's intake of air, water, or fuel. Engineers use advanced electrical instruments to help them troubleshoot, perform maintenance, and monitor heating and cooling systems.

Stationary engineers are also required to perform repairs and routine maintenance when necessary. This involves overhauling or replacing defective parts, including gaskets, valves, and bearings. Routine maintenance tasks include lubricating bearings and other moving parts, replacing old air filters, and cleaning grease and dirt from equipment. Stationary engineers also work with furnaces or boilers, which require routine inspection and maintenance.

Throughout the workday, a stationary engineer will use logbooks or computer software to record data regarding maintenance, repair, and safety issues.

Duties and Responsibilities

- Adjusting controls
- Inspecting equipment to detect malfunctions or the need for repair, adjustment or lubrication
- Maintaining the operation of boilers, air-conditioning and refrigeration equipment, diesel engines, turbines, generators, pumps, condensers and compressors
- Keeping a record about the operation and maintenance of the equipment
- Insuring equipment is running economically
- Monitoring computer-controlled systems by reading output
- Reading meters, gauges or automatic recording devices

OCCUPATION SPECIALTIES

Boiler Operators

Boiler Operators tend and operate automatically fired boilers to produce steam supplying heat and power for buildings and industrial processes.

Diesel and Gas Engine Operators

Diesel and Gas Engine Operators operate stationary diesel and gas engines that supply power for generators and other plant equipment.

WORK ENVIRONMENT

Physical Environment

Stationary engineers commonly work in large buildings such as hospitals, shopping malls, corporate headquarters, or government offices. They can also work in chemical or industrial facilities. These environments can present several hazards, so proper safety precautions must be followed at all times.

Plant Environment

Stationary engineers also work in manufacturing environments such as factories. These environments are typically well ventilated and well lit, but they contain several hazards, such as dust, loud noise, and moving machinery. Some factories may also use or produce dangerous chemicals.

Relevant Skills and Abilities

Organization & Management Skills
- Making decisions
- Paying attention to and handling details
- Performing duties which change frequently

Research & Planning Skills
- Developing evaluation strategies

Technical Skills
- Working with machines, tools or other objects

Human Environment

Stationary engineers work alongside other engineers, as well as supervisors and the employees of the buildings they maintain. In smaller buildings, a stationary engineer may work alone. Technological Environment Stationary engineers work with an assortment of technologies, ranging from small hand tools to large machinery. They often work with computer and electronic systems associated with refrigeration, air conditioning, and heating.

EDUCATION, TRAINING, AND ADVANCEMENT

High School/Secondary

Most employers require that an applicant have a high school diploma or the equivalent. There are several high school courses relevant to the profession that can help students develop a strong background in stationary engineering, including mathematics and mechanical drawing. Many high schools offer extracurricular training at machine shops or automobile shops, where students can learn the fundamentals of engine mechanics.

Suggested High School Subjects
- Applied Math
- Applied Physics
- Blueprint Reading
- Chemistry
- Computer Science
- Electricity & Electronics

- English
- Heating/Air Cond./Refrigeration
- Machining Technology
- Mechanical Drawing
- Metals Technology
- Physics
- Shop Math

Famous First

The first boiler inspection law enacted by a state was approved in 1864 by the state of Connecticut. The law authorized the governor to appoint an Inspector of Boilers to check all steam boilers, like the one pictured, used for manufacturing or mechanical purposes in order to ensure their safety.

College/Postsecondary

Some employers require that an applicant have a postsecondary degree from a college or university. Relevant areas of study for jobs in stationary engineering include industrial technology and mechanical engineering. Stationary engineers also gain knowledge and experience from formal apprenticeships and on-the-job training.

Training for a job in stationary engineering is a long process. Individuals typically begin their careers as helpers who work alongside more experienced technicians and engineers. Under the supervision of these experienced workers, new workers gain knowledge, improve their skills, and increase their eligibility for advancement.

Stationary engineers can also train through formal apprenticeship programs. The International Union of Operating Engineers offers apprenticeship sponsorships for stationary engineers. An apprenticeship commonly lasts four years and includes eight thousand hours of on-the-job training, as well as six hundred hours of technical instruction in a traditional classroom setting. During an apprenticeship, individuals learn about a wide variety of subjects pertaining to stationary engineering. These subjects include the fundamentals of air quality, the operation and maintenance of equipment, and how to balance and control HVAC systems.

Related College Majors
- Electromechanical Technology
- Heating, Air Conditioning & Refrigeration Mechanics & Repair

Adult Job Seekers

Stationary engineers typically work full time during regular business hours. Engineers working in buildings that operate around the clock may be required to work overnight shifts. Many of these buildings are open weekends and holidays as well. These job requirements should be taken into consideration.

If an individual has no background in systems engineering, they should enroll in a technical or vocational school that offers training. Schools offer programs that last anywhere from several weeks to several months. These schools are also a great place to network with experienced people from the field.

Professional Certification and Licensure

Certain states require licensure for stationary engineers, often with different class categories. Classes specify the type and size of equipment the stationary engineer is authorized to operate. In order to obtain a license, a stationary engineer must be eighteen years old, pass a written exam, and be able to demonstrate his or her knowledge and skills. If an engineer relocates to another state, he or she may be required to apply for a new license in that state. If a worker did not go through a formal apprenticeship, it is recommended that he or she apply for a license.

Additional Requirements

Stationary engineers work with very complex machines. The job requires strong knowledge of machine maintenance, repair, and operation. Engineers should be in good physical shape to perform the necessary tasks of the job, such as kneeling, reaching, and standing for long periods. Stationary engineers should also be very detail oriented, as the machinery they work with can be very dangerous.

Fun Fact

Stationary Engineers are so called because originally they worked on a boiler or other piece of equipment that was fixed in one place – or stationary. However, it also includes railroad engineers and marine engineers who ran furnaces of great ocean liners.

Source: The Building Engineering Training blog by stationary engineer Steve Larsen.
http://buildingengineertraining.com/stationary-engineers/

EARNINGS AND ADVANCEMENT

Stationary engineers advance by being placed in charge of larger or more powerful equipment. Generally, stationary engineers advance to these jobs as they obtain higher licenses. Earnings depend on the geographic location of the employer, the type of industry and the employee's experience and skills. In 2013, mean annual earnings of stationary engineers were $56,190. The lowest ten percent earned less than $34,320, and the highest ten percent earned more than $81,560.

Stationary engineers may receive paid vacations, holidays, and sick days; life and health insurance; and retirement benefits. These are usually paid by the employer.

Metropolitan Areas with the Highest Employment Level in this Occupation

Metropolitan area	Employment [1]	Employment per thousand jobs	Hourly mean wage
New York-White Plains-Wayne, NY-NJ	2,630	0.50	$38.07
Chicago-Joliet-Naperville, IL	1,440	0.39	$33.63
Minneapolis-St. Paul-Bloomington, MN-WI	880	0.49	$27.73
Los Angeles-Long Beach-Glendale, CA	710	0.18	$31.64
Washington-Arlington-Alexandria, DC-VA-MD-WV	630	0.27	$32.26
San Francisco-San Mateo-Redwood City, CA	590	0.56	$35.77
Oakland-Fremont-Hayward, CA	420	0.42	$36.71
Buffalo-Niagara Falls, NY	410	0.77	$23.86
Philadelphia, PA	390	0.21	$25.74
Newark-Union, NJ-PA	390	0.40	$23.98

[1]Does not include self-employ ed. Source: Bureau of Labor Statistics

EMPLOYMENT AND OUTLOOK

There were approximately 38,000 stationary engineers employed nationally in 2012. Employment of stationary engineers is expected to grow slower than the average for all occupations through the year 2022, which means employment is projected to increase 0 percent to 6 percent. This is due to greater automation and computerized control of equipment, thus reducing the number of jobs needed. Job opportunities will be best for those with apprenticeship training or vocational school courses in computerized controls.

Employment Trend, Projected 2012–22

Total, All Occupations: 11%

Stationary Engineers and Boiler Operators: 3%

Plant and System Operators (All): -1%

Note: "All Occupations" includes all occupations in the U.S. Economy. Source: U.S. Bureau of Labor Statistics, Employment Projections Program

Related Occupations
- Chemical Equipment Operator
- Heating & Cooling Technician
- Power Plant Operator
- Water Treatment Plant Operator

Inset: Military Occupations
- Compressed Gas Technician
- Marine Engine Mechanic
- Power Plant Electrician
- Power Plant Operator
- Powerhouse Mechanic

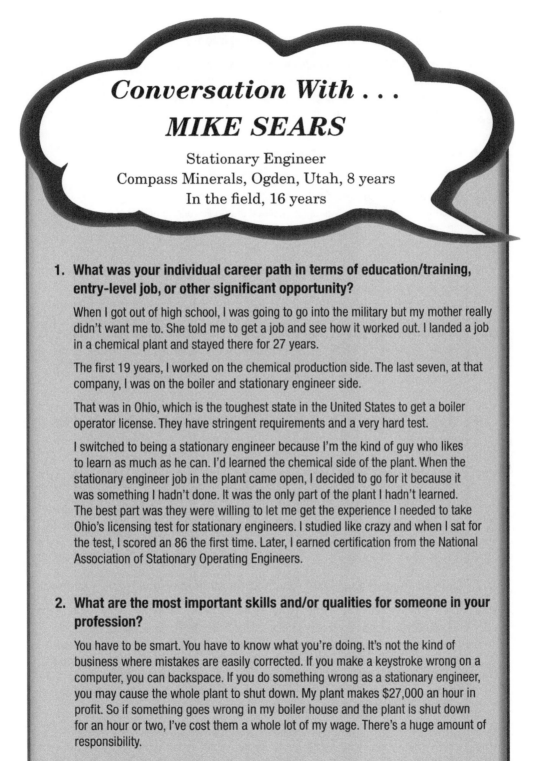

Conversation With . . .
MIKE SEARS

Stationary Engineer
Compass Minerals, Ogden, Utah, 8 years
In the field, 16 years

1. What was your individual career path in terms of education/training, entry-level job, or other significant opportunity?

When I got out of high school, I was going to go into the military but my mother really didn't want me to. She told me to get a job and see how it worked out. I landed a job in a chemical plant and stayed there for 27 years.

The first 19 years, I worked on the chemical production side. The last seven, at that company, I was on the boiler and stationary engineer side.

That was in Ohio, which is the toughest state in the United States to get a boiler operator license. They have stringent requirements and a very hard test.

I switched to being a stationary engineer because I'm the kind of guy who likes to learn as much as he can. I'd learned the chemical side of the plant. When the stationary engineer job in the plant came open, I decided to go for it because it was something I hadn't done. It was the only part of the plant I hadn't learned. The best part was they were willing to let me get the experience I needed to take Ohio's licensing test for stationary engineers. I studied like crazy and when I sat for the test, I scored an 86 the first time. Later, I earned certification from the National Association of Stationary Operating Engineers.

2. What are the most important skills and/or qualities for someone in your profession?

You have to be smart. You have to know what you're doing. It's not the kind of business where mistakes are easily corrected. If you make a keystroke wrong on a computer, you can backspace. If you do something wrong as a stationary engineer, you may cause the whole plant to shut down. My plant makes $27,000 an hour in profit. So if something goes wrong in my boiler house and the plant is shut down for an hour or two, I've cost them a whole lot of my wage. There's a huge amount of responsibility.

3. What do you wish you had known going into this profession?

You're going to work a lot of rotten hours and you're going to work in a dangerous environment at times. When you have a boiler that's angry, it can be intense. It's not to be taken lightly. But I was glad that I got into it. It's a good solid living and has provided a very good life for me.

4. Are there many job opportunities in your profession? In what specific areas?

From what I've seen, statistically, my industry is going to grow by maybe 5-10 percent. Most of the jobs will open because of people retiring or otherwise leaving the field.

5. How do you see your profession changing in the next five years, what role will technology play in those changes, and what skills will be required?

There will always be a need for stationary engineers and boiler operators. If you get into the industry, you will pretty much always be able to have a job. The industry is changing because of fracking and everyone switching from coal- and oil-fired boilers to natural gas. That has changed the balance of jobs in the business.

6. What do you enjoy most about your job? What do you enjoy least about your job?

I'm not the kind of guy who likes to pat himself on the back but when you're a stationary engineer, you are pretty much revered. It doesn't end with the boiler plant here, it begins with the boiler plant. So if the boiler plant says do this, others say, well, that's what you do. I like that. I don't like the hours. When you come off after 12 hours and your boiler has had an attitude for the past six hours, you come off stressed. That's the bad part.

7. Can you suggest a valuable "try this" for students considering a career in your profession?

You could take a short course at a trade school. They're like three weeks long. It won't give you all the hours you need for a test like Ohio's but it would help. Some places have co-op positions that could give you some experience. Or you could take an entry-level job, like coal-unloading, where you'd work around boilers and you could maybe see about becoming an apprentice stationary engineer. You definitely won't come out of high school doing what I do now.

SELECTED SCHOOLS

Many technical and community colleges offer programs in or related to the work of a stationary engineer. Commercial trade schools are also an option. Students are advised to consult with their school guidance counselor or research area post-secondary schools to find the right program.

MORE INFORMATION

International Union of Operating Engineers
Director of Research and Education
1125 17th Street, NW
Washington, DC 20036
202.429.9100
www.iuoe.org

National Association of Power Engineers, Inc.
1 Springfield Street
Chicopee, MA 01013
413.592.6273
www.powerengineers.com

National Association of Stationary Operating Engineers
39 W. Alexis Rd. Ste. 101
Toledo, OH 43612
419.708.2258
www.nasoe.org

Patrick Cooper/Editor

Telecommunications Equipment Installer/Repairer

Snapshot

Career Cluster: Electronics; Maintenance & Repair; Technology

Interests: Traveling, working with your hands, solving problems, working with tools

Earnings (Yearly Average): $54,030

Employment & Outlook: Slower than Average Growth Expected

OVERVIEW

Sphere of Work

Telecommunications equipment installers and repairers, also known as telecom technicians, set up, maintain, service, and repair networks and devices that carry communication signals, including Internet connections. These signals are carried over telephone lines and fiber-optic cable. Telecom technicians perform their work in homes, commercial facilities, and office buildings. Technicians

may take devices that require significant work to a repair shop. Technicians also perform installations of telecom equipment.

Work Environment

Work environments for telecommunications equipment installers and repairers vary for each job. Offices, commercial facilities, and homes predominate. Depending on the job, workers may have to climb ladders or use trucks with lift buckets to reach telephone wires and rooftops. Technicians also work in communication centers, where telephone calls are routed. Job locations and repair shops are usually well lit. Field workers spend some time traveling to and from clients. Working high off the ground in utility trucks can be dangerous, and safety guidelines should be followed. Telecom technicians also work with electrical components that can pose safety risks.

Profile

Working Conditions: Work Indoors
Physical Strength: Light to Medium Work
Education Needs: On-The-Job Training, Technical/Community College
Licensure/Certification: Usually Not Required
Physical Abilities Not Required: No Heavy Labor
Opportunities For Experience: Military Service
Holland Interest Score*: REI, RES

* See Appendix A

Occupation Interest

Each day of work can present a telecommunications equipment installer and repairer with a different problem, so technicians must be able to apply skills and knowledge in varying circumstances. The profession typically attracts individuals who enjoy solving problems and working with their hands outside of an office environment. A telecommunications equipment installer and repairer must be willing to stay abreast of new technologies, tools, and repair methods. Driving to and from clients is often required, so a repairer should enjoy traveling.

A Day in the Life—Duties and Responsibilities

Telecom technicians repair and maintain telecommunications systems that keep the public connected. These systems include telephone networks, switchboards, computer equipment, and radios. Field repairers will travel to a client's location, which may be a home, office, or commercial building, to perform maintenance and repairs. Some technicians will work at the central offices of telephone companies and Internet service providers.

When a client calls for a repair, a technician will travel to the location with tools and other necessary equipment. In order to help diagnose the problem, the worker will examine telephone wires both inside and outside the house, which may require him or her to inspect lines attached to telephone poles. For Internet malfunctions, the worker will test the connection using basic troubleshooting techniques and electronic devices. Technicians who work with radio technology service both stationary equipment on transmission towers and mobile equipment in vehicles. If the worker decides that a repair cannot be performed on location, he or she will either call in more technicians or bring the equipment back to a repair shop for service.

Technicians who work at central offices maintain and service telephone exchanges. Exchanges are systems that connect telephone calls. Workers test connections on exchanges to ensure that the communication links are functioning correctly. These exchanges can sometimes feature complex digital components.

Duties and Responsibilities

- Installing, rearranging, replacing and removing the complex switching and dialing equipment used in central offices
- Testing, repairing and maintaining all types of local and toll switching equipment that automatically connects lines when customers dial numbers
- Locating problems by using testboards or by entering instructions into a computer terminal

OCCUPATION SPECIALTIES

Central Office Technicians

Central Office Technicians install, test, analyze defects and repair telecommunications circuits and equipment in central telecom company offices.

PBX Installers and Repairers

PBX Installers and Repairers install, analyze and repair defects in telecommunications switchboards, network systems, and Voice Over Internet applications.

Station Installers and Repairers

Station Installers and Repairers—also known as home installers and repairers—set up and repair telecommunications equipment in customers' homes and businesses. For example, they set up modems to install telephone, Internet, or cable television services.

WORK ENVIRONMENT

Physical Environment

Telecom technicians typically work in repair shops and on site at the offices of telecom/telephone companies. Field repairers work at a variety of locations, including offices and homes, in all weather. Their duties can involve working off the ground on telephone poles, ladders, and lift trucks.

Human Environment

Telecommunications equipment installers and repairers collaborate with supervisors and colleagues. They also work closely with clients and often work to make sure clients have a clear understanding of how their telecommunications systems work.

Relevant Skills and Abilities

Communication Skills
- Speaking effectively

Interpersonal/Social Skills
- Being able to work independently
- Cooperating with others
- Working as a member of a team

Organization & Management Skills
- Making decisions
- Paying attention to and handling details
- Performing duties that change frequently

Research & Planning Skills
- Developing evaluation strategies
- Using logical reasoning

Technical Skills
- Performing technical work
- Working with machines, tools or other objects

Technological Environment

Telecom technicians work with a wide range of tools and technologies. Technicians use basic hand tools, including screwdrivers and wire cutters, as well as specialized equipment such as spectrum analyzers and polarity probes. Telecommunications equipment includes electronic components and color-coded wires. Those who work in the field also use vans, ladders, and lift trucks.

EDUCATION, TRAINING, AND ADVANCEMENT

High School/Secondary

Employers typically require applicants to have a high school diploma or an equivalent certificate. Any high school courses involving electronics, computers, or mathematics will give future telecommunications equipment repairers a good understanding of industry fundamentals.

Suggested High School Subjects

- Applied Communication
- Applied Math
- Blueprint Reading
- Computer Science
- Electricity & Electronics
- English
- Shop Math
- Shop Mechanics
- Welding

Famous First

The first radio telephone service for commercial use was launched in 1920, between Los Angeles and Santa Catalina Island, California. A radio link connected the two locations via telephone lines. The service ran for three years, when it was replaced by a cable in order to provide privacy to users. Operators of the original service pictured.

College/Postsecondary

Most employers require applicants to have completed relevant postsecondary training.
Technicians who work at central offices are usually required to have a degree in a relevant field. Vocational, technical, and trade schools offer postsecondary training programs. Training programs in electronics repair, computer science, and communication technology will greatly benefit an aspiring telecommunications equipment repairer. Typically, these associate's degree programs last two years, but an individual interested in more advanced work in the telecommunications industry may want to consider a four-year program.

Related College Majors

- Computer Engineering Technology
- lectrical, Electronic & Communications Engineering Technology
- Instrument Calibration & Repair

- Instrumentation Technology

Adult Job Seekers

Anyone interested in a profession in the telecommunication industry should build up a strong background of knowledge and skills. The best way to do this is through a formal associate's degree training program at a technical, trade, or vocational school. For individuals with no experience in the trade, a formal training program is essential. Researching reputable schools is important before enrolling. Being a telecommunications equipment installer and repairer covers a wide range of knowledge and skills, so an individual should approach his or her training with a broad perspective. Since telecommunications technology is always developing, a technician needs to be willing to keep learning throughout his or her career.

Professional Certification and Licensure

Commonly, employers provide telecommunications equipment installers and repairers with on-the-job training. More experienced workers or supervisors train new hires. Training can last anywhere from a few weeks to several months. Some employers will send new hires and experienced workers alike to training sessions to learn about new technologies, products, and repair methods. Equipment manufacturers will sometimes send a representative to companies to train employees on new products.

Certification is required for individuals interested in performing more complex tasks and for specialization in a specific area of telecommunications. Employers dictate which employees need certification. Organizations like the Telecommunications Industry Association (TIA) offer certification programs for repairers in various areas, including telecommunications infrastructure standards and land mobile communications standards. Manufacturers also offer certification on equipment they produce.

Individuals interested in advancing their career should seek out certification. The more certifications an employee has, the greater his or her chance of higher pay and promotions.

Additional Requirements

Telecommunications equipment installers and repairers must possess great dexterity to handle the wires, cables, tools, and electronic components used in the industry. Since most telecommunication wires are color coded, workers must also be able to distinguish colors well. Those who plan to work in the field should be in good physical shape and able to endure climbing, kneeling, and long periods on their feet. Repairers should also have good communication skills in order to collaborate with colleagues, supervisors, and clients.

EARNINGS AND ADVANCEMENT

Earnings of telecommunications equipment repairers vary by employer and location. Median annual earnings of telecommunications equipment installers and repairers were $54,030 in 2013. The lowest ten percent earned less than $30,070, and the highest ten percent earned more than $75,690.

Union contracts determine paid holidays and vacations based on seniority. Other benefits include paid sick leave; group life, medical, and dental insurance; vision care; accidental benefits; educational benefits; retirement and disability pensions; a savings plan and an employee stock ownership plan.

Metropolitan Areas with the Highest
Employment Level in this Occupation

Metropolitan area	Employment [1]	Employment per thousand jobs	Hourly mean wage
New York-White Plains-Wayne, NY-NJ	7,930	1.51	$32.62
Chicago-Joliet-Naperville, IL	7,610	2.06	$26.62
Los Angeles-Long Beach-Glendale, CA	7,300	1.84	$26.69
Atlanta-Sandy Springs-Marietta, GA	6,880	2.98	$25.17
Dallas-Plano-Irving, TX	5,750	2.68	$23.49
Houston-Sugar Land-Baytown, TX	3,470	1.26	$23.23
Tampa-St. Petersburg-Clearwater, FL	3,130	2.72	$21.50
Fort Lauderdale-Pompano Beach-Deerfield Beach, FL	2,900	3.96	$26.67
Phoenix-Mesa-Glendale, AZ	2,870	1.61	$27.87
Washington-Arlington-Alexandria, DC-VA-MD-WV	2,800	1.18	$29.89

[1]Does not include self-employ ed. Source: Bureau of Labor Statistics

EMPLOYMENT AND OUTLOOK

Telecommunications equipment installers and repairers held about 217,000 jobs in 2012. Employment is expected to grow slower than the average for all occupations through the year 2022, which means employment is projected to increase 1 percent to 7 percent. Although the need for installation work will grow as companies seek to upgrade their telecommunications networks, there will be a declining need for maintenance work because of increasingly reliable equipment. Most job openings will occur as workers transfer to other occupations or leave the labor force.

Employment Trend, Projected 2012–22

Total, All Occupations: 11%

Installation, Maintenance, and Repair Occupations (All): 10%

Telecommunications Equipment Installers and Repairers: 4%

Note: "All Occupations" includes all occupations in the U.S. Economy. Source: U.S. Bureau of Labor Statistics, Employment Projections Program

Related Occupations
- Biomedical Equipment Technician
- Computer Service Technician
- Electrical Line Installer & Repairer
- Electrician
- Electronic Equipment Repairer
- Office Machine Repairer
- Telecommunications Line Installer/Repairer
- Telephone Installer & Repairer
- Television & Radio Repairer

Related Occupations
- Communications Equipment Repairer
- Communications Manager

Conversation With . . .
ROBERT H. PICKNELL, CETma

Senior Technician
Advanced Communications and Electronics, Inc.
Albuquerque, NM
In the industry, 20 years

1. What was your individual career path in terms of education/training, entry-level job, or other significant opportunity?

I've always had a fascination with electricity and electronics, but it wasn't until later in life that I had the discipline to educate myself and to see entry-level jobs as opportunities for advancement.

I started out as a volunteer at an easy listening and inspirational radio station in the Midwest and worked as an on-air announcer for a few hours every week. When the General Manager/Engineer found out I was interested in electronics, I started working with him. Upon his departure, I became the station's first paid, part-time engineer.

That's when I started taking night classes for computer networking. I moved to another company and became an engineer for seven radio stations. That company held twice-annual conferences for their engineers, where I learned a lot by being around all those years of experience, as well as about the importance of networking. Having the ability to call other people for help and ideas was invaluable.

This eventually led me to the two-way radio and microwave communications field of electronics. For 11 years, I have worked for a company that handles about half of the 911 dispatch centers around the state of New Mexico. This job affords me the opportunity to work in various aspects of the electronics industry, including telecommunications, two-way radios, and microwave communications.

2. What are the most important skills and/or qualities for someone in your profession?

The ability to articulate, both verbally and in writing, what you need to say; the desire to want to learn more about your field; and the desire to work. When times are tough for a company, it's difficult to justify keeping an employee whose only apparent desire is to be paid top-dollar to play solitaire on a computer.

3. What do you wish you had known going into this profession?

That mentors are critical. People in this vast field of electronics are willing to be mentors to those willing to learn, and each mentor usually has one or two areas that they are strong in. If possible, find several.

That education is not static. You must be willing to continue your education throughout your entire life.

That education comes in many forms. Classroom education is good to build a foundation and to learn the fundamentals. But there's also on-the-job training; trade publications for keeping abreast of changes; manufacturer websites and training programs that help you stay current and relevant; and trade certifications and memberships.

4. Are there many job opportunities in your profession, in what specific areas?

With cell phones, home computers, and world communications, the electronics industry has exploded and the need for technicians has never been greater than it is today.

The electronics industry covers nearly all aspects of life and fields of interest. A few areas that are growing rapidly include telecommunications—cell phones, satellites, DSL, cable, broadcast communications, computers; automotive, and power—wind, solar, nuclear and gas and oil.

5. How do you see your profession changing in the next five years, what role will technology play in those changes, and what skills will be required?

If recent history is any measure of things to come, we can expect this industry to expand exponentially for the foreseeable future. A firm understanding of the fundamentals, and in this case of electricity and electronics, will be required if you wish to do more than just replace modules using an instruction manual.

6. What do you enjoy most about your job? What do you enjoy least about your job?

Variety is, without a doubt, the one thing I most like about my job. I seldom know exactly what I will be doing from day-to-day. I have to be able to "think outside the box" on a consistent basis.

I least enjoy dealing with customer support. It can be extremely frustrating, but I do have to say it has helped me tremendously to learn to deal with different types of people and attitudes.

7. Can you suggest a valuable "try this" for students considering a career in your profession?

Do an internship. When I was a teenager and wanted to be a truck driver, my parents got me to meet with a truck driver and his "rig." I spoke with him regarding his carrier choice, asked lots of questions, and got to ride in his truck. It didn't take me long to realize that while driving a truck across the county may be a great job for others, it was not for me. Take the time to research a career; it's much easier to change direction at 20 than it is at 40.

SELECTED SCHOOLS

Many technical and community colleges offer programs in telecommunications technology. Commercial trade schools are also an option. Students are advised to consult with their school guidance counselor or research area post-secondary schools to find the right program.

MORE INFORMATION

Communication Workers of America
501 3rd Street NW
Washington, DC 20001
202.434.1100
www.cwa-union.org

National Coalition for Telecommunications Education and Learning
www.nactel.org

Telecommunications Industry Association
2500 Wilson Boulevard, Suite 300
Arlington, VA 22201
703.907.7700
www.tiaonline.org

United States Telecom Association
607 14th Street, NW, Suite 400
Washington, DC 20005-2164
202.326.7300
www.usta.org

Patrick Cooper/Editor

Vending Machine Repairer

Snapshot

Career Cluster: Maintenance & Repair

Interests: Electrical repair, machine maintenance, mechanics, electronics

Earnings (Yearly Average): $32,840

Employment & Outlook: Average Growth Expected

OVERVIEW

Sphere of Work

Vending machine repairers, also known as vending machine technicians, operators, or route drivers, perform a broad range of maintenance and repairs on a variety of vending machines, including soda, coffee, and snack machines. Technicians also often stock the vending machine, collect the money from inside, and change labels as necessary. Knowledge of mechanics and electronics is required. Vending machine repairers determine if a machine needs to be removed for

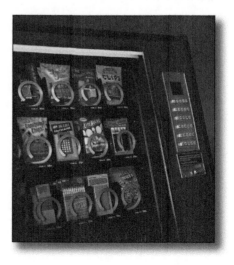

major repairs or replaced. Many repairers will transport the machines themselves.

Work Environment

Vending machine repairers work in a wide range of environments, commonly indoors. They work anywhere vending machines are found, including office buildings, arcades, laundromats, schools, shopping malls, and more. They also spend a lot of time on the road, driving to the various places where their company's vending machines are located. Major repairs are done at the vending company's location, where a repair workshop is typically found. Vending machines are also often stored in these locations.

Profile

Working Conditions: Work Indoors
Physical Strength: Medium Work
Education Needs: No High School Diploma, On-The-Job Training, High School Diploma or G.E.D.
Licensure/Certification: Required
Physical Abilities Not Required: N/A
Opportunities For Experience: Apprenticeship, Part-Time Work
Holland Interest Score*: RCE

* See Appendix A

Occupation Interest

Being a vending machine repairer means having to frequently drive to various locations and work on a range of machines. This profession attracts individuals who have a background in machinery, electronics, and mechanical repair. Vending machine repairers are great problem solvers who are able to assess and repair a malfunction in a short period of time. They should enjoy traveling and working with their hands.

A Day in the Life—Duties and Responsibilities

Vending machine repairers have a scheduled route that they follow. Commonly, vending machine companies assign repairers to a specific region where they are in charge of restocking, collecting money, and performing preventative maintenance and repairs. When a repairer arrives at a location, he or she examines the machine to ensure everything is working properly. This includes the mechanical and electrical components.

When checking drink-dispensing machines, such as coffee machines, repairers make sure the electrical, heating, and refrigeration components are working correctly. They go over all of the components that create the different coffee drinks and make sure they are mixing the drinks properly. For snack-vending machines, repairers ensure the keypad and motorized dispensers are working correctly and accurately. Workers must clean and lubricate inner components as well as clean the outside of the machine. They must also confirm all local health and sanitation regulations are being met.

If a repair needs to be made, the worker will assess if he or she is able to take care of it on-site or if the machine needs to be taken to the vending company's repair shop for more extensive repair work. Repairers use a variety of handheld tools to inspect and fix vending machines on-site. Some workers also stock the vending machines and make sure the items are labeled correctly. Repairers must fill out relevant paperwork concerning repair costs, inventory, and money collected.

Duties and Responsibilities

- Preparing machines for installation following manufacturer's instructions
- Testing new machines to make sure that everything works
- Making electrical and water connections necessary to install machines
- Maintaining machines by cleaning and adjusting mechanical parts
- Inspecting and repairing broken machines
- Filling out reports, preparing cost estimates and ordering parts
- Stocking machines with merchandise

WORK ENVIRONMENT

Physical Environment

Vending machine repairers work wherever vending machines are found. This includes commercial buildings, schools, hospitals, and shopping malls. They also work in vending-machine repair shops, commonly located at their company's headquarters. A lot of time is spent in vehicles traveling to different locations.

Relevant Skills and Abilities

Organization & Management Skills
- Paying attention to and handling details

Technical Skills
- Performing technical work
- Working with machines, tools or other objects
- Working with your hands

Human Environment

Vending-machine repair requires strong communication skills. Workers communicate with clients, other repairers, and their superiors to ensure work is done correctly. While on a job, a repairer usually works alone but is in frequent contact with company headquarters.

Technological Environment

Repairers utilize a wide range of handheld tools, including circuit testers, wrenches, multimeters, and pliers. At the repair shop, they can use heavier tools, such as drills, saws, and grinders. Electronic components such as circuit boards and magnetic card readers are also handled.

EDUCATION, TRAINING, AND ADVANCEMENT

High School/Secondary

Most employers require a worker to have a high school diploma or the equivalent, although some do not. Regardless of education, a repairer should have a strong background in mechanics. Some high schools may offer courses in subjects that are beneficial for potential repairers, such as mechanics, machine repair, refrigeration, and electricity.

Suggested High School Subjects
- Appliance Repair Technology
- Applied Math
- Electricity & Electronics
- English
- Heating/Air Cond./Refrigeration
- Physical Science
- Shop Math
- Shop Mechanics

Famous First

The first vending machine to dispense food from bulk was the Automatic Clerk, invented in 1897 by T. S. Wheatcraft of Rush, Pennsylvania. The machine, pictured, which dispensed hot peanuts in bags, was housed in a wooden cabinet six feet high. Inside were a heater and a weighing device as well as mechanical equipment for delivering the peanuts.

College/Postsecondary

Most vending companies do not require an applicant to have a college degree. However, there are numerous courses and programs offered by community, vocational, and technical colleges that can help an individual gain the knowledge and skills needed for vending-machine repair. Contemporary vending-machine technology utilizes numerous electrical components, such as scrolling messages, multilevel pricing, and inventory tracking. To repair these diverse components, a worker must have a strong knowledge of electrical repair. Some community colleges offer beneficial programs, such as associate of applied science degrees in electrical construction.

There are more than fifty electrician-training schools in the United States that can teach an individual the skills needed to become a vending machine repairer. These schools typically offer one- to two-year programs that cover the fundamentals of electrical repair through formal classroom instruction and hands-on practice. Such programs cover the fundamentals of electrical schematics, electrical safety, and tools. Once an individual completes a program, he or she is certified to become an apprentice electrician. Vending companies are more likely to employ someone who has completed such a program, and some employers even look to these electrician-training schools for potential hires.

Adult Job Seekers

Starting off in the vending-machine repair profession requires a lot of commitment to training. Those with no background in electrical or refrigeration repair should consider the amount of training they will need to be successful in the position. Attending an electrician school or a technical school is a great way to gain the knowledge and skills needed. Job-placement programs at these schools will help an individual transition to the profession. These schools are also a good way to make connections and do some networking with other professionals in the industry.

Professional Certification and Licensure

Many vending machine repairers are required to become certified electricians. Commonly, the electrician schools provide certification at the completion of programs. Experienced electricians can get certified through the National Automatic Merchandising Association (NAMA), which offers a NAMA Certified Executive (NCE) certification to repairers who have a minimum of eight years experience. NAMA also offers vending-technician certification. To gain NAMA credentials, an individual must pass an exam and meet certain requirements.

Additional Requirements

Because vending-machine technology is always changing, a repairer needs to have a commitment to learning. The only way to advance in the profession is to be willing to study developing technologies. Because they interact with clients, supervisors, and other workers, a repairer needs to be personable and open to collaboration. Great attention to detail is necessary for success.

Fun Fact

The first reference to a vending machine is from the first century, when a coin inserted in a slot produced a measured amount of holy water.
Source: http://www.vendingmachinesunlimited.com/blog/10-fun-facts-vending-machines/

EARNINGS AND ADVANCEMENT

Earnings depend on the size and geographic location of the employer, the type of equipment repaired and the employee's level of training and skill. Most vending machine repairers are paid hourly wages. Median annual earnings of vending machine repairers were $32,840 in 2013.

Vending machine repairers may receive paid vacations, holidays, and sick days; life and health insurance; and retirement benefits. These are usually paid by the employer.

EMPLOYMENT AND OUTLOOK

Nationally, there were about 35,000 vending machine repairers employed in 2012. Employment is expected to about as fast as the average for all occupations through the year 2022, which means employment is projected to increase 7 percent to 12 percent. Workers with some background in electronics should have the best job prospects. Most job openings will occur to replace workers who transfer to other occupations or retire.

Related Occupations
- Electronic Equipment Repairer
- Home Appliance Repairer
- Locksmith

Conversation With . . . DARYL MOWRER

Vendnet, Parts and Service Manager, Des Moines, IA
In the vending repair field, 20 years

1. What was your individual career path in terms of education/training, entry-level job, or other significant opportunity?

I grew up working on farm equipment, took electronics classes in high school, and worked in several machine shops making and repairing all kinds of stuff out of steel. When I was 23, I went into the Peace Corps for two years and worked in The Caribbean Agricultural Research and Development Institute on St. Kitts. One of the main things I did was build peanut thrashers that two people could pick up and carry around a field. Before that, the old ladies and kids would pull down the peanuts and pick them up in the field, unless the monkeys got to them first. I went on to work at Garst Seed Company, where I worked integrated electronics into a combine so you could harvest two rows of corn, 17 feet long, and the combine could tell you what it weighed and how many bushels an acre that particular variety of corn would yield.

During that time I got an associate's degree in electronics. I also lost my brother, who was killed in a tractor-train wreck. He was a farmer and I did a lot of work with him on the family farm. I decided to take a different path and came here. I started out fixing electronics components such as control boards and dollar bill validators, then moved to the service department. I moved around in the company a couple of times, and now manage the parts and service department.

Our company builds everything from coffee machines to frozen food machines. We also build intelligent dispensing machines, primarily hooked up through the Internet, some that are used in schools to vend lunch meals so they can offer discounts and such to kids who aren't as well off as others. Usually they have card readers that read the kid's lunch card. We use the same type of machine for EMS and fire departments with ambulances so they can store drugs and supplies. These machines can require up to three different security steps for entry, so the machine knows who is getting the drugs, their PIN number, and, if controlled substances are involved, there may be fingerprint readers. We also work with companies like Google, Yahoo and Apple, dispensing maintenance products like computer keyboards and mice. This way, they don't have somebody manning the maintenance department for routine items. One of our newer products is a machine for medical scrubs. Hospital workers use an employee ID to access scrubs and get charged if they're not returned.

2. What are the most important skills and/or qualities for someone in your profession?

You need to have good mechanical aptitude and basic computer skills. If you can read electrical diagrams or schematics, that's a plus. You need to be able to stay calm; sometimes our customers get pretty anxious because they need their machines to make a living and they need them up and running.

3. What do you wish you had known going into this profession?

I wish I'd known how challenging it is, because I would have done it sooner. I love a challenge, and I learn something new every day. Also, I should mention that I lost my left leg in a bad motorcycle accident many years ago, and have a prosthetic leg and hydraulic knee. Disabilities aren't going to keep you out of this field. We do things like put Braille on keypads, for instance, so blind people are able to do this work.

4. Are there many job opportunities in your profession? In what specific areas?

There are only a handful of full-time vending repair companies around the country, and those are in cities. But our company is on the leading edge of technology for vending machines, and with the diverse uses we've developed there's going to be more and more need for guys to service the machines. Think about the scrubs machine outside a surgery area: if that machine goes down, it needs to be fixed right away.

5. How do you see your profession changing in the next five years, what role will technology play in those changes, and what skills will be required?

Technology is changing dramatically and rapidly. Instead of driving around with a big truck to look at inventory, you can look at a computer and know exactly what was sold. So there are opportunities for analysts and computer geeks as well. We have engineering interns to give them a taste of what the engineering is about in this industry.

6. What do you enjoy most about your job? What do you enjoy least about your job?

I enjoy the challenge, and the diversity of things I get to do. I work with a really good group of people. I also enjoy helping people who are having problems get them fixed. I least enjoy the angry customers over the phone, but I try to turn that into an opportunity to help.

7. Can you suggest a valuable "try this" for students considering a career in your profession?

The National Automatic Merchandising Association has a show or two every year, and if you're really interested you could go see all the new technology and different products that go along with vending. It's pretty cool stuff.

SELECTED SCHOOLS

A college degree is not necessary to work as a vending machine repairer. For those interested in the field, however, taking courses at a technical or community college or a commercial trade school may provide an advantage. Students are advised to consult with their school guidance counselor or research area post-secondary schools to find the right program.

MORE INFORMATION

American Amusement Machine Association
450 E. Higgins Road, Suite 201
Elk Grove, IL 60007
847.290.9088
www.coin-op.org

National Automatic Merchandising Association
20 North Wacker Drive, Suite 3500
Chicago, IL 60606-3102
312.346.0370
www.vending.org

Patrick Cooper/Editor

What Are Your Career Interests?

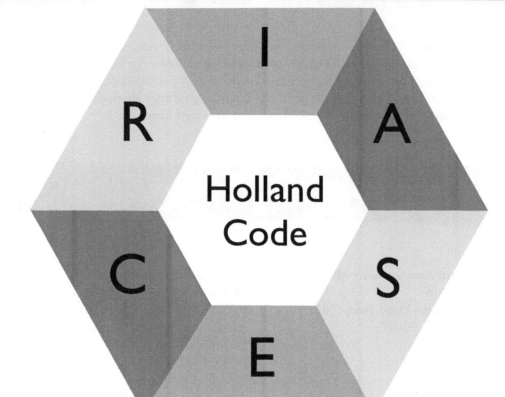

This is based on Dr. John Holland's theory that people and work environments can be loosely classified into six different groups. Each of the letters above corresponds to one of the six groups described in the following pages.

Different people's personalities may find different environments more to their liking. While you may have some interests in and similarities to several of the six groups, you may be attracted primarily to two or three of the areas. These two or three letters are your "Holland Code." For example, with a code of "RES" you would most resemble the Realistic type, somewhat less resemble the Enterprising type, and resemble the Social type even less. The types that are not in your code are the types you resemble least of all.

Most people, and most jobs, are best represented by some combination of two or three of the Holland interest areas. In addition, most people are most satisfied if there is some degree of fit between their personality and their work environment.

The rest of the pages in this booklet further explain each type and provide some examples of career possibilities, areas of study at MU, and co-curricular activities for each code. To take a more in-depth look at your Holland Code, take a self-assessment such as the SDS, Discover, or a card sort at the MU Career Center with a Career Specialist.

Realistic *(Doers)*

People who have athletic ability, prefer to work with objects, machines, tools, plants or animals, or to be outdoors.

Are you?		Can you?	Like to?
practical	independent	fix electrical things	tinker with machines/vehicles
straightforward/frank	ambitious	solve electrical problems	work outdoors
mechanically inclined	systematic	pitch a tent	be physically active
stable		play a sport	use your hands
concrete		read a blueprint	build things
reserved		plant a garden	tend/train animals
self-controlled		operate tools and machine	work on electronic equipment

Career Possibilities
(Holland Code):

Air Traffic Controller (SER)	Dental Technician (REI)	Laboratory Technician (RIE)	Property Manager (ESR)
Archaeologist (IRE)	Farm Manager (ESR)	Landscape Architect (AIR)	Recreation Manager (SER)
Athletic Trainer (SRE)	Fish and Game Warden (RES)	Mechanical Engineer (RIS)	Service Manager (ERS)
Cartographer (IRE)	Floral Designer (RAE)	Optician (REI)	Software Technician (RCI)
Commercial Airline Pilot (RIE)	Forester (RIS)	Petroleum Geologist (RIE)	Ultrasound Technologist (RSI)
Commercial Drafter (IRE)	Geodetic Surveyor (IRE)	Police Officer (SER)	Vocational Rehabilitation
Corrections Officer (SER)	Industrial Arts Teacher (IER)	Practical Nurse (SER)	Consultant (ESR)

Investigative *(Thinkers)*

People who like to observe, learn, investigate, analyze, evaluate, or solve problems.

Are you?		**Can you?**	Like to?
inquisitive	intellectually self-confident	think abstractly	explore a variety of ideas
analytical	Independent	solve math problems	work independently
scientific	logical	understand scientific theories	perform lab experiments
observant/precise	complex	do complex calculations	deal with abstractions
scholarly	Curious	use a microscope or computer	do research
cautious		interpret formulas	be challenged

Career Possibilities
(Holland Code):

Actuary (ISE)	Chemical Engineer (IRE)	Geologist (IRE)	Physician, General Practice (ISE)
Agronomist (IRS)	Chemist (IRE)	Horticulturist (IRS)	Psychologist (IES)
Anesthesiologist (IRS)	Computer Systems Analyst (IER)	Mathematician (IER)	Research Analyst (IRC)
Anthropologist (IRE)	Dentist (ISR)	Medical Technologist (ISA)	Statistician (IRE)
Archaeologist (IRE)	Ecologist (IRE)	Meteorologist (IRS)	Surgeon (IRA)
Biochemist (IRS)	Economist (IAS)	Nurse Practitioner (ISA)	Technical Writer (IRS)
Biologist (ISR)	Electrical Engineer (IRE)	Pharmacist (IES)	Veterinarian (IRS)

Artistic *(Creators)*

People who have artistic, innovating, or intuitional abilities and like to work in unstructured situations using their imagination and creativity.

Are you?	original	Can you?	Like to?
creative	introspective	sketch, draw, paint	attend concerts, theatre, art
imaginative	impulsive	play a musical instrument	exhibits
innovative	sensitive	write stories, poetry, music	read fiction, plays, and poetry
unconventional	courageous	sing, act, dance	work on crafts
emotional	complicated	design fashions or interiors	take photography
independent	idealistic		express yourself creatively
Expressive	nonconforming		deal with ambiguous ideas

Career Possibilities
(Holland Code):

Actor (AES)	Copy Writer (ASI)	Interior Designer (AES)	Medical Illustrator (AIE)
Advertising Art Director (AES)	Dance Instructor (AER)	Intelligence Research Specialist	Museum Curator (AES)
Advertising Manager (ASE)	Drama Coach (ASE)	(AEI)	Music Teacher (ASI)
Architect (AIR)	English Teacher (ASE)	Journalist/Reporter (ASE)	Photographer (AES)
Art Teacher (ASE)	Entertainer/Performer (AES)	Landscape Architect (AIR)	Writer (ASI)
Artist (ASI)	Fashion Illustrator (ASR)	Librarian (SAI)	Graphic Designer (AES)

Social *(Helpers)*

People who like to work with people to enlighten, inform, help, train, or cure them, or are skilled with words.

Are you?	cooperative	Can you?	Like to?
friendly	generous	teach/train others	work in groups
helpful	responsible	express yourself clearly	help people with problems
idealistic	forgiving	lead a group discussion	do volunteer work
insightful	patient	mediate disputes	work with young people
outgoing	kind	plan and supervise an activity	serve others
understanding		cooperate well with others	

Career Possibilities
(Holland Code):

City Manager (SEC)	Historian (SEI)	Park Naturalist (SEI)	Teacher (SAE)
Clinical Dietitian (SIE)	Hospital Administrator (SER)	Physical Therapist (SIE)	Social Worker (SEA)
College/University Faculty (SEI)	Psychologist (SEI)	Police Officer (SER)	Speech Pathologist (SAI)
Community Org. Director	Insurance Claims Examiner	Probation and Parole Officer	Vocational-Rehab. Counselor
(SEA)	(SIE)	(SEC)	(SEC)
Consumer Affairs Director	Librarian (SAI)	Real Estate Appraiser (SCE)	Volunteer Services Director
(SER)Counselor/Therapist	Medical Assistant (SCR)	Recreation Director (SER)	(SEC)
(SAE)	Minister/Priest/Rabbi (SAI)	Registered Nurse (SIA)	
	Paralegal (SCE)		

Enterprising *(Persuaders)*

People who like to work with people, influencing, persuading, leading or managing for organizational goals or economic gain.

Are you?
self-confident
assertive
persuasive
energetic
adventurous
popular

ambitious
agreeable
talkative
extroverted
spontaneous
optimistic

Can you?
initiate projects
convince people to do things
  your way
sell things
give talks or speeches
organize activities
lead a group
persuade others

Like to?
make decisions
be elected to office
start your own business
campaign politically
meet important people
have power or status

Career Possibilities
(Holland Code):

Advertising Executive (ESA)
Advertising Sales Rep (ESR)
Banker/Financial Planner (ESR)
Branch Manager (ESA)
Business Manager (ESC)
Buyer (ESA)
Chamber of Commerce Exec
  (ESA)

Credit Analyst (EAS)
Customer Service Manager
  (ESA)
Education & Training Manager
  (EIS)
Emergency Medical Technician
  (ESI)
Entrepreneur (ESA)

Foreign Service Officer (ESA)
Funeral Director (ESR)
Insurance Manager (ESC)
Interpreter (ESA)
Lawyer/Attorney (ESA)
Lobbyist (ESA)
Office Manager (ESR)
Personnel Recruiter (ESR)

Politician (ESA)
Public Relations Rep (EAS)
Retail Store Manager (ESR)
Sales Manager (ESA)
Sales Representative (ERS)
Social Service Director (ESA)
Stockbroker (ESI)
Tax Accountant (ECS)

Conventional *(Organizers)*

People who like to work with data, have clerical or numerical ability, carry out tasks in detail, or follow through on others' instructions.

Are you?
well-organized
accurate
numerically inclined
methodical
conscientious
efficient
conforming

practical
thrifty
systematic
structured
polite
ambitious
obedient
persistent

Can you?
work well within a system
do a lot of paper work in a short
  time
keep accurate records
use a computer terminal
write effective business letters

Like to?
follow clearly defined
  procedures
use data processing equipment
work with numbers
type or take shorthand
be responsible for details
collect or organize things

Career Possibilities
(Holland Code):

Abstractor (CSI)
Accountant (CSE)
Administrative Assistant (ESC)
Budget Analyst (CER)
Business Manager (ESC)
Business Programmer (CRI)
Business Teacher (CSE)
Catalog Librarian (CSE)

Claims Adjuster (SEC)
Computer Operator (CSR)
Congressional-District Aide (CES)
Cost Accountant (CES)
Court Reporter (CSE)
Credit Manager (ESC)
Customs Inspector (CEI)
Editorial Assistant (CSI)

Elementary School Teacher
  (SEC)
Financial Analyst (CSI)
Insurance Manager (ESC)
Insurance Underwriter (CSE)
Internal Auditor (ICR)
Kindergarten Teacher (ESC)

Medical Records Technician
  (CSE)
Museum Registrar (CSE)
Paralegal (SCE)
Safety Inspector (RCS)
Tax Accountant (ECS)
Tax Consultant (CES)
Travel Agent (ECS)

BIBLIOGRAPHY

Electronics and Precision Equipment

Bowles, Roger. *Biomedical Equipment Technicians.* Waco, TX: Texas State Technical College Publishing, 2008.

Buckwalter, Len. *Avionics Training: Systems, Installation, Troubleshooting.* Leesburg, VA: Avionics Communications, 2005.

Careers in Focus: Electronics. New York: Ferguson/Infobase, 2009

Careers in Focus: Technicians. New York: Ferguson/Infobase, 2001.

DeLaurier, Dennis. *Electronic Technician Level 1.* Manor, TX: Crescent Multimedia, 2014.

Hitz, C. Breck, et al. *Introduction to Laser Technology,* 4th ed. Piscataway, NJ: IEEE Press, 2012.

Khandpur, Raghbir Singh. *Troubleshooting Electronic Equipment.* New York: McGraw Hill, 2007.

Lowe, Doug. *Electronics All-in-One for Dummies.* Hoboken, NJ: Wiley, 2012.

Ribbens, William B. *Understanding Automotive Electronics.* Boston: Newnes, 2003.

Rosenthal, Morris. *Computer Repair with Diagnostic Flowcharts,* 3rd ed. New York: Foner Books, 2013

Rowh, Mark. *Opportunities in Electronics Careers.* New York: McGraw Hill, 2007.

Rudman, Jack. *Electronic Equipment Maintainer.* Syosset, NY: National Learning Corp., 2014.

Rudman, Jack. *Electronic Technician.* Syosset, NY: National Learning Corp., 2005.

The Way Things Work: Telecommunications. Wynnewood, PA: Schlessinger Media, 2003.

Energy Systems

Brumbaugh, James E. *HVAC Fundamentals.* Indianapolis, IN: Audel/Wiley, 2004.

Erlich, Robert. *Renewable Energy: A First Course.* Boca Raton, FL: CRC Press, 2013.

Frost, Harold J., et al. *Stationary Engineering,* 4th ed. Orland Park, IL: American Technical Publishers, 2008.

NCCR. *HVAC Level 1 Trainee Guide,* 3rd ed. Upper Saddle River, NJ: Prentice Hall, 2007.

Tostvein, G. Mark. *Energy System Design and Operation: A Unified Method.* New York: McGraw Hill, 2012.

Whitman, Bill, et al. *Refrigeration and Air Conditioning Technology.* Boston: Cengage, 2012.

Mechanics and Heavy Equipment

Anderson, Gary D. *Motion Control Basics: Troubleshooting Skills for CNC & Robotics.* Seattle, WA: CreateSpace Publishing, 2014.

Avotek. *Introduction to Aircraft Maintenance.* Weyers Cave, VA: Avotek, 2012.

Brumbach, Michael E., and Jeffrey A. CLade. *Industrial Maintenance.* Boston: Cengage, 2013.

Clark, Massimo. *Modern Motorcycle Technology.* Minneapolis, MN: Motorbooks, 2010.

Halderman, James D., et al. *Introduction to Automotive Service.* Upper Saddle River, NJ: Prentice Hall, 2012.

Hunn, Peter. *Small Engines and Outdoor Power Equipment.* Minneapolis, MN: Cool Springs Press, 2014.

Huzij, Robert, et al. *Heavy Equipment Systems.* Boston: Cengage, 2008.

McDonnell, Greg, and Jerry Pinkepank. *Locomotives: The Modern Diesel and Electric Reference.* Richmond Hill, ON: Boston Mills Press, 2011.

Norman, Andrew, and John Corinchock. *Diesel Technology: Fundamentals, Service, Repair.* Tinley Park, IL: Goodheart-Wilcox, 2006.

Richardson, Duncan. *Plant Equipment and Maintenance Engineering Handbook.* New York: McGraw Hill, 2014.

Yost, Spencer. *How to Rebuild and Restore Farm Tractor Engines.* Osceola, WI: MBI, 2000.

Other

Briere, Danny and Pat Hurley. *Home Theater for Dummies.* Hoboken, NJ: Wiley, 2008.

Evans, Allan, et al. *Technology in Action.* Upper Saddle River, NJ: Prentice Hall, 2013.

Ingram, Jimmie and Richard Goudie. *Full-Line Vending Machine Snapshot.* n.p.: e-Business Media, 2012.

Kleinert, Eric. *Troubleshooting and Repairing Major Appliances.* New York: McGraw Hill, 2012.

INDEX